# The 1031 TAX ADVANTAGE for REAL ESTATE INVESTORS

## Timothy S. Harris
## Linda Monroe

**McGraw-Hill**

New York   Chicago   San Francisco   Lisbon
London   Madrid   Mexico City   Milan   New Delhi
San Juan   Seoul   Singapore   Sydney   Toronto

The *McGraw·Hill* Companies

1 2 3 4 5 6 7 8 9 0 DOC/DOC 0 9 8 7 6

ISBN–13:   978–0–07–147896–0
ISBN–10:      0–07–147896–5

This publication is designed to provide accurate and authoritative information in regard to the subject matter covered. It is sold with the understanding that neither the author nor the publisher is engaged in rendering legal, accounting, or other professional service. If legal advice or other expert assistance is required, the services of a competent professional person should be sought.

—From a Declaration of Principles jointly adopted by Committee of the American Bar Association and a Committee of Publishers.

McGraw-Hill books are available at special quantity discounts to use as premiums and sales promotions, or for use in corporate training programs. For more information, please write to the Director of Special Sales, McGraw-Hill Professional, Two Penn Plaza, New York, NY 10121–2298. Or contact your local bookstore.

**Library of Congress Cataloging-in-Publication Data**
Harris, Timothy S.
    The 1031 Tax Advantage for Real Estate Investors / by Timothy S. Harris, and Linda Monroe.
        p. cm.
    Includes bibliographical references and index.
        ISBN 0–07–147896–5 (pbk. : alk. paper) 1. Real property, Exchange of.
2. Real estate investment. 3. Commercial real estate. I. Monroe, Linda. II. Title.

HD1395.H37 2006
332.63'24—dc22                                                    2006028082

# Dedication

This book is dedicated to the outstanding, hardworking, and wonderful employees at TIMCOR Exchange Corporation. They have helped us, taught us, made us laugh, and enriched us in innumerable ways. Their friendships and loyalty will always be remembered fondly.

# Contents

Preface   vii
Acknowledgments   ix
Introduction   xi
Frequently Asked Questions   xv

PART 1: 1031 EXCHANGE BASICS   1

1   The Value of Exchanges   3
2   Terminology   13
3   Basic Tax Concepts   21
4   Qualifying Property and Qualifying Use   27
5   Vesting Issues and Entity Structures That May
    Affect Exchanges   39
6   Role of the Qualified Intermediary   51

PART 2: 1031 EXCHANGES AND FINANCIAL
        MATTERS   63

7   Exchanges Involving Related Parties   65
8   How Much Do I Need to Reinvest?—Exchange Value, Boot,
    and Boot Netting   71
9   Seller Financing and Its Implications for an Exchange   79
10   Identification of Replacement Property   87
11   Treatment of Early Release Money, Earnest Money
    Deposits, and Prorations   99

PART 3: COMPLEX ISSUES IN 1031 EXCHANGES   107

12   Tenancies in Common; Delaware Statutory Trusts; and Oil,
    Gas, and Mineral Rights   109

13  Personal Residences—Combining Sections 121
    and 1031   117
14  Refinancing Exchange Property   121
15  "Construction" ("Build to Suit") Exchanges   125
16  Reverse Exchanges—Parking Transactions   137
17  Personal Property Exchanges   153


PART 4:  MISCELLANEOUS 1031 EXCHANGE
         ISSUES   157

18  Reporting Your Exchange to the IRS and
    Related Matters   159
19  Involuntary Conveyances—IRC Section 1033 Issues   167
20  Miscellaneous Exchange Issues   171


Final Thoughts   175


Appendix A    Section 1031 Exchange of Property Held for
              Productive Use or Investment   177

Appendix B    Rev. Proc. 2000–37, 2000–2 CB 308, 9/18/2000,
              IRC Sec(s). 1031   183

Appendix C    Rev. Proc. 2002–22, 2002–1 CB 733, 03/19/2002,
              IRC Sec(s). 1031   193

Appendix D    Rev. Proc. 2005–14, 2005–7 IRB 528 01/27/2005,
              IRC Sec(s). 121   207

Appendix E    Rev Rul. 2004–86, 2004–33 IRB 191, 07/20/2004,
              IRC Sec(s). 7701   219

Appendix F    §121 Exclusion of Gain from Sale of Principal
              Residence   231

Appendix G    §280A Disallowance of Certain Expenses in
              Connection with Business Use of Home,
              Rental of Vacation Homes, etc.   239


Index   247

# Preface

We have been involved with a qualified intermediary company for many years, in various legal and managerial capacities. During that time, we have processed, with the assistance of a dedicated staff, tens of thousands of exchanges. We have had occasion to speak with literally thousands of investors, real estate agents, and closing agents, as well as their accountants, attorneys, and financial advisors, both individually and in groups, both large and small.

The issues covered by this book are ones that we have encountered frequently among taxpayers and their advisors. Regardless of whether someone is merely contemplating a 1031 exchange or is already engaged in the process, we find that the same questions, problems, and issues recur, again and again.

We have attempted to present this information in what we hope is an unintimidating, reader-friendly, and nontechnical manner, principally for the benefit of the typical investor who is not an attorney, an accountant, or a financial professional. While we found the research and writing to be very rewarding and satisfying, the challenge has been to find effective ways to explain complex tax and legal issues in terms that readers with no legal or tax background can understand.

We hope you find our efforts to be useful and profitable. We encourage you to avail yourself of the advantages of Section 1031. You will find that it offers you a terrific opportunity to build wealth for yourself and your family.

# Acknowledgments

The authors wish to acknowledge the excellent suggestions and comments from Dale Bowling and Douglas Shively, which were invaluable in putting this manuscript together. Deserving of special thanks are Lani Harris and Stephen Monroe, who listened to us when we needed them and exhibited immense patience as this project was coming together. In addition, we wish to thank Aron Harris, who assisted us in putting some final touches on the manuscript.

Tim Harris wishes to remember C. Timothy Corliss, for whom TIMCOR Exchange Corporation was named, and who taught him much about the real estate industry. He also wishes to thank Sorrell Trope for teaching him to think and act like a lawyer. Finally, he wishes to remember Harvey Harris, who was instrumental in his life in so many ways, and an inspiration to the growth of TIMCOR.

Linda Monroe has many family and friends too numerous to name, who have been supportive and caring during this project. Special appreciation goes to Sherry Lewis, who has been a terrific colleague over so many years, and to her dearest friend, Janet Burns, who inspired her with courage and a sense of humor through adversity, and who reminds her so often of the importance of appreciating and enjoying every precious day, notwithstanding the hectic press of daily obligations. Finally, acknowledgement must go to Tim Harris, a mentor and a wonderful friend, who has been so supportive of my career as an attorney, and who gave me the opportunity to learn and to participate in the growth of TIMCOR.

# Introduction

There is a wonderful, yet often poorly understood, provision in the Internal Revenue Code (the federal tax code) that allows you to sell your property and defer payment of your taxes. Does that sound too good to be true? The Code section we are talking about is Section 1031. There are very few provisions in the Code that are so favorable to taxpayers. This book is intended to help you take advantage of Section 1031.

The book is divided into several parts. We have tried to apply some logic to the order of the various portions. Nonetheless, you need not read it cover to cover like a novel. We anticipate that it will be more useful as a reference tool. As a result, we have tried to make the table of contents and index very thorough, so that you can easily find the specific topics that are relevant to your own situation.

We start with frequently asked questions. These are typical questions that we have heard countless times from clients, regardless of their background, education, or level of financial sophistication. They are the questions that arise most often, and they are applicable to a wide variety of situations. If you are contemplating undertaking a 1031 exchange, you will probably find that these questions address some of your concerns and issues.

The answers to our frequently asked questions then give references to the applicable chapters of the book where you can find additional information. We have also included endnotes with legal references at the end of each chapter for readers who may want to read source materials for themselves.

Part 1 covers the basics—always a good way to start. Chapter 1 begins with a simple example demonstrating the value, in dollars and cents, of using Section 1031. It then offers some history of the law. Chapter 2 defines certain key words used in exchanges. This is both important and useful. Chapter 3 goes over some basic tax concepts that all real estate investors need to know. (This is a must read!) Chapter 4 discusses the critical concept of what property qualifies for 1031 treatment. This area of the law is one that seems to raise many questions among clients. Chapter 5 deals with how to take title to property and discusses the various types of entities that investors use for holding their property. Chapter 6 covers the role of the qualified intermediary (QI). If you are planning to do a 1031 exchange, you undoubtedly will be retaining the services of a QI. It is very important that you know how to select a competent QI before you begin.

Part 2 for the most part deals with money, but it also discusses other issues that are peculiar to 1031 exchanges. Chapter 7 covers the situation in which a taxpayer is selling to or buying from a relative. If you are in this situation, you must read this chapter and learn the special rules that apply to you and your relatives. Chapter 8 discusses the critical question of how much money you must reinvest in your exchange. It also explains the concept of taxable *boot*. Chapter 9 brings in the frequently encountered subject of seller financing as it relates to exchanges. Chapter 10 deals with the very critical rules surrounding identification of the replacement property. Finally, Chapter 11 explains how to use exchange funds for a deposit on the replacement property.

Part 3 encompasses issues arising in more complex exchanges. Chapter 12 discusses the very popular tenancy-in-common investments (TICs). There are some tips for unwary investors who may find these types of offerings to be of interest. Chapter 13 looks at the interaction of the sale of a personal residence (IRC Section 121) and Section 1031. This is a fairly common situation that creates opportunities with which taxpayers may wish to acquaint themselves. Chapter 14 addresses the refinancing of property involved in an exchange. Chapter 15 deals with using exchange proceeds to make improvements to your replacement property. Chapter 16 covers the complex area of exchanges done in reverse order, and the special problems that arise. Chapter 17 touches on the subject of exchanges of personal property, which includes any property that is not real estate. This is important, for example, for someone who is considering selling a business, farm machinery, or other equipment.

Part 4 covers tangential issues. Chapter 18 provides information on reporting your exchange with your tax return. Chapter 19 discusses a related Code section that has similar but not identical rules. This is Section 1033, which may apply in the case of casualty losses and eminent domain. Chapter 20 deals with miscellaneous exchange issues that arise from time to time.

Finally, we have included seven appendices that provide some of the statutory and tax materials referred to in the book. Although these items may not be of general interest, they are valuable resources, especially if you wish to discuss Section 1031 with a tax advisor, attorney, or real estate agent who does not have a detailed knowledge of 1031 law.

We sincerely hope you will find this book an informative and useful reference tool.

# Frequently Asked Questions

## The Basics

1. Where did the name "1031 Exchange" come from?
   Section 1031 is the section of the Internal Revenue Code that allows for deferral of taxes when like-kind property is exchanged.

2. Have 1031 exchanges been around very long?
   They have been in the Code since 1921. Although the U.S. Congress has modified the procedure for these exchanges several times, they have actually been available to investors for over 85 years. (See Chapter 1.)

3. If the property I am selling is in one state, can I use the money to buy property in another state?
   Yes. The law applies throughout the entire United States, and also in the U.S. Virgin Islands and Guam. You may reinvest just about anywhere, except in a foreign country. This is a great tool for investors who are relocating to another state. It also makes sense if you believe that one real estate market has gotten overpriced, and that there are better opportunities in a different market. (See Chapter 4.)

4. Are there timing limitations for completing a 1031 exchange?
   Yes, there are several, three of which are absolutely critical to a successful exchange: (1) you must enter into an agreement with a qualified intermediary prior to selling any property, (2) you have 45 days from your closing to identify the property you wish to buy, and (3) you

have 180 days from your closing to complete all purchases. These deadlines are inflexible, and failure to comply with them will cause your exchange to fail. (See Chapters 6 and 10.)

5. Can I do an exchange using my personal residence?
   Generally, no. Section 1031 applies only to investment property. However, sometimes a personal residence can be converted to an investment property, and sometimes a property is partially a personal residence and partially an investment property. (See Chapter 13.)

6. Can I buy an apartment building and live in one of the units?
   Yes. However, you must allocate your purchase price, apportioning it between your 1031 investment in replacement property and the portion you will use personally. The same rule applies if you are selling a building and you live in one of the units. The property will qualify under both Sections 121 and 1031; you get the best of both worlds! (See Chapter 13.)

7. If I sell an apartment building, must I buy another apartment building?
   That is not necessary. Most qualifying real property can be exchanged for any other qualifying real property. So if you sell an apartment building, you may acquire another one, or you may acquire, for example, an office building, vacant land, industrial property, or commercial property. (See Chapter 4.)

8. Can I buy a new building before I sell one that I already own?
   Yes. This is called a *reverse exchange*. It is an exchange that is done in reverse order. However, all of the same rules and regulations apply. One big advantage is that you know exactly what you are buying and do not have the worry of locating a suitable replacement property. A reverse exchange is more complex and more expensive, but it is an effective alternative for some investors, in the right circumstances. (See Chapter 16.)

## Money Issues

9. How much do I have to spend on my replacement property?
   If you want to avoid paying any taxes, you must use all of your cash proceeds and replace all of your mortgage debt. If you don't reinvest

the entire amount, you may still complete a partial exchange, but you may have to pay some tax. (See Chapter 8.)

10. Why can't I just reinvest my profit?
    Because of the way in which our tax laws work, you are deemed to withdraw your profit first and your basis second. In a 1031 exchange, you have to replace your entire net sales price to fully defer paying any tax. (See Chapter 8.)

11. Can I add money to my exchange proceeds to buy a bigger property?
    Yes, definitely. This is usually a good investment strategy. One big advantage of real estate investing is the use of leverage (mortgage debt). The amount of debt you can qualify for is a function of the amount of equity (cash) you start with. By adding outside money to your exchange proceeds, you can use Section 1031 to grow your wealth even faster. (See Chapter 1.)

12. Can I buy more than one property?
    Yes. You can use your exchange proceeds to purchase multiple replacement properties. By buying multiple properties, you diversify your real estate holdings. You can do this with different types of properties, or with properties in different locations. Either way, you end up with a better investment portfolio and a greater chance to enhance your wealth. (See Chapter 4.)

13. Can I sell two properties and combine them in a single exchange?
    Yes. You can also sell two or more properties and combine the money to buy one or more replacement properties. This is a good investment strategy. Sometimes the more expensive the property you purchase, the better the return on investment (ROI). There are sometimes better economies of scale in operating a larger property. Sometimes you can get better leverage. (See Chapter 4.)

14. May I use exchange money to cover my closing costs?
    Yes, you may. Many typical closing costs, such as real estate commissions, escrow and legal fees, title fees, and recording costs, are deductible as part of your exchange, and therefore you may use exchange proceeds to pay them. However, some costs, such as loan fees, taxes, and rental prorations, cannot be paid with exchange funds without creating tax liability. (See Chapter 18.)

15. Can I take some cash out when I sell my property?

    Yes, you may. However, any money you take out is called *boot* and is taxable to you. Sometimes investors need, or simply wish, to use some of their cash proceeds for purposes other than immediate reinvestment. This will not disqualify your transaction. However, the cash must be taken directly from the closing agent; it cannot be received from the qualified intermediary. (See Chapter 8.)

16. If I want to cancel my exchange after I sell my property, how soon can I get my money back?

    That is a question requiring a complex answer. It depends upon where in the exchange process you are. One very important rule to remember, however, is that there are severe restrictions on your exchange proceeds until your exchange is completed. You cannot access any of your exchange proceeds within the first 45 days after you close your sale, except for the purposes of acquiring a replacement property. (See Chapter 8.)

17. How do I report the 1031 exchange to the IRS and when?

    An exchange must be reported on a Form 8824, which is filed in conjunction with your normal tax return. However, you cannot file until you have completed your exchange. This form, like all tax forms, can be downloaded from the IRS Web site: www.irs.gov. It is a two-page form with three pages of instructions. It requires you to have all of your sale and purchase information (dates, amounts, and so on). If you normally complete your own tax return, this form should not be too difficult. Still, the authors normally recommend that you retain a professional to assist you. (See Chapter 18.)

## Qualifying Property

18. How long do I have to hold a property before I can sell it?

    You have to acquire your replacement property with the intent to hold it as an investment and not resell it. Section 1031 is intended for investors who intend to hold for the longer term, not for people who want to "flip" properties to make a quick profit or for dealers or contractors who are in the business of buying and selling property. Of course, intent is hard to prove, but if you hold property for only a short time, be prepared to explain your reasons to the IRS in the event of an audit. (See Chapter 4.)

19. How long do I have to wait after my exchange before I can move into the property I acquired?

    You have to acquire your replacement property with the intent to hold it as an investment and not with the intent to use it as your personal residence. If you move into it within the first year or two after you acquire it, you may be inviting an IRS audit. (See Chapters 4 and 13.)

20. Can I build on property that I already own?

    You certainly may, but *not* as part of a 1031 exchange. You cannot use exchange proceeds to pay for construction on property that you already own. The essence of an exchange is disposing of one property and acquiring a new one in replacement. However, there is a type of exchange, called a *construction exchange*, that will allow you to improve property that you are planning to acquire. (See Chapter 15.)

21. Does a vacation home qualify as 1031 exchange property?

    A vacation home that is used as a rental property and not for personal enjoyment will qualify; a vacation home that is used for your own vacation will not qualify. Remember that the definition of a qualifying property requires that the property be held as an investment. A house or condo in a resort area can make a great investment. You may be able to have limited use of it, while earning enough revenue to cover all expenses. The authors have found there to be a very active 1031 market in ski lodges and beach area condos. (See Chapter 4.)

22. Can I buy a replacement property and add my children onto the deed?

    When you add children to the title on property, you are technically making a gift to them, and therefore you should check with your tax advisor. You also must ensure that the percentage of ownership that you retain is sufficient to satisfy your exchange requirement. (See Chapter 4.)

23. Can I sell property owned by my corporation and buy property in my own name?

    No. There is an exchange rule called the *same taxpayer* rule. The same taxpayer who sells the old property must also buy the new property. With some exceptions, entities are treated by the IRS as different taxpayers. (See Chapter 5.)

24. Can a taxpayer pay down the mortgage on real estate already owned using exchange proceeds?

    No. The 1031 statute requires that the taxpayer *acquire* replacement property with the exchange proceeds. Reducing a debt does not qualify as the purchase of replacement property. Having a reasonable amount of leverage on investment real estate is generally a good strategy. Rather than using the money to pay down debt on an existing property, you would probably be better off acquiring a second replacement property in your exchange. (See Chapter 8.)

25. Can I lease my investment property to a relative?

    Yes, but you have to act at arm's length with your tenant/relative. You must treat the property as an investment and charge a fair market rent. If you are planning to acquire a home for one of your children to live in without paying rent, it does not qualify. (See Chapter 4.)

## Identification Questions

26. Can the qualified intermediary be flexible about identification dates?

    No. The property must be identified within the 45-day deadline. To manufacture or accept backdated or falsified documents in order to make it appear that a property identification was timely is against the law. Taxpayers and qualified intermediaries are both required to obey the law. The 45-day identification period in Section 1031 is not a flexible time period, despite what you may have heard. There are exceptions where there has been a declared natural disaster, but those are extremely rare. (See Chapter 10.)

27. What are the consequences of backdating my property identification?

    In a 1999 case, the taxpayers claimed to have orally identified properties to one another, and then schemed to backdate a written identification. The IRS held their exchange to be invalid. The court found their testimony about their property identification to be incredible. They were ordered to pay $1,030,663 in taxes and were assessed a fraud penalty of $772,997. (See Chapter 10.)

28. Can an identification form be signed by someone with a power of attorney?

    The Section 1031 Regulations require that the identification form be signed by the taxpayer. Under normal rules of agency, a person who is duly authorized to sign documents on behalf of a taxpayer may bind the taxpayer. Thus, this is probably acceptable, but it is always safer to have the exchangor sign personally. (See Chapter 10.)

29. What if I am not intending to acquire a 100 percent interest in the replacement property—for instance, suppose I intend to buy only a 5 percent interest?

   If you are buying only a fractional share, as a tenant in common with others, including in a sponsored TIC (see Chapter 12), you must specify the percentage you intend to acquire on your identification form. Otherwise, what you ultimately acquire will be inconsistent with what you identified (a 5 percent interest versus a 100 percent interest), causing the exchange to fail. Of course, if you identify a 65 percent interest, and you ultimately acquire a 67 percent interest, the difference is *de minimus* and will probably have no effect in the event of an audit. (See Chapter 10.)

30. Do I have to buy one of the identified properties, or can I buy something else if the identified properties don't work out?

   Only a property that has been validly identified in a timely manner may be received as qualified replacement property to complete a bona fide exchange. Otherwise, all exchangors would simply identify "the Empire State Building, the White House, and the Golden Gate Bridge," and then buy whatever they wanted, rendering the concept of the 45-day identification period utterly meaningless. (See Chapter 10.)

31. Can I change my list of identified properties?

   Certainly. The identification list may be changed or revoked at any time up until midnight of your forty-fifth day. The revocation or amendment must be done with the same formality as the original identification, i.e., it must be in writing, signed, and timely delivered. The list cannot be changed after the end of the forty-five day identification period. (See Chapter 10.)

32. Is having a signed sales contract within the 45-day window the same as identifying a property?

   Technically no, although that might qualify as an identification made to the seller. A better practice is to identify the property to the qualified intermediary. Also, if the exchangor has already identified three other properties, and this is a fourth property, the exchangor would have to qualify under either the 200 percent rule or the 95 percent rule in order to include this property in the exchange. (See Chapter 10.)

33. What if the property I identify is sold or taken off the market?

    If your identification date has not passed, you can simply identify something else. However, once your forty-fifth day has passed, you are limited in your exchange to the properties that you identified. For that reason, it is wise to list more than one property, so that you have some backups if you are unable to acquire your first-choice property. (See Chapter 10.)

# The 1031
## TAX ADVANTAGE
### *for*
## REAL ESTATE
## INVESTORS

# PART 1

# 1031 EXCHANGE BASICS

C H A P T E R

# The Value of Exchanges

*How does the use of 1031 exchanges help you build your wealth?*

The following example demonstrates the advantages offered by Section 1031. It shows the value of compounding tax deferral over a 10-year period by taking advantage of this powerful wealth-preserving tool, which is readily accessible to all taxpayers.

Our two fictional taxpayers, Mr. Sharp and Mr. Bumble, are both residents of Pleasantville, U.S.A. Table 1–1 illustrates their respective experiences in real estate investment. (For the sake of simplicity, all of the transactions described here require no real estate commissions and no sale expenses.)

In Year 1, Mr. Sharp and Mr. Bumble both make initial $500,000 investments in real property, each making a down payment of $125,000 (25 percent), and each obtaining a loan of $375,000 (75 percent). As of Year 4, each of them has experienced appreciation of 20 percent ($100,000) in his Pleasantville property. Each is able to sell his property for $600,000. But at this point, their fortunes change, and their financial paths diverge.

Mr. Sharp is lucky (or smart, or both). He has a savvy tax advisor who informs him of the benefits of Section 1031. Mr. Sharp does not *sell* his property; he *exchanges* it for another. Unfortunately for Mr. Bumble, neither his real estate agent nor his accountant is familiar with Section 1031. He merely sells the property, pays his taxes, and then buys a new property.

## TABLE 1–1  Example of Exchange Compared to Purchase and Sale

| | Mr. Sharp Exchange | | Mr. Bumble Sale and Purchase | |
|---|---|---|---|---|
| **Year 1** | | Taxes Due | | Taxes Due |
| Acquire Property 1 | | | | |
| Down payment | $125,000.00 | | $125,000.00 | |
| New debt | $375,000.00 | | $375,000.00 | |
| Total price | $500,000.00 | | $500,000.00 | |
| **Year 4** | | | | |
| Sell Property 1 for 20% gain | | | | |
| Price | $600,000.00 | | $600,000.00 | |
| Depreciation taken | $30,000.00 | | $30,000.00 | |
| Adjusted basis | $470,000.00 | | $470,000.00 | |
| Realized gain | $130,000.00 | | $130,000.00 | |
| Federal tax due @15% | | $0.00 | | $19,500.00* |
| Cash available to reinvest | $225,000.00 | | $205,500.00 | |
| Acquire Property 2 | | | | |
| Down payment | $225,000.00 | | $205,500.00 | |
| New debt | $675,000.00 | | $616,500.00 | |
| Purchase price | $900,000.00 | | $822,000.00 | |
| **Year 7** | | | | |
| Sell Property 2 for 20% gain | | | | |
| Price | $1,080,000.00 | | $986,400.00 | |
| Depreciation taken | $54,000.00 | | $50,000.00 | |
| Adjusted basis | $716,000.00 | | $772,000.00 | |
| Realized gain | $364,000.00 | | $214,400.00 | |
| Federal tax due @15% | | $0.00 | | $32,160.00* |
| Cash available to reinvest | $405,000.00 | | $337,740.00 | |
| Acquire Property 3 | | | | |
| Down payment | $405,000.00 | | $337,740.00 | |
| New debt | $1,215,000.00 | | $1,013,220.00 | |
| Purchase price | $1,620,000.00 | | $1,350,960.00 | |
| **Year 10** | | | | |
| Sell Property 3 for 20% gain | | | | |
| Price | $1,944,000.00 | | $1,621,152.00 | |
| Depreciation taken | $94,000.00 | | $81,000.00 | |
| Adjusted basis | $946,000.00 | | $1,269,960.00 | |
| Realized gain | $998,000.00 | | $351,192.00 | |
| Federal tax due @15% | | $0.00 | | $52,678.80* |
| Cash available to reinvest | $729,000.00 | | $555,253.20 | |
| Acquire Property 4 | | | | |
| Down payment | $729,000.00 | | $555,253.20 | |
| New debt | $2,187,000.00 | | $1,665,759.60 | |
| Purchase price | $2,916,000.00 | | $2,221,012.80 | |
| **Total federal taxes paid** | | **$0.00** | | **$104,338.80†** |

* This is a very simplified example, intended for illustration only.
† The depreciation shown is an estimate, and is rounded. In an actual transaction, there would be additional tax due as a result of depreciation recapture, and most states have taxes due as well.

At the closing of their respective sales in Year 4, they both have sale proceeds of $225,000 cash (remember, there are no commissions and no sale expenses). But Mr. Bumble must pay federal capital gains taxes of $19,500 from that amount. The tax is 15 percent of the capital gain of $130,000, which includes the $100,000 appreciation plus the depreciation taken of $30,000.

Mr. Sharp is able to reinvest his entire $225,000, leveraging that equity to obtain a new 75 percent loan ($675,000). Thus, he is able to acquire a new property selling for $900,000. Mr. Bumble, using his $205,500 of after-tax cash with the same leverage percentage (75 percent), is able to acquire only a property selling for $822,000.

By the end of Year 7, after another 20 percent appreciation in their Pleasantville properties, both of our investors again elect to sell. Mr. Sharp does another exchange; Mr. Bumble, still uninformed, does not. Mr. Sharp realizes proceeds on his sale of $405,000 ($225,000 equity + $180,000 appreciation). He is able to reinvest that amount and acquire his third property for $1,620,000, with another new 75 percent ($1,215,000) loan.

Mr. Bumble realizes cash proceeds on his sale of $369,900 ($205,500 equity + $164,400 appreciation). But he must again pay a 15 percent capital gains tax of $32,160 on his gain of $214,400 ($164,400 appreciation + $50,000 depreciation), leaving him only $337,740 for his next property. He buys a new building for $1,350,960, again obtaining a 75 percent loan.

Happily for both taxpayers, the properties in Pleasantville continue to rise in value. By the end of Year 10, they have risen another 20 percent! Again, both taxpayers decide to sell. At this point, Mr. Sharp finds himself with equity of $729,000. He repeats the Section 1031 process and is able to afford a fourth property, this one valued at $2,916,000.

Mr. Bumble, on the other hand, is still using the same uninspired tax advisors, who have failed to educate themselves or him about the benefits of Section 1031. He remains in the dark about the ability to defer his taxes. He realizes sales proceeds of $607,932. But after he pays his capital gains taxes, he has only $555,253 to reinvest. He buys his fourth property for $2,221,013. Mr. Sharp is now nearly $695,000 ahead of Mr. Bumble. Of course, Mr. Bumble has had the dubious pleasure of paying more than $100,000 in federal capital gains taxes up until now, while Mr. Sharp has paid no capital gains taxes at all.

It is easy to see from this very simple story how two taxpayers, starting out with exactly the same amount of cash and with the same opportunity for growth, experienced very different outcomes because one of them took advantage of the compounding power of Section 1031 to build equity and wealth for his family.

Of course, this is a simplified example. It assumes that there are no commissions or expenses of sale, that no state income taxes are due, and that depreciation is taken but is not subject to recapture, which we will explain a little later. None of those assumptions are likely to hold true in the real world. We are also assuming that all encumbrances are "interest only," so that there is no paydown of principal during the life of the loans, which could have a small effect on the outcome.

In reality, if you are subject to state income taxation and depreciation recapture (discussed later in this book), the results are even more favorable to Mr. Sharp, and more disadvantageous to Mr. Bumble, than this example shows.

## If This Is So Terrific, Why Isn't Everyone Doing Exchanges?

If Section 1031 is such a great deal, why wouldn't everyone want to do an exchange? Often, the answer is that many taxpayers, like Mr. Bumble, are simply unaware of Section 1031's existence. People who are educated about 1031 exchanges do them routinely. They merely have to have a property that has appreciated in value and the desire to replace it with another investment.

However, conditions are not always ripe for doing an exchange. The laws and regulations governing Section 1031 are demanding, onerous, and strict. They are not always logical, and they are not very flexible. They restrict a taxpayer's access to his or her money, and they prescribe the ways in which it can be spent. They are not always well understood, and if they are not properly adhered to, they can lead to unpleasant surprises at tax time. We will explain the advantages and disadvantages as we continue. But first, a bit of background would be appropriate.

## Background and Overview of Exchanges

Federal taxation of income in the United States is governed by the Internal Revenue Code. The Internal Revenue Code is divided into many chapters, subchapters, and sections. (Except as otherwise noted, all references in this book to the Code refer to the Internal Revenue Code, and all references to Section 1031 refer to Internal Revenue Code Section 1031.) Ordinary income, such as the salary you earn from employment or interest paid on your bank accounts, is taxed at various rates. However, gains from the sale of assets, such as shares of stock or real estate, commonly referred to as *capital gains*, may qualify to be taxed at different rates. These rate differences are based on policy decisions made by the U.S. Congress to encourage people to invest in our economy. An entire industry has grown up around Section 1031. Smart investors regularly utilize Section 1031 to defer taxes on the sale of their real estate investments.

The primary purpose of this book is to explain and clarify the "why's" and the "how's" of Section 1031. In addition, we will discuss a relatively new aspect of 1031 exchanges: some real estate professionals have begun buying investment-quality properties and then selling fractional interests in those properties to 1031 investors. This book will also address the concepts and potential benefits of this type of ownership. Two trade organizations have been established to represent the interests of companies in these areas: the Federation of Exchange Accommodators (www.1031.org) and the Tenant-in-Common Association (www.ticassoc.org).

## The Basic Concept

Internal Revenue Code Section 1031 allows for the deferral of the tax that would ordinarily be due as a result of gain on the sale of qualifying properties, provided that the transaction is structured as an *exchange*. There are several *necessary elements*, all of which must be present for an exchange under Section 1031:

- The properties involved must *qualify*.
- An *exchange* must occur—there must be a reciprocal and interdependent transfer of those qualifying properties, rather than a sale followed by a purchase.
- The taxpayer must comply with all relevant timing requirments;
- The *same taxpayer* must be involved both at the beginning and at the end of the transaction.
- The taxpayer must have *no actual or constructive receipt of the sales proceeds*.

## Overview of Tax Law

U.S. tax laws are enacted by Congress and codified into the Internal Revenue Code. Individual states also have their own tax laws, which can vary to a considerable degree. For the most part, this book will focus only on federal tax law. However, it is important to be aware that in addition to this, there are minor variations from state to state in the laws governing exchanges. Indeed, readers who are contemplating an exchange are encouraged to consult with their accountants or attorneys regarding how an exchange might affect their individual circumstances and if there are any applicable local tax laws.

The Internal Revenue Service, which is a part of the Department of the Treasury, has the duty of interpreting and enforcing our federal tax laws. After a particular code section is legislated into existence, the IRS will sometimes issue interpretative regulations concerning that code section. The IRS may, from time to time, issue a Revenue Ruling (Rev. Rul.), Revenue Procedure (Rev. Proc.), Private Letter Ruling (PLR), Technical Advice Memorandum (TAM), Notice, and/or Bulletin to address specific taxpayer issues. These are usually published at taxpayers' request and involve specific fact patterns. In addition, taxpayers may contest the outcome of an IRS audit in one of several federal courts, which may result in opinions and decisions interpreting the language of various Code sections. All of this output together makes up the body of U.S. tax law. Except as specifically noted from time to time, most of the focus of this book will be on exchanges of real property. However, like-kind exchanges can also be done with personal property, which we address in Chapter 17.

## Applicable Federal Statutes

Internal Revenue Code Section 1031 provides for the deferral of capital gains taxes on the sale of *qualifying property*, provided the taxpayer complies with the section's requirements. As we saw in the example comparing Mr. Sharp and Mr. Bumble, by deferring the payment of his or her taxes, the savvy investor has more funds with which to purchase more property or more expensive or better-located property.

Keep in mind, however, that Section 1031 does not allow taxpayers to avoid taxes. This permissible *tax deferment* is more in the nature of an interest-free loan from the government. If and when the taxpayer ultimately sells the property acquired in an exchange, the accumulated deferred tax will, in most instances, have to be paid.

The predecessor statute to Section 1031 was first enacted by Congress as Section 202(c) of the Revenue Act of 1921. This legislation was enacted soon after the adoption of the Sixteenth Amendment to the U.S. Constitution in 1913, which for the first time authorized the imposition of income-based taxes. The purpose of Section 202(c) was to exempt from taxation transactions in which the taxpayer received no cash. Shortly thereafter, Congress amended that section to exclude securities transactions (those involving the purchase and sale of stocks and bonds) from the exemption.

The foregoing Code section was renumbered in the Revenue Act of 1928 as Section 112(b)(1). In the recodification of the Internal Revenue Code in 1954, that section was again renumbered and became Section 1031, which is how it is identified today. (Clearly this Code section has a long history.)

There are many federal court decisions interpreting various aspects of these laws as well. The section has been very popular with real estate investors, the real estate industry, and companies that, for business reasons, need to relocate their plants and offices. Like most tax provisions that exempt or defer recognition of taxable income, Section 1031 is not so popular with the Internal Revenue Service.

## The Starker Case

A major milestone with respect to tax-deferred exchanges resulted from the Appellate Court decision in *T. J. Starker v. United States* 602 F2d 1341 (9th Cir 1979). Prior to that time, it was generally understood that an exchange required the *simultaneous* relinquishment and acquisition of "like-kind" property. The Starker case, involving the sale and exchange of timberland, held for the first time that Section 1031 could be used to defer taxes in a situation where the exchange of properties was not concurrent or simultaneous.

Mr. Starker and his son and daughter-in-law sold their Oregon timberland to Crown Zellerbach Corporation. In exchange, Crown Zellerbach promised "to acquire and deed over to the Starkers other real property in

Washington and Oregon . . . within five (5) years or pay any outstanding balance in cash." It also agreed to add a 6 percent "growth factor" to the outstanding balance annually. The IRS sought to disallow this exchange as not complying with the statutory requirements of Section 1031. But the court sided with the Starkers and against the position taken by the IRS.

Partly as a consequence of the taxpayer victory in *Starker*, the Internal Revenue Service prevailed on Congress to amend Section 1031 by inserting tighter time limits for completion of an exchange. In the Deficit Reduction Act of 1984, Section 1031 was revised to add two specific timing requirements: (1) a 45-day identification period and (2) a 180-day exchange period, both of which we will explore in great detail later in the book. The 1984 amendment sanctioned the use of nonsimultaneous exchanges (which to this day are still frequently referred to as "Starker exchanges"). In addition, the 1984 amendment also added a prohibition on exchanging partnership interests.

## Enactment of Treasury Regulations

The next major change in Section 1031 occurred in 1991, when the Department of the Treasury promulgated extensive regulations "interpreting" or "clarifying" the provisions of Section 1031. This was a very important development for investors, exchange intermediaries, and other real estate professionals in this field. Following the general format of Treasury Regulations, these are denominated as "Regulation 1.1031 . . . ," with the portion inserted after the "1031" indicating a subsection reference. These regulations will be cited and discussed in greater detail throughout the book. The adoption of these regulations added greater certainty for the companies engaged in structuring these transactions for taxpayers, as well as for taxpayers and their advisors.

In 2004, the American Jobs Creation Act amended Code Section 121 as it relates to Section 1031. Section 121 deals with the exclusion of gain on the sale of a personal residence. The 2004 amendment requires a taxpayer who initially acquired his or her personal residence in a 1031 exchange and subsequently converted it from investment to personal use to hold such personal residence for five years (rather than two years) to obtain the benefits of Section 121. (See Chapter 13 for more detailed information.)

## Coverage of Section 1031: Operative in the Entire United States and Some Territories

Because Section 1031 is a federal law, it is applicable to exchanges in all 50 states. Some states have slight modifications to the basic provisions of the law (such as Georgia, which until recently required replacement property to be located within that state). Some states, such as Colorado, Hawaii, and Vermont, for example, may require collection of a withholding tax on real estate sales, with an exemption available for exchanges.

*Authors' Note:* If you are planning to do an exchange, check with a local tax advisor for any special state law requirements. There are also special provisions allowing for exchanges of property located in the U.S. Virgin Islands and in Guam.

## Disadvantages of an Exchange

Despite the good news, there are downsides to 1031 exchanges. The rules and regulations of Section 1031 are technical tax law and require strict adherence. There are more steps and more documents involved in a 1031 real estate exchange than there are in a "regular" real estate transaction. In close cases, a determination of the taxpayer's intent is critical to establish the right motivation and qualifications. Therefore, it is important that your intent to exchange be evidenced in writing as early in the process as possible. In both the agreement to list the property for sale with the broker and the actual purchase and sale agreement with the buyer, the seller's intent to engage in a 1031 exchange should be clearly stated. In the purchase and sale agreement, the buyer should be obligated to cooperate (cooperation clause) with the seller/exchangor, without additional cost to the buyer.

Compliance with short time deadlines can be a problem for some investors. Many taxpayers have difficulty identifying a replacement property within the allowed 45-day identification period. Some exchangors find their perfect replacement property before they have sold their existing property. They are then forced to do a reverse exchange, which is even more costly and more complicated. (Reverse exchanges are explained more fully in Chapter 16.)

Some taxpayers want to use their 1031 sale proceeds for construction projects that cannot be completed within the 180-day exchange period allowed. Other taxpayers want to use their exchange proceeds to construct improvements on property that they already own (not allowed). Some taxpayers simply want or need to use their real estate equity for other purposes that do not comply with the Section 1031 requirements. In addition, the tax deferral rules are automatic, so if a taxpayer has a capital loss or loss carryover (such as from a prior sale of stock or other property), he or she may find it is advantageous to *avoid* utilizing Section 1031.

A 1031 exchange will not work in every case. However, when a 1031 exchange is appropriate, taxpayers should structure their transactions so that they are in full compliance with all the requirements.

## The "Gray Areas"

Some areas of tax law are crystal clear; others are relatively murky. In the 1031 field, it is no different. Throughout this book you will see references to the "gray areas" of Section 1031 law. Although there are specific and definitive requirements for accomplishing a successful exchange, there are also some areas where the IRS guidance is not so clear, or where there is ambiguity as to exactly which actions will comply and which will not.

# Terminology

In order to understand the intricacies of the exchange process, it is important that you become familiar with certain basic terminology that is unique to the exchange industry. Many of these terms are used in the Treasury Regulations (sometimes referred to in this book as "Regs") published under Section 1031 [Reg. 1.1031(a) et seq.]. These terms will be used extensively, and the material will be much easier to follow if you are familiar with them.

These terms are not listed in alphabetical order. We have placed them in the order in which you are likely to encounter them. The first few deal with property. The next group covers different types of exchanges. The following group deals with terms used in structuring an exchange. The final few are items that will arise after your sale closes. All of the terms are discussed in much greater detail in subsequent chapters.

## Qualifying Property

The *qualifying property* is the type of property that qualifies under Section 1031 for purposes of an exchange. The statutory definition in the Code is: "Property held for investment, or for productive use in a trade or business." It cannot be property held primarily for resale, and it cannot be your personal residence. It is also sometimes referred to as *like-kind* property. It can be either real or personal property, or a combination of both.

## Relinquished Property

The *relinquished property* is the qualifying property that is being sold or trans-ferred by the taxpayer in the exchange. It is the property that the taxpayer wishes to replace. It is also sometimes referred to as the *downleg* or "Phase I" property. There can be multiple relinquished properties in an exchange.

## Replacement Property

The *replacement property* is the qualifying property that is being acquired by the taxpayer in the exchange. It is also sometimes referred to as the *upleg* or "Phase II" property. There can be multiple replacement properties in an exchange.

## Exchange

An *exchange* is the reciprocal, interdependent transfer of one or more relinquished properties for one or more replacement properties. The recip-rocal nature of the transfers is the essence of an exchange. (This definition is well illustrated by three separate and significant tax cases.[1–3]) Section 1031 requires an exchange of qualifying properties, not merely a sale followed by a purchase.

## Like-Kind Exchange

As you will see, not only must a transaction be structured as an exchange to allow favorable tax treatment, but the properties involved in the exchange must be deemed to be of *like kind*. Whether one asset is deemed like kind to another depends in part on whether it is real or personal property. (The concept of *like kind* is addressed more fully in Chapter 4.)

## Exchangor

The *exchangor* is the taxpayer/real estate investor engaging in an exchange.

## Delayed Exchange

The *delay* refers to the timing difference between the respective dates of the sale and the subsequent purchase in an exchange. The majority of exchanges are *delayed exchanges.* However, an exchange of properties can also be *concurrent* or *simultaneous* and still qualify. A delayed exchange may also be referred to as a *forward exchange,* to distinguish it from a *reverse exchange.*

## Reverse Exchange

Normally, a taxpayer sells the relinquished property before buying a replacement. However, sometimes the taxpayer finds the "perfect" replacement property before selling the existing property. Section 1031 and Rev. Proc. 2000–37 make provision for this "reverse-order" exchange. A *reverse exchange* is a transaction in which a taxpayer acquires replacement property before selling the relinquished property.

## Deferred Exchange

The term *deferred* refers to the deferral of tax on the sale. A *deferred exchange* may be *concurrent,* meaning that the taxpayer relinquishes and replaces qualifying property on the same day, delayed, or reverse. A 1031 exchange is not tax-free or tax-exempt. It is, however, tax-deferred.

## Constructive Receipt

A taxpayer may not have either actual or constructive receipt of the exchange funds during the exchange process. Actual receipt of money is an easy concept to understand. *Constructive receipt* refers either to receipt of the sale proceeds by an agent of the taxpayer, such as an attorney, accountant, or real estate agent, or to circumstances in which the taxpayer controls the sale proceeds without having actual or physical possession of them, such as if they are deposited directly into a bank account in the taxpayer's name. To be valid, 1031 exchanges must be structured to avoid the taxpayer's ever having constructive receipt of his or her funds. Actual or constructive receipt of exchange proceeds will invalidate an exchange.[4,5]

## Qualified Intermediary

A *qualified intermediary* is a person or company who acts as an independent middleman to facilitate the exchange process by selling the relinquished property and acquiring the replacement property on behalf of the taxpayer. The qualified intermediary, or QI, is also referred to as the *accommodator* or *facilitator*.

## Safe Harbors

*Safe harbors* are methods of conducting or structuring a 1031 deferred exchange that satisfy the requirements of Treasury Reg. 1.1031(k)–1(g). These methods involve utilizing a qualified intermediary, qualified escrow account, or qualified trust; security devices; and the payment of interest. Safe harbor exchanges avoid having a taxpayer deemed to be in actual or constructive receipt of exchange funds.

## Disqualified Person

This term is defined in Treasury Reg. 1.1031(k)–1(k). It refers to someone who is an agent of the taxpayer, is related to the taxpayer, or has a preexisting business relationship with the taxpayer. The 1031 Regulations proscribe certain activities between the exchangor and a disqualified person during the exchange process. A disqualified person cannot act as the qualified intermediary.

## Boot

*Boot* is cash or other property, including debt relief, received by the taxpayer in an exchange that is not like kind to the relinquished property. Boot may also arise as a result of the payment of transaction costs unrelated to the purchase or sale of an asset, such as real property taxes, loan fees, credit card bills, or repairs.

## Mortgage Boot

*Mortgage boot* is created if all the available cash is used in the exchange, but a lower-balance mortgage is placed on the replacement property. Mortgage boot can be offset by additional cash paid in order to avoid having to pay capital gains taxes. The opposite does not work; one cannot offset cash received with additional debt.

## Escrow

In some jurisdictions, real estate transactions and closings are processed by companies set up exclusively for that purpose. These are called *escrow* companies; they are very common in California and other western states. They are not law offices, and the people who process the transactions usually are not attorneys. They are more or less the counterparts of closing attorneys, who typically handle real estate transactions in jurisdictions that do not use escrow companies. Escrow companies may be independent companies, or they may be connected to real estate brokers, title companies, or even some banks.

## Closing

As used in this book, the term *closing* refers to the date and/or event when the "benefits and burdens" of ownership of a property are transferred from one owner (the seller) to another (the buyer).[6,7] The *closing date* of a transaction is the critical date that commences the identification period and the exchange period (defined later in this chapter) in a 1031 exchange. The term *closing* also has a common meaning, which is the time and place when the parties, in nonescrow jurisdictions, meet to sign the closing documents (usually at an attorney's office), but that is not the meaning to be applied with reference to Section 1031.

## Identification Period

The *identification period* is the statutory 45-day period for identifying potential replacement properties. It starts on the date of the closing of the relinquished property, and it ends on the date that is 45 calendar days later.[8]

## Exchange Period

The *exchange period* is the 180-day period allowed by law for completing a 1031 exchange. It starts on the date of the closing of the relinquished property, and it ends on the date that is 180 calendar days later.[9]

However, there is a special additional rule that can shorten the exchange period. The taxpayer must complete his or her exchange prior to filing his or her income tax return for the year of the sale transaction. If a relinquished property closing occurs between October 17 and December 31, the 180-day exchange period will carry past April 15, the traditional date on which individual income tax returns are due. Therefore, the tax- payer must either complete the exchange by that date or obtain an extension for filing the return.[10]

See Figure 2–1 for a graphic of how an exchange is typically structured.

**Step 1.** Mr. Smart (exchangor) will enter a contract to sell his vacant land (Property A) to Mrs. Doe. Mr. Smart or his representatives will contact a qualified intermediary to begin the exchange process. Once the exchange is in place, the parties are allowed to close on Property A.

**Step 2.** The money paid for Property A will be transferred to the qualified intermediary to hold while Mr. Smart looks for a new property to purchase.

**Step 3.** When Mr. Smart signs a contract on his replacement property (Property B), the qualified intermediary should be notified to prepare the second half of the 1031 exchange documentation and have the funds ready to be sent to the closing office in order to complete the purchase transaction.

**Completed.** If all the money was used to purchase Property B, the 1031 exchange should be complete and Mr. Smart has successfully exchanged his vacant land for a new apartment building while deferring all of his capital gains taxes.

## Endnotes

1. *Florida Industries Investment Corp. et al.*, TC Memo 1999–346 (October 19, 1999), aff'd. 252 F3d 440 (3/23/2001), where the Tax Court, in denying the validity of the taxpayer's exchange, states: "Transactions that take the form of a cash sale followed by a reinvestment cannot, in substance, qualify as an exchange . . . ."

2. *Coastal Terminals, Inc. v. United States,* 320 F2d 333, 337 (4th Cir 1963), where the court stated: "The purpose of Section 1031(a), as shown by its legislative history, is to defer recognition of gain or loss when a direct exchange of property between the taxpayer and another party takes place; a sale for cash does not qualify as a nontaxable exchange even though the cash is immediately reinvested in like property."

3. *Swaim v. U.S.,* 651 F2d 1066 (5th Cir 1981). There is no exchange where purchase is delayed, despite exchange intent language in the contract; the court found the transactions not to be "contractually interdependent."

4. *Dobrich v. Commissioner*, 188 F3d 512 (9th Cir 1999), where exchange treatment was denied to taxpayers and fraud penalties were imposed on egregious facts.

5. *Baxter v. Commissioner,* 816 F2d 493 (9th Cir 1987); though not a 1031 case, this thoroughly discusses the concept of constructive receipt.

6. *Benedict et al. v. U.S.,* 881 F.Supp 1532 (3/31/95) gives an excellent analysis of the "benefits and burdens" test as it relates to determination of the date of sale.

7. *James W. Keith et ux v. Commissioner*, 115 TC 605, 611 (2000) discusses the "benefits and burdens" test to determine when a sale is completed.

8. Reg. 1.1031(k)–1(b)(2)(i).

9. Reg. 1.1031(k)–1(b)(2)(ii).

10. *Christensen v. Commissioner*, 142 F3d 442 (9th Cir 1997); exchange treatment was denied by the court when taxpayers did not complete their exchange by April 15 and did not seek an extension to file their tax return.

C   H   A   P   T   E   R

# Basic Tax Concepts

*What do you need to know if you have never bought or sold real estate before?*

In order to decide whether you are an appropriate candidate to utilize the benefits of Section 1031, you need a basic understanding of certain tax concepts. This chapter explains seven related tax terms in detail. Except for *carryover basis*, all of these are applicable to standard real estate transactions, whether or not you are doing an exchange. We discuss these tax terms in the order in which they will generally arise in a real estate transaction. These terms are critical to a general understanding of exchanges.

These tax concepts are used to establish whether you have a gain or a loss on the sale of your property. Gain (commonly called "profit") or loss is the difference between the *net sale price* (called the *amount realized*) and the *adjusted tax basis* of the property being sold.[1] If you anticipate that you will have a gain on the sale of qualifying property, you wish to defer payment of the taxes that would otherwise be due on that gain, and you are willing to reinvest the sale proceeds in qualifying replacement property, you are a good candidate to engage in a 1031 exchange.

## Net Sale Price

The *net sale price* is the contract or gross sale price reduced by the expenses necessitated by the sale. The net sale price is also referred to as the *amount realized.*[2] Typical expenses of sale would include the brokerage commission, title charges, escrow or closing fees, legal fees, and recording fees, among others. It is important to understand that the amount of the mortgage balance due *is not* subtracted in this calculation. The net sale price determines how much needs to be reinvested when doing a 1031 exchange. We may from time to time refer to this as the *exchange value.*

## Basis

The *basis,* also known as the *cost basis*, is typically the price paid for an asset at the time of its purchase.[3] Having a higher basis at the time of a sale generally results in paying a lower amount of tax, while having a lower basis will result in paying a greater amount of tax. For example, if you purchased a diamond three years ago for $1,000, then your basis in the diamond is $1,000 (high basis). If you now sold the diamond for $1,100, you would have a gain of $100. If instead you had bought the diamond 20 years ago for $200 (low basis) and now sold it for $1,100, your gain would be $900, and the tax owed would be higher.

## Adjusted Basis

The tax basis of any asset, such as real estate, for example, can increase or decrease over time. These changes in the original basis lead to a new or *adjusted basis*. This is the basis of the asset at any given time after the original acquisition. Adjusted basis is the original cost basis, *decreased* by the amount allowable for depletion, exhaustion, and wear and tear (*depreciation*) and *increased* by the amount of any additional investment made to improve or preserve the value of the asset.[4]

Table 3–1 shows a simple example of the calculation of adjusted basis.

**TABLE 3–1   Adjusted Basis**

| **Relinquished Property** | |
| --- | --- |
| 1. Original purchase price | $100,000 |
| 2. Less: Depreciation taken | (20,000) |
| 3. Additional capital investment added (new roof, copper piping) | 50,000 |
| 4. Adjusted basis (Line 1 minus Line 2, plus Line 3) | **$130,000** |

In the example shown in Table 3–1, the owner, Doug, purchased his building three years ago for $100,000. He has taken depreciation of $20,000, and he has made capital improvements in the amount of $50,000 to add value to the property. Therefore, Doug presently has an adjusted basis in his property of $130,000.

## Capital Gain/Capital Loss

A *capital gain* or *capital loss* is generated from the sale of a capital asset, such as a real estate investment. A capital gain or loss can be considered long-term or short-term, depending on how long the taxpayer owned the asset.[5] A short-term gain or loss results from the sale of an asset held for *no more than* one year. A long-term gain or loss results from the sale of an asset held for *longer than* one year. Long-term gains and losses are netted against each other, and short-term gains and losses are netted against each other. The maximum federal tax rate on long-term capital gains is currently 15 percent.[6] Short-term gains are taxed at ordinary income tax rates. There may also be state income taxes that are applicable.

## Carryover Basis

Code Section 1012 provides that the basis of property is its purchase price (its original cost), unless otherwise provided. For property acquired in a 1031 exchange, however, the basis to be employed is not the purchase price, but something called the *carryover basis*. The adjusted basis from the property that is sold (the relinquished property) is used to calculate the basis of the property that is acquired (the replacement property). Under Treasury Regulation 1.1031(d)–1(a), in an exchange where there is no boot received, the basis of the replacement property is the basis "carried over" from the relinquished property, which carryover basis may be increased by the amount of any additional consideration added by the taxpayer in the exchange at the time of the acquisition. Please refer to Table 3–2 for another example.

Recall the example in Table 3–1, where Doug originally paid $100,000 for Property A. Assume that three years later, as a result of improvements made to the property, it has an adjusted basis of $130,000 and has appreciated to a fair market value of $350,000. Assume that there is no mortgage debt.

**TABLE 3–2    Carryover Basis**

| Relinquished Property | |
| --- | --- |
| 1. Original purchase price | 100,000 |
| 2. Additional capital investment (new roof, copper piping) | 30,000 |
| 3. Adjusted basis (Line 1 plus Line 2) | **$130,000** |
| 4. Sale price | $350,000 |
| 5. Capital gain (Line 4 minus Line 3) | $220,000 |

| Replacement Property | |
| --- | --- |
| 6. Purchase price | $500,000 |
| 7. Carryover basis from above | $130,000 |
| 8. Additional capital added (consideration paid above sale price of Relinquished Property) | $150,000 |
| 9. New adjusted basis (Line 7 plus Line 8) | **$280,000** |

If Doug sold Property A, he would have a long-term capital gain of $220,000 ($350,000 minus $130,000). But instead of selling, Doug does a 1031 exchange, trading up and acquiring replacement Property B for $500,000. He will have a carryover basis in Property B of $280,000 [determined by adding $130,000 (his adjusted basis of relinquished Property A) and $150,000 (the additional consideration Doug added above the sale price of his relinquished property: $500,000 minus $350,000)].

In an exchange where there *is* boot received, the basis of property acquired in an exchange is the basis of the relinquished property, decreased by the amount of cash received by the taxpayer and increased by the amount of gain (or decreased by the amount of loss) recognized by the taxpayer in the exchange.[7] If the exchangor's mortgage on the relinquished property is assumed by the buyer of that property, it is treated as money received by the taxpayer (it is debt relief). This is called *boot netting*. (See Chapter 8 for more specific details.)

Sometimes a taxpayer acquires more than one replacement property. When multiple properties are acquired in an exchange, the carryover basis from the relinquished property is allocated among the replacement properties according to their respective fair market values. It can get even more complicated if you have multiple relinquished properties and multiple replacement properties.[8]

## Stepped-Up Basis

Basis can also change as a result of death. A *stepped-up basis* occurs when the owner of an asset dies and the asset is inherited by another party. The new basis will be the fair market value of the asset as of the date of death. An immediate sale of the property by the heir would therefore usually result in no gain or loss (and thus no need to do an exchange).[9]

Again using the facts of Table 3–1, Doug paid $100,000 for his property, and it currently has an adjusted basis of $130,000. If it can now be sold for $350,000, then Doug would have a capital gain of $220,000 if he were to sell. However, if Doug were to die without selling the property, and it is instead acquired by his heir, the heir would have a stepped-up basis of $350,000. If Doug's heir were then to sell the subject property immediately, he or she might have no gain to report and no tax to pay.

## Depreciation Recapture

Property owners are allowed a tax deduction for the "exhaustion, [and] wear and tear" of their property. We call this *depreciation*. Taxpayers engaging in 1031 exchanges need to be aware of special rules governing recapture of the depreciation deduction when their real estate is sold. Depreciation is governed by IRC Section 167. Taxpayers are often unaware that the depreciation taken in prior years must be *recaptured* as ordinary income in the tax year in which the sale of a depreciated asset occurs.[10] This can have a potentially large dollar impact if the asset has been held for many years, and thus the accumulated depreciation taken is substantial. (The actual rules and computations are complex and beyond the scope of this book. Discuss this issue with a tax advisor when applicable.)

The tax rate for recaptured depreciation is 25 percent—significantly higher than the tax rate for ordinary capital gains. Thus, if the taxpayer realizes a capital gain on the disposition of a depreciated asset, all or part of the gain must be reported as recaptured income, subject to tax at the higher recapture rate.[11]

The amount that must be recaptured is equal to the *lesser* of

- The total depreciation allowable on the asset (except that for home offices; this applies only to depreciation for periods after May 6, 1997)
- The total gain realized[12]

That means that if the total gain realized is more than the amount that must be recaptured, the excess may be reported as capital gain, at the maximum 15 percent rate, provided the asset has been held for more than one year. If the total depreciation deduction is greater than the gain realized, the entire amount of gain will be taxed at 25 percent.

All of the gain realized, including the recaptured depreciation, can be deferred if the taxpayer undertakes a 1031 exchange.[13] Nevertheless, there is a possible pitfall for the unwary. If the taxpayer elects to acquire a replacement property that cannot be depreciated (e.g., vacant land), the recaptured depreciation from the relinquished property cannot be deferred. It will still be subject to the higher recapture rate, notwithstanding the fact that the taxpayer met all the other requirements of a valid 1031 exchange.[14]

## Endnotes

1. IRC Section 1001(a), "Computation of Gain or Loss."
2. IRC Section 1001(b).
3. IRC Section 1012, which defines *basis*.
4. IRC Sections 1011 and 1016, which define *adjusted basis*.
5. IRC Section 1222.
6. IRC Section 1(h).
7. IRC Section 1031(d).
8. Reg. 1.1031(j)–1(c).
9. IRC Section 1014.
10. IRC Section 1250(a).
11. IRC Section 1(h)(1)(X).
12. IRC Section 1250(a)(1)(A).
13. IRC Section 1250(d)(4)(A).
14. IRC Section 1250(d)(4)(C).

CHAPTER

# Qualifying Property and Qualifying Use

*How do I know if my property will qualify for a 1031 exchange? And what can I buy in its place?*

These are two of the most common questions that arise. Only certain kinds of property will qualify for 1031 exchange treatment. Even with a qualifying property, how you use it can make a difference.

Qualifying property, for the purpose of Section 1031, is property that is either used in a trade or business or held for investment.[1] In order to qualify for an exchange, one must have a *qualifying property* and that property must be put to a *qualifying use*. Understanding which types of property qualify for 1031 exchange treatment and which do not is extremely important.

## Types of Property

Property is generally divided into two kinds: real property and personal property. Generally, *real property* is defined as land or structures affixed to land. Common examples are houses and condominiums, apartment buildings, warehouses, office buildings, and vacant land. It can also include mineral and timber rights.

*Personal property*, on the other hand, is generally movable. Examples are trucks, airplanes, railcars, livestock, and business equipment. Of course, some personal property is intangible, such as copyrights, stocks, bonds, and contract rights. Nearly all property that is not classified as real property is considered personal property. The same definition of qualifying property is applicable to personal property exchanges as to real property exchanges (i.e. property held for productive use in a trade or business, or for investment). (In Chapter 17, you will find a brief discussion of personal property exchanges.)

## Real Property

Real property is usually defined by the law of the state in which that property is situated. Occasionally, however, what qualifies as real property for state law purposes is not regarded as such by federal court rulings in tax cases. The kinds of property that can create questionable results are water and timber rights, oil and gas leases, and growing crops. There are a number of fact-specific rulings in these areas. As a general proposition, however, any qualifying real property can be exchanged for any other qualifying real property.[2]

## Types of Real Property Interests

Real property can be further divided into three classifications.

- **Fee Interests.** A *fee* interest, sometimes referred to as a *fee simple* interest, is not limited by time. A fee interest can involve subsurface rights,
  such as oil and mineral rights; surface rights; and even airspace rights.
  A fee interest is what is most typically acquired when one buys a piece
  of property.
- **Leasehold Interests.** A *leasehold* interest is a right to use a parcel of
  land or a portion of it (like an apartment or office space) for a limited
  period of time. A leasehold interest can have a term as short as a few
  days or be month-to-month, or it can represent a right to possession with
  a term extending for many years. Ordinarily leases are not like kind to
  fee title to real property. A typical leasehold would be considered
  personal property, although it represents an interest in real property—it
  has a dual nature. The IRS has determined that leases for terms of at least

30 years are considered real property and are like kind to fee title.[3,4] A 20-year lease that includes, in addition, two 5-year options to extend would similarly qualify. Be aware, however, that shorter-term leases may also be used in exchanges. A person can exchange property subject to a 10-year lease for replacement property that is also subject to a 10-year lease.[5]

- The question arises as to how similar the respective lease terms must be for the properties to be considered like kind. It is probable that a 3-year lease is not like kind to a 15-year lease, but a 14-year lease may be like kind to a 17-year lease. This is one of those gray areas mentioned earlier. When contemplating an exchange where this issue arises, a conversation with a knowledgeable tax advisor is necessary and appropriate.

- **Easements.** Easements may also qualify as 1031 property. An *easement* is a right to use a portion of a parcel belonging to someone else, usually for a specific and limited purpose. Most of us are familiar with power line easements belonging to utility companies, a neighbor's easement for a driveway, or an underground easement for extracting minerals.[6-9] In some limited cases, even easements may be exchanged. Consultation with a real estate attorney is recommended if you believe this situation may apply to you.

### Personal Property

Unlike real property, personal property is generally movable. Examples are trucks, airplanes, railcars, livestock, and business equipment. Qualifying personal property can be exchanged only for like-kind qualifying personal property. The like-kind requirement for personal property is much narrower and more restrictive than the requirement for real property. Only assets of the same asset class or product class are considered like-kind personal property. For example, a truck may be exchanged for a comparable truck, and a computer may be exchanged for another computer. But a truck can never be like kind to a computer, nor a horse to an airplane. (Chapter 17 explores this subject in more detail.)

## Qualifying Property

Many types of property will *qualify* for the purposes of accomplishing an exchange. Any property held for investment or used in a trade or business should qualify. Typically, an exchange will involve a rental house or condominium, an apartment building, an office building, a retail store or shopping center, or even unimproved land. An exchange can also involve an undivided fractional interest in any of the foregoing as well.

Exchanges may involve real property, personal property, or both. Some examples involving both real and personal property would be hotels and motels, or perhaps a manufacturing business where the sale includes both types if property—both land and buildings and the business fixtures, furniture and equipment. In those cases, the exchangor must separately enumerate and value the items of real and personal property being traded in order to ensure that he or she acquires like-kind replacement property of each relinquished property type of sufficient value to have a successful exchange.

In a very recent and novel case that was decided in favor of the taxpayer, gold mines were swapped for coal mines.[10] The issue was not whether you could exchange one mine for another. You could. However, because the coal mines were subject to supply contracts, there was a question as to whether they were like kind to mines that were not subject to such contracts. The court decided that the contract restrictions affected only the grade or quality of the asset and did not alter its class. So, in the event that you own a gold mine, be aware that you can do an exchange!

## Property That Does Not Qualify

Not all property will qualify. Property that is held not for investment, but rather for personal use and enjoyment, will not qualify. The best example of this is your personal residence.[11] Foreign-located property or property acquired for a quick resale will not meet the "held for investment" requirement and will not qualify (see the section "Holding Periods and Investment Intent" later in the chapter).

Section 1031(a)(2) specifically enumerates certain other types of assets that cannot be exchanged. They are:

1. Stock in trade or other property held primarily for resale[12]
2. Stocks, bonds, and notes
3. Other securities or evidences of indebtedness or interest
4. Interests in partnerships

5. Certificates of trust or beneficial interests
6. Choses in action

Section 1031(a)(2) further explains that one cannot exchange an interest in real estate for shares of stock in a real estate investment trust (REIT), or an interest in real estate for an interest in a partnership or LLC that owns real estate.

As previously mentioned, 1031 exchanges are often referred to as "like-kind exchanges." Reg. 1.1031(a)–1(b) defines *like kind* as having "reference to the nature or character of the property and not to its grade or quality." It goes on to state that whether real property is "improved or unimproved is not material, for that fact relates only to the grade or quality of the property and not to its kind or class."

For purposes of Section 1031, qualifying property is defined as property used in a trade or business or held for investment; this definition arises from another section of the Internal Revenue Code, Section 1231(b). As stated earlier, any qualifying real property can be exchanged for any other qualifying real property. Examples of this include an apartment building exchanged for vacant land and a rental house exchanged for an office building. These differences involve only the grade or quality of the property, not its kind or class.

Section 1031 also requires that qualifying property be located in the United States. Since Section 1031 is federal law, exchanges of properties located in different states are acceptable. Exchanges of foreign property for U.S. property or foreign property for foreign property do not work. The IRS has ruled that property located in the U.S. Virgin Islands is like kind to property located within the United States for exchange purposes.[13] More recently, the IRS has also held that property in Guam and the Northern Marianas Islands could be exchanged.[14]] (However, as of this writing, property located in Puerto Rico or American Samoa does not qualify.)

Exchanges are not limited to tangible property. In an interesting but uncommon ruling, the IRS ruled that a taxpayer could exchange its FCC *radio* broadcast station license for an FCC *television* broadcast station license.[15] The IRS has also ruled that trades of player contracts owned by professional football teams would be considered exchanges of like-kind property.[16] (However, as noted earlier, except in specific instances, this book will focus for the most part on real property exchanges.)

## Qualifying Use

Does a vacation home or second home fall within the purview of the qualifying property definition? The question raises the second factor necessary for qualification, which is a *qualifying use*. Just as with a personal residence, if the property does not generate any rental income, or if it is not held primarily for the production of rental income, it is not going to qualify as property used in a trade or business. It does not have a qualifying use.

But can one make the argument that the second home is held for investment or held for appreciation in value? The IRS approved an exchange in which the taxpayers exchanged property that they claimed to use approximately 10 days per year for a like property.[17] The taxpayers did not rent out their property, but testified that it was held strictly for appreciation in value and "personal enjoyment of the community." This last reference in quotes is a bit confusing. The Tax Court has ruled that where the replacement property consisted of a two-week timeshare, intended at the time for *personal use*, it would not qualify.[18]

Whether or not a vacation or second home qualifies under Section 1031 is determined using a facts and circumstances test. This is another one of those gray areas. The IRS will always look at the taxpayer's intent at the time of purchase. It will look at the amount of actual use by the taxpayer and his or her family, compared to the amount of time the property was rented out or offered for rent. The IRS will also look at the taxpayer's other real estate investments and activities. In one case, the taxpayer testified that he purchased his mother's personal residence from her both to help her and with the intent to "turn a profit on the deal."[19] The court found that the taxpayer's primary purpose in purchasing the house was to make a profit. This was not an exchange case, but nonetheless the reasoning is applicable.

Taxpayers who intend to engage in a 1031 exchange where either the relinquished property or the replacement property is used as a vacation or second home should be prepared to prove that their primary intent in holding the property was for appreciation in value. They should document their use of the property, or lack thereof. They should also expect to be audited on this issue.

IRC Section 280A deals with the deductibility of certain expenses when the taxpayers' personal residence also has a business use, but this section is also relevant in connection with determining the qualification of vacation home property for 1031 purposes. Subsection (d) defines personal use of the dwelling unit as use for more than 14 days per year or more than 10 percent of the time it is used as a rental unit, which is a good guideline to use if you own this type of property.

## Options to Buy Property

An option to buy real estate is generally considered a contract right involving real property. Therefore, it can be exchanged.[20,21] However, depending upon whether the option is characterized as real or personal property, the like-kind aspect can become an issue. If an option is deemed to be real property in the state in which the underlying property is located, the option itself can be exchanged for a fee interest. For example, in Colorado, there is a statute that specifically provides that an option to purchase real property is an interest in real property.[22] However, if an option is characterized as personal property in the state in which the property is situated, it is very likely that it can be exchanged only for another option to purchase real property.

# Multiple Property Exchanges

More than one replacement property can be purchased with the exchange money. An exchange can involve more than one relinquished property and more than one replacement property. One exchange can include multiple relinquished properties with one replacement or one relinquished property with multiple replacements. An exchange can also involve a combination of multiple properties on both legs of the transaction.[23]

It is imperative to determine at the outset if an exchange involving multiple relinquished properties is truly a single exchange or a series of several separate exchanges. If there is only one exchange, then the identification period will begin with the closing date of the first property sold. The amount of replacement property to be identified and the method of identification (as you will see in Chapter 10) will be limited accordingly.

When multiple replacement properties are acquired in an exchange, the basis of each must be determined. The adjusted basis of the relinquished property will be allocated among the several replacement properties according to their respective fair market values.[24,25] The same general rule applies when there are both multiple relinquished properties and multiple replacement properties. The computation is a two-step process, where the first step requires computing the aggregate adjusted basis of all relinquished properties. The second step requires allocation of the determined carryover basis to the replacement properties.

## Example

Arline owns two properties, each of which has substantial equity. Arline wishes to exchange into two larger properties with more leverage. Assume the following facts:

|  | Relinquished Property A | Relinquished Property B |
|---|---|---|
| Fair market value: | $1,000,000 | $1,500,000 |
| Debt: | $300,000 | $500,000 |
| Equity: | $700.000 | $1,000,000 |
| Adjusted Basis: | $150,000 | $200,000 |

Arline is selling properties with an aggregate fair market value of $2,500,000, aggregate adjusted bases of $350,000, and aggregate debt of $800,000.

Now assume that Arline identifies two replacement properties to purchase, Property C and Property D, with an aggregate fair market value of $5,500,000, as shown here. She must allocate her basis in the two new properties proportionally to their values. As a consequence, the carryover bases in these properties will be determined as follows:

|  | Replacement Property C | Replacement Property D |
|---|---|---|
| Fair market value: | $2,500,000 | $3,000,000 |
| Debt: | $1,700,000 | $2,100,000 |
| Equity: | $800,000 | $900,000 |
| Carryover Basis: | $159,091 | $190,909 |
| New adjusted basis: | $1,659,091 | $1,690,909 |

There can also be multiple exchanges involving a mixture of real and personal property. In this situation, the assets are first segregated into classes of like-kind property called *exchange groups*,[26] then they are treated as if there were separate exchanges between each grouping of assets. This scenario is not uncommon for exchangors who are active in the hotel or motel field, or those who are buying and selling businesses involving different kinds of equipment.[27,28]

## Holding Periods and Investment Intent

Recall that qualifying property is property that is *held* for productive use in a trade or business, or for investment. Note the emphasis on the word *held*. Remember that this definition is applicable to both the property that is being sold and the property that is to be purchased.

A frequent concern of taxpayers is the length of time that a property must be held if it is to qualify for exchange treatment. Unfortunately, there is no definitive answer. This is another of those many gray areas of 1031 law. Basically, the taxpayer must hold the property for a sufficient length of time to demonstrate "investment intent." The IRS has ruled that a taxpayer who acquired a ranch solely for the purpose of exchanging it for another ranch did not satisfy the holding period requirement, and as to him, the exchange failed.[29]

Here is the authors' rough rule of thumb on holding periods:

- *Less than one year.* There is a high risk that the exchange could be found invalid, requiring you to pay all the tax you thought you had deferred, plus interest and penalties, if any.
- *More than two years.* The risk of invalidity is low. The IRS has ruled that a rental house acquired with the intent to sell immediately would not qualify; but when the request for a ruling was resubmitted with the facts changed so that the taxpayer would hold the house for at least two years, the IRS issued a favorable ruling on the exchange.[30]
- *Between one and two years.* There is some risk that the exchange could be disallowed.

This issue is really a dual one. First, a determination must be made as to whether the relinquished property has been held long enough to qualify under the statutory definition. If the exchangors are already under contract to sell the subject property before they even acquire title (in other words, if they are "flipping" the property), it is difficult to argue that they had investment intent at the time of acquisition.

Second, how long must the taxpayer hold onto the replacement property after the exchange for that property (and thus the entire exchange) to qualify? In an IRS audit, the taxpayer has the burden of proof to establish the validity of the transaction reported on the tax return. If the taxpayer has sold the replacement property shortly after its acquisition, the taxpayer's intent may be suspect. If the taxpayer can establish a valid business reason for such a short holding period for the replacement property, however, the transaction may indeed qualify for exchange treatment. This is a "facts and circumstances" test.

The taxpayer's intent regarding the holding period is viewed as of the date of acquisition of the replacement property. Since intent is a subjective state of mind, proof of intent can be difficult. A reasonable explanation for a short holding period might be that since the acquisition, the taxpayer has been unable to rent the replacement property and is suffering a financial hardship as a result. Likewise, a taxpayer could discover facts about the property that make it undesirable for that investor to continue to hold it for its intended use (say it has mold).

Another example where a good argument could be made to support a short holding period might be a case in which the taxpayer originally intended to operate his business from the property. Upon filing an application for a business license, he discovers that he cannot obtain the license because the zoning has recently been changed and no longer allows that type of business use.

A more problematic scenario is the so-called receipt of an unsolicited "offer too good to refuse." It does happen from time to time, but if a taxpayer finds himself or herself in that situation, he or she should be prepared to document all the facts to show that the intent as of the date of acquisition was to retain and use the property for an extended period of time.[31]

## Endnotes

1. IRC Section 1031(a)(1).
2. Reg. 1.1031(a)–1(a) states: "Under section 1031(a)(1), property held for productive use in a trade or business may be exchanged for property held

for investment. Similarly, under section 1031(a)(1), property held for investment may be exchanged for property held for productive use in a trade or business."

3. See Treas. Reg. 1.1031(a)–1(c).

4. PLR 9149018.

5. *Cary A. Everett*, TC Memo 1978–53 (2/13/78), where the court approved an exchange of three timber leases of six-year, six-year, and three-year duration for leases of ten-year duration. The court also discussed the issue of whether the taxpayer was holding property for sale, since he had also granted an option to sell to a third party.

6. Rev. Rul. 55–749, 1955–2 CB 295; the IRS concluded that where, under the law of that state, perpetual water rights are considered an interest in real property, they could be exchanged for a fee interest in land.

7. Rev. Rul. 72–549, 1972–2 CB 472; the IRS found that a permanent right-of-way easement granted to an electric utility could be exchanged for an apartment building.

8. PLR 200203042 (January 19, 2002); the IRS ruled that a perpetual conservation easement, which was deemed an interest in real property under local law, could be exchanged for a ranch.

9. PLR 8334026 approved the exchange of a conservation easement for adjoining marshland.

10. *Peabody Natural Resources* (2006) 126 TC No. 14.

11. PLR 8915012 (1/5/88); the IRS ruled that a house intended to be used as a personal residence would not qualify.

12. See the extensive examination of factors to determine the seller's intent in *Neal T. Baker Enterprises, Inc. v. Commissioner,* TC Memo 1998–302 (8/19/1998).

13. PLR 200040017.

14. Reg.1.935–1T.

15. Technical Advice Memorandum (TAM) 200035005 (5/11/00).

16. Rev. Rul. 71–137, 1971–1 CB 104.

17. PLR 8103117.

18. *Dewey v. Commissioner*, TC Memo 1993–645 (12/30/93).

19. *Jefferson v. Commissioner,* 50 TC 963 (9/26/68).

20. *Starker v. U.S.,* 602 F2d 1341 (CA9 1979).

21. *Biggs v. Commissioner*, 632 F2d 1171 (CA5 1980).

22. CRS 38–25–111.
23. Reg. 1.1031(j)–1 governs exchanges of multiple properties.
24. Reg. 1.1031(j)–1(c).
25. Rev. Rul. 68–36, 1968–1 CB 357.
26. Reg. 1.1031(j)–1(a).
27. See PLR 200109022 for a complicated multiple property exchange program approved by the IRS.
28. See PLRs 9627014 and 9447008, which deal with exchanges of groups of vehicles.
29. Rev. Rul. 77–297, 1977–2 CB 304.
30. PLR 8429039 (4/17/84).
31. See *Loren F. Pallus, et ux et al. v. Commissioner*, TC-Memo 1996–419 (9/17/96) for an excellent analysis by the court on the issue of whether property was held for investment or for resale.

C  H  A  P  T  E  R

# Vesting Issues and Entity Structures That May Affect Exchanges

*Does it matter how I take title to the property I am buying? Can I buy using an LLC? What if my wife and I set up a living trust to hold our property?*

One requirement for a valid 1031 exchange is the so-called same taxpayer requirement. For individuals, this is generally not a major issue. When a taxpayer is using an entity, however, it is necessary to take care. The form that the real estate transaction takes (not just its substance) is important in a 1031 exchange.

## Vesting Generally

*Vesting* is an important concept in real estate generally, and in 1031 exchanges specifically. Vesting is the manner in which title to property is held. To *vest* is to place ownership in, or to give control of an asset to, a specific person or entity. 1031 law limits taxpayers' ability to change vesting during the course of an exchange.

Each state has its own real property laws, which will govern the manner in which title can be taken to some extent. Common ways in which *individuals* may vest title to their property include the following:

• A single person
• Husband and wife as joint tenants
• Husband and wife as community property
• Husband and wife as tenants by the entirety
• Tenants in common

Real estate can also be owned by *entities*. Corporations, partnerships, limited partnerships, limited liability companies (LLCs), estates, and trusts are all considered "persons" under the law. They have most of the same rights and capacities that individuals have. Entities are created under enabling statutes of the various states. Those state laws govern the rights, abilities, and obligations of these entities. The entities can own real or personal property in their own names; that is, property may be vested in their names. Individuals create and utilize entities for a variety of tax and nontax reasons. Corporations and other entities even create other entities, often called *subsidiaries*, to engage in real estate activities. Legally, entities are "persons" that are separate and distinct from their shareholders, members, or partners, as the case may be. Entities can also do 1031 exchanges.

For taxpayers who own property in any type of entity, there are special planning considerations that can affect if and how an exchange can be done. A few common property-holding entities, such as trusts, partnerships, and limited liability companies, are called *pass-through* entities because income and expenses (like rental income or a utility expense) are not taxed to the entity that owns the asset; instead, they are reported pro rata by the owners of the entity. An S corporation is also a pass-through entity, but a C corporation is not.

Each U.S. taxpayer, whether an individual or an entity, is defined by a taxpayer identification number that is used on that taxpayer's tax returns, whether it be the social security number or some other federal tax identification number. Just as each natural person has a unique social security number, each taxable entity has a unique taxpayer identification number.

The most important thing to remember when evaluating vesting in connection with your exchange is that the ownership vesting on your relinquished property and the ownership vesting on your replacement property must be the same. This is because the taxpayer who is doing the exchange must be both the seller of the relinquished property and the buyer of the replacement property. For example, if Wendy owns her relinquished property in her own name, she cannot acquire replacement property in the Wendy Corporation. That would be a different taxpayer.

## Timing on Vesting Changes

A vesting change, as used here, refers to a change in how the taxpayer is acquiring the replacement property relative to the way the relinquished property was vested at or immediately prior to the time of sale. As a general rule, there cannot be a change in taxpayers. In addition, if there is a vesting change immediately before the closing of a sale or immediately after the closing of a purchase, the exchange may be jeopardized. For example, if Wendy held title to property in the name of her corporation, deeded the property to herself as an individual, and then sold the property in an exchange, she, as an individual, may not have held title long enough for the property to qualify for 1031 treatment. Wendy's corporation, not Wendy, was the owner of the investment, reporting the property income on its own separate tax return and taking the deductions. The courts have occasionally allowed exchanges on properties immediately after acquisition from related entities.[1,2] However, the reader is urged to exercise caution in making any such changes.

Likewise, if Wendy acquires her replacement property in her corporation, which is the way she owned and sold her relinquished property, but then she immediately deeds it to herself as an individual or to another entity, she will not be reporting the (income and expenses of the) new property to the IRS as the same taxpayer.[3,4]

Avoid changing the vesting on property bought or sold during the exchange process. (This sounds deceptively simple, but in practice it often creates problems for taxpayers.) Any vesting change must not involve a change in the actual taxpayer doing the exchange.

## Changes Involving Spouses

Typically a husband and wife will hold title as joint tenants, tenants in common, tenants by the entirety, or community property. But property can also be the separate property of one spouse or the other. If a husband and wife both own the relinquished property, then they should *both* acquire the replacement property. If only one owned the relinquished property, that same one should acquire the replacement property solely in his or her name.

Sometimes credit problems or other issues will prevent one of the spouses from being able to acquire title to a property. This can potentially create problems in a 1031 context. In a Private Letter Ruling, the IRS ruled that where both spouses sold a piece of property, then divorced, and only the husband purchased replacement property, the wife was taxed on 50 percent of the gain because she did not acquire any replacement property.[5]

Moreover, a husband and wife cannot sell their relinquished property and then acquire title to replacement property in the name of a corporation—that is a different taxpayer. They will not own the replacement property; rather, they will be acquiring an interest in the stock of a corporation that actually owns the property. The stock of a corporation is not like kind to the real property that they sold. The husband and wife must hold direct title to the replacement property in their individual names, exactly as they sold.

## Effect of the Death of the Taxpayer during the Exchange

If a taxpayer, having commenced an exchange, dies after the closing of his or her relinquished property, the taxpayer's estate must complete the exchange to avoid taxation.[6,7] The individual heirs of the deceased exchangor cannot complete the exchange, because they did not sell the relinquished property. The heirs are not the same taxpayer as the deceased exchangor.[8]

## Permissible Vesting Changes

The foregoing notwithstanding, certain entities can be ignored for 1031 exchange purposes. The most typical of these are single-member limited liability companies ("LLCs") and revocable grantor trusts, often called "living trusts." This is not so much a gray area as it is a confusing one. Both revocable grantor trusts and some, but not all, single-member LLCs are considered *disregarded entities* by the IRS, because the IRS allows the qualifying taxpayer to so elect.[9] These are not considered separate entities for federal tax purposes. Thus, title to your replacement property may be acquired in the name of a single-member LLC even if you sold the relinquished property in your own name. And a husband and wife could sell as joint tenants or community property and then acquire replacement property in their revocable living trust, or vice versa.

Also, two or more tenants in common may sell relinquished property and then acquire separate replacement properties because tenants in common do not constitute a recognizable entity. *Tenancy in common* is a way for two or more people to hold title to property, but it is not a separate tax entity like an LLC or a corporation. Tenants in common each file their own individual tax returns under their own tax identification numbers or social security numbers.

## Partnerships

People who own an interest in a partnership are called "partners." Partnerships come in two varieties, general partnerships and limited partnerships. The following discussion applies to both types. Sometimes taxpayers own property as tenants in common, but refer to themselves colloquially as "partners." There is a critical tax difference between a partnership (an entity) and a tenancy in common (a manner of holding title, but not an entity). Sometimes title is vested one way, but the owners have been reporting the income and expenses to the IRS in a different manner. This discrepancy needs to be discussed with a competent tax advisor before commencing an exchange.

## Partnerships May Do Exchanges

As stated earlier, a partnership is not taxed as an entity; instead, the income and expenses of the partnership are passed through to the individual partners and reported on their individual tax returns (Form 1040). However, for the purpose of a 1031 exchange, a partnership is a recognized legal entity, separate from its individual partners, with its own taxpayer identification number. It consists of two or more people who join together for the purpose of carrying on a business, financial operation, or venture in a noncorporate setting. A partnership is an entity in which people commonly acquire and own property.

A partnership may certainly take advantage of the provisions of Section 1031. For example, if a partnership has owned an apartment building for several years, it may elect to exchange it for another apartment building in a better neighborhood or with more rental units. The exchangor in this case is the partnership itself. The exchange documents will be executed by the general partner(s), acting on behalf of the entity. The partnership will file a Form 8824 with its informational return, Form 1065, to report the exchange. The partners do not report the exchange on their individual returns.

## Distinction between Partnerships and the Individual Partners

Be aware that there is a difference between a partnership that owns real estate and the partners in that partnership who own the partnership interests. The partnership has a *direct* ownership interest in the underlying real estate (it is vested on title), while the partners are considered to have an *indirect* ownership interest in the real estate (they are not on title; they own interests in the partnership). An individual partner may *not* exchange his or her interest in a particular partnership for an interest in a different partnership. This is strictly prohibited by Section 1031(a)(2)(D).

An issue often arises when partners have held their real estate investment in a partnership format for some time and have reached a point where they want to separate their interests and acquire different properties, or when some partners want to "cash out." Partnerships will frequently elect to dissolve after they have already contracted to sell their property. In partnership dissolution, the partnership distributes to each partner his or her pro rata interest in each of the partnership's assets. This creates a problem if one or more of the partners were contemplating engaging in a 1031 exchange. Typically, the dissolving partnership distributes the partnership assets to the partners on a pro rata basis; the individual partners take their proportionate shares of the partnership property as tenants in common and then immediately sell the subject property to the buyer with whom the partnership is already under contract. The 1031 compliance problem is that the individual partners did not hold the subject property for any length of time, but rather acquired it with the intent to sell it (to the already-contracted-with buyer). The IRS has yet to rule on whether it will tack the partnership holding period onto the individual partners' ownership and allow a 1031 exchange under these circumstances. At present, this is a very risky approach. In one TAM (Tax Advice Memorandum), the IRS ruled against distribution and immediate sale.[10]

However, there is a contrary opinion from the IRS. In this case, under threat of condemnation, a partner negotiated a sale to the condemning authority; one month later, the partnership distributed property to the partners, and 18 days after that, the individual partners entered into an agreement for sale to the condemning authority. The IRS upheld the transaction.[11]

In another case, a partnership sold relinquished property, but had replacement property deeded directly to partners in liquidation of their partnership interests. This was found *not* to be a valid exchange.[12]

## Corporations

A corporation is another type of recognized legal entity. It is like a partnership, but it has shareholders instead of partners. Regular corporations are called C corporations, while smaller corporations with special rules are called S corporations. The tax rules governing corporations are very complicated and are beyond the scope of this book. Also, the tax consequences of dissolving a corporation are much more complicated than those of dissolving a partnership.

A corporation may also take advantage of the provisions of Section 1031. In large corporations, it is common to exchange retail locations, manufacturing plants, or other types of properties used in the trade or business. However, a corporate shareholder may not exchange his or her shares in a corporation for shares in a different corporation. This is strictly prohibited by Section 1031(a)(2)(B). Nor can a shareholder exchange his or her shares in a corporation for a direct interest in real property. As a very general rule, a corporation is not a particularly advantageous way for individuals to own real estate.

## Limited Liability Companies

A limited liability company ("LLC") is a relatively new type of entity. People who own interests in an LLC are called "members." An LLC may have one member or multiple members. If there are two or more members, it is generally taxed and treated like a partnership, although in some circumstances it can be taxed like a corporation. An LLC is a type of entity in which people commonly acquire and own real property. It is not treated as an entity for federal tax purposes unless the members elect to have it taxed like a corporation.

In addition, states have varying laws with respect to the creation and taxation of LLCs. An LLC may also take advantage of the provisions of Section 1031.

There are special rules for single-member limited liability companies (SMLLCs). Their status as an entity is *disregarded* by the IRS.[13] A husband and wife who hold their ownership in an LLC as their community property, and who are the sole members, may elect to be taxed either as a disregarded entity or as a partnership.[14] Inasmuch as LLCs are creatures of state law and not federal law, it is important to check with a lawyer in the state in which you want to form the LLC to see what special rules may exist, especially with respect to single-member LLCs and husband-and-wife LLCs.

A single-*asset* LLC is not necessarily the same as a single-*member* LLC. Single-asset LLCs are popular among lending institutions when lending on investment real estate assets. They are referred to as *special-purpose entities*, or *SPEs*, because they often exist for the sole purpose of holding a single asset and are considered "bankruptcy remote." Essentially, that means that if the owner of the LLC files for bankruptcy, the asset owned by the SPE will not be subject to the same restrictions as other assets of the bankrupt person, and the lender will therefore have less risk of loss.[15]

A conflict may arise when several individuals are joining together to purchase one asset as tenants in common in order to satisfy their individual 1031 requirements, and the lender is insisting that the asset be owned by a single LLC. This issue can become the subject of much negotiation.

The IRS has allowed one way to avoid the problem.[16] An exchange was approved where the replacement property was acquired by multiple parties, but each party took title to his or her own interest in his or her separately formed LLC, rather than all of them taking title in one larger LLC.

## Trusts

There are various types of trusts. They are created for a variety of different reasons. Land trusts are a special case and will be discussed separately in a later section of this chapter. A common estate-planning type of trust is the revocable living trust. Generally, the person who created this type of trust will use his or her own social security number when dealing with trust assets. As long as the grantor (or both grantors in the case of a husband and wife) is still living, the trust will be disregarded for tax purposes and is treated as if the trust assets were owned directly by the grantor(s).

After the death of the grantor, these trusts generally become irrevocable, and they then have different tax consequences (including a requirement that they have separate tax identification numbers and must file their own tax returns). Other types of trusts include life insurance trusts, charitable remainder trusts, testamentary trusts, and qualified personal residence trusts. (A tax advisor should be consulted if a trust other than a simple grantor-type trust is to be involved in an exchange.) In most cases, these latter kinds of trust are not disregarded entities. If they sell property in an exchange, they must acquire replacement property in their own name.

## Tenancies in Common (TICs)

A tenancy in common is a method of owning a fractional share or partial share of property with another person or entity. The more traditional type of tenancy in common consists of two or more individuals, each owning a specific percentage interest in real property, in an arrangement that is not a partnership or other legal entity, although they may informally refer to one another as their "partners." The ownership need not be equal; the respective owners' percentages could be 50–50, 25–35–40, or even 90–5–5. The number of tenants in common is not limited to any set amount. In a tenancy in common situation, one or more or even all of the owners can enter into one or more exchanges and then purchase replacement property together or separately.

For example, Alicia and Carlos could sell a property in which they owned 60 percent and 40 percent, respectively. They could buy one replacement property together, or each of them could acquire separate replacement properties. This type of tenancy in common generally involves a group of individuals, all of whom know each other and cooperate to manage their property. However, see Chapter 12 for a further discussion of professionally organized and managed tenancies in common, typically referred to today as "TICs."

## Additional Nonentity Types of Ownership

Joint tenancy, or joint tenancy with right of survivorship, is a type of vesting similar to tenancy in common. In this type of vesting, however, if an owner dies, his or her interest is automatically passed on to the remaining, living owner(s). Joint tenants are not required to be married or related to one another.

Some states, primarily those that were once under Mexican ownership (Texas and California, for example), have a form of ownership called *community property*. A husband and wife who acquire property together in a community property state hold it in that form of vesting. It is similar but not identical to joint tenancy. A tenancy by the entirety is another way for a husband and wife to hold property. The difference is in how each individual spouse can deal with his or her interest. Each state has its own laws covering the various types of vesting available in that state. If a taxpayer owning property in any of these manners wants to do an exchange, that person may acquire replacement property in his or her own name.

## Cooperative Apartments

A cooperative apartment (a *co-op*) is a special structure established to hold ownership of some apartment buildings in some states. It is very similar to a condominium. Co-ops are found most commonly in New York City and a few other jurisdictions. Ownership of a co-op is evidenced by a stock certificate, not a grant deed. However, the IRS allows co-op ownership to be treated as a real property interest, not an interest in corporate stock. A co-op interest may be exchanged for fee title to real estate.[17,18]

## Land Contracts

A land contract is a security device wherein a seller contracts to sell his or her property to the buyer and actually delivers possession to the buyer, but with the understanding that title (a deed) will not be delivered until the property is fully paid for. How is this form of ownership treated by the IRS for 1031 purposes?

Under federal tax law, the date on which a sale actually occurs may depend on the facts and circumstances of the particular transaction. There are several cases that spell out the factors that the courts look at in order to make the proper determination.[19–21]

In most cases, the date on which the parties execute the land sales contract and/or possession is delivered to the buyer should be the date used for purposes of commencing the 45-day identification period and the 180-day exchange period. When a seller has previously entered into a land sales contract with a buyer, that seller should not assume that he or she can commence the 1031 exchange at the later date when he or she actually transfers title, but should use the earlier date when the contract is signed and possession is actually delivered. Sellers using a land sales contract might also consider reporting their sale under IRC Section 453 (Installment Sales) rather than attempting to utilize Section 1031.

## Land Trusts

Land trusts are a special method of holding title to real property. In Rev. Rul. 92–105, the IRS ruled that a taxpayer's interest in an Illinois land trust constituted an interest in real property that would qualify for a 1031 exchange. The ruling notes that several states have land-holding trusts similar to those in Illinois, including California, Florida, Hawaii, Indiana, North Dakota, and Virginia. It goes on to state that the ruling also applies to "similar arrangements" wherein (1) the trustee holds title to the property, (2) the beneficiary has the exclusive right to direct or control the trustee, and (3) the beneficiary has the exclusive right to the earnings and proceeds from the property and the obligation to pay the taxes and obligations of the property.

## TICs, DSTs, and REITs

Tenancies in common (TICs), Delaware statutory trusts (DSTs), and real estate investment trusts (REITs) are additional ways in which title to real property or other assets may be held. There are various business reasons for selecting one of them over the others. (Transactions involving exchanges using these types of ownership are covered in Chapter 12.)

*Authors' Note:* Keep in mind that the various types of vesting can have different implications for a party contemplating doing a 1031 exchange. Consult a knowledgeable professional if you have questions about your specific facts and circumstances.

## Endnotes

1. *Bolker v. Commissioner,* 760 F2d 1039 (9th Cir 1985).
2. *Miles H. Mason,* TC Memo aff'd. 880 F2d 420 (11th Cir 1989).

3. *Magneson v. Commissioner,* 753 F2d 1490 (9<sup>th</sup> Cir. 1985), wherein the court upheld an exchange that was immediately followed by a transfer of title.
4. *Bonny B. Maloney,* 93 TC 89 (1989), wherein the court upheld an exchange immediately followed by a transfer of title.
5. PLR 8429004.
6. Rev. Rul. 64–161; *In re Goodman's Estate,* 199 F2d 985 (3rd Cir 1952).
7. *Estate of Gregg v. Commissioner,* 69 TC 468 (1977).
8. *Estate of Jayne v. Commissioner,* 61 TC 744 (1974).
9. Reg. 301.7701–3(a).
10. TAM 9645005 (11/08/96), where, in a 1033 context, the IRS held that a partner in a joint venture could not defer gain when property was distributed to him the day before a condemnation sale's closing.
11. PLR 9022037, also a 1033 case.
12. TAM 9818003.
13. Reg. 301.7701–2(c)(2).
14. Rev. Proc. 2002–69 (10/09/02).
15. PLR 199911033 (3/22/99).
16. PLR 98070013 (2/13/98).
17. PLR 8810034.
18. PLR 200137032.
19. *Keith v. Commissioner,* 115 TC 605, 611 (2000); this ruling held that a sale occurs when the benefits and burdens of ownership transfer from seller to buyer.
20. See *Dettmers v. Commissioner,* 430 F2d 1019 (6th Cir 1970), which focuses on the transfer of the "benefits and burdens" of ownership to determine if a sale has occurred.
21. *Grodt & McKay Realty, Inc.,* 77 TC 1221 (1981) focuses on the transfer of the "benefits and burdens" of ownership to determine if a sale has occurred.

# Role of the Qualified Intermediary

*Once you have decided to do an exchange, how do you get started?*

Most taxpayers who engage in a 1031 exchange use the services of a qualified intermediary. Understanding the qualified intermediary's role in the exchange is very important. Picking a competent qualified intermediary is critical.

## Types of Safe Harbors

It is important to conduct an exchange using a safe harbor. A safe harbor ensures that your exchange will comply with all the IRS rules and regulations. Treasury Regulation 1.1031(k)–1(g) establishes four so-called safe harbors, or 1031 structures, "the use of which will result in a determination that the taxpayer is not in actual or constructive receipt of money or other property."

*Authors' Note:* It is theoretically possible to do a "non-safe harbor" exchange that complies with the Code, but does not necessarily comply with these regulations. However, it is certainly not recommended.

One safe harbor covers arrangements that secure or guarantee a taxpayer's exchange funds before they are used to acquire the replacement property. The regulations under Section 1031 state that the exchangor's money may be secured with a mortgage or deed of trust (presumably on property owned by the party holding the funds), by a standby letter of credit (which may be drawn on only in the event of default), or a by third-party guarantee.[1]

A second safe harbor has to do with qualified escrow accounts and qualified trust accounts established to hold the taxpayer's funds. In a qualified escrow account, the escrow holder cannot be the taxpayer or a disqualified person. The qualified escrow account must restrict the taxpayer's access to the funds. (This is explained more fully later in this chapter.) In a qualified trust account, the trustee cannot be the taxpayer or a disqualified person. The trust agreement must restrict the taxpayer's access to his or her funds.

A third safe harbor has to do with the payment of interest, or a growth factor, to the taxpayer. This type of safe harbor is discussed in more detail in Chapter 20.

## Qualified Intermediary as Safe Harbor

The fourth safe harbor, and the most common, sets forth the requirements for exchanges using qualified intermediaries. This is a simple way to ensure that the taxpayer has no actual or constructive receipt of the exchange proceeds, which includes actual receipt by an agent of the taxpayer. Examples of agents of the taxpayer include his or her attorney, accountant, and real estate broker. In order to avoid having the qualified intermediary be deemed an agent of the taxpayer, the regulations mandate what the intermediary can and cannot do. As long as both the taxpayer and the qualified intermediary comply with the safe harbor provisions of the 1031 Regulations, the intermediary will not be considered the agent of the exchangor. The qualified intermediary can be neither the taxpayer nor a disqualified person.

The qualified intermediary, pursuant to the current regulations,

> enters into a written agreement with the taxpayer (the "exchange agreement") and, as required by the exchange agreement, acquires the relinquished property from the taxpayer, transfers the relinquished property, acquires the replacement property, and transfers the replacement property to the taxpayer.[2]

These are the statutory obligations of the qualified intermediary.

Note that the starting point is a written agreement between the parties. Properly documenting the exchange is critical to achieving an exchange that satisfies all of the legal and technical requirements.[3,4]

Notwithstanding this rather straightforward language, the qualified intermediary is not required to take title to any real estate. However, the qualified intermediary must "orchestrate" the series of property transfers. There can be direct deeding between the titled parties. There are IRS Revenue Rulings that provide authority for deeding from the seller of the replacement property directly to the exchangor/taxpayer.[5] This rule has at least two further benefits, in addition to its administrative ease: it avoids the cost of double documentary or transfer taxes when recording deeds, and it also avoids having the qualified intermediary appear in the chain of title, thereby preventing possible liability arising from any environmental or other kinds of problems with the replacement property.

Although the qualified intermediary does not usually "go on title," it must still become a party to the exchange. As the taxpayer, your rights under the contract to sell the relinquished property or to purchase the replacement property must be assigned to the qualified intermediary, and the other parties to the respective transactions must be notified of those assignments.

In practice, the principal activities of your qualified intermediary are threefold:

- To advise the taxpayer on the general rules and regulations surrounding exchanges
- To enter into a written agreement with the taxpayer that contains the restrictions set forth in Treasury Reg. 1.1031.(k)–1(g)(6)
- To hold the exchange proceeds during the exchange period

Although this is not strictly required, in most cases the exchanging party will also make his or her identification to the qualified intermediary.

Please notice also what your qualified intermediary does not do. *It does not give you legal or tax advice.* In fact, it is prohibited from doing so. That is the purview of your CPA, your attorney, or other financial advisors.

## Orchestration and Documentation of the Exchange

The qualified intermediary's role in an exchange transaction includes functions that are vital to the transaction's success: guidance and consultation, documentation, and accounting for funds. To create appropriate documentation, the intermediary must gather all relevant real estate documents from the taxpayer's real estate agent, attorney, title company, escrow company, or other closing agent. The intermediary reviews the transaction documents to ensure that the same taxpayer is both the seller and the buyer. The title commitment and the deed should match, both as to the legal description of the property and as to the vesting of the parties. If there is a leasehold interest involved, the term of the lease needs to be examined to determine that it is long enough (at least 30 years to qualify as real property). The qualified intermediary will also discuss any other exchange issues that arise after reviewing the exchangor's real estate documents, such as holding periods and qualifying property questions..

Based on the receipt and review of the transactional documents, the intermediary will then prepare an exchange agreement to comply with its statutory duty. There may be other documents prepared in connection with the exchange. You should thoroughly understand everything that you are asked to sign.

## Processing Exchange Funds

Another critical function of the qualified intermediary is to account for the taxpayer's funds. Upon closing of the sale of the relinquished property, the closing agent should send the qualified intermediary a HUD–1 closing statement, together with the taxpayer's net sale proceeds. Depending on the arrangement between the intermediary and the exchangor, the funds may be deposited in an interest-bearing account or otherwise safely invested in some type of highly liquid account. The qualified intermediary may be called upon to make earnest money deposits or to pay expenses incurred in connection with the acquisition of the replacement property. Ultimately, the exchangor's funds will be used to purchase one or more replacement properties. In some cases, unspent exchange proceeds may remain at the conclusion of the exchange (boot), and these must be remitted to the taxpayer; there may also be withholding taxes to pay. In any case, the intermediary will prepare and provide a final accounting to the taxpayer before closing the file.

## The Exchange Process—What to Expect

Although not all qualified intermediaries will have identical procedures, the following are the typical steps in an exchange:

- *Selection of a qualified intermediary.* Select a qualified intermediary to handle the exchange transaction.
- *Initiation of the exchange.* This may be accomplished by a phone call or a written communication with the qualified intermediary. It may come from you directly or from your representative.

*Authors' Note:* We recommend that you make direct contact with the qualified intermediary of your choice. The reason for this is twofold: you will be sure that the qualified intermediary has accurate information, and you will also know that the qualified intermediary is actually aware of your transaction. Taxpayers often assume that their real estate agent or closing agent got their exchange started, and then find to their dismay that there is a last-minute hassle to get things done.

The qualified intermediary will do a preliminary screening by asking specific questions to ensure that the transaction appears to qualify as a 1031 exchange, and will offer guidance concerning any potential hazards disclosed in that initial communication.

- *Communication with the closing agent for the relinquished property.* The qualified intermediary will communicate with the closing agent and obtain relevant documents. Typically these will include the purchase and sale contract, the preliminary title report or title commitment, and a copy of the proposed deed, which will convey title to the buyer.
- *Exchange documents.* The qualified intermediary will prepare an exchange agreement between itself and you, the taxpayer, assigning your interest in the contract to the qualified intermediary.. It will also draft a Notice of the Assignment, which must be signed by you, the qualified intermediary, and the buyer.

- *W–9 form.* You will usually be required to provide the qualified intermediary with your taxpayer identification number. (Without this, the qualified intermediary will not be able to credit you with any interest on your exchange funds.)
- *Transfer of exchange proceeds to qualified intermediary.* Following the closing, the closing agent will transmit the sale proceeds to the qualified intermediary, by check or wire.
- *Identification of replacement property.* (This is a *very critical* step in the exchange.) On or before the forty-fifth day after the close of your relinquished property transaction, a written identification of potential replacement properties must be delivered to the qualified intermediary or another nondisqualified person. Most qualified intermediaries will provide a special form designed for this purpose. Delivery may be made in person, via facsimile, by U.S. mail, or by messenger. *This step is* always necessary *unless the taxpayer has closed on all replacement properties in connection with the exchange* before *the forty-fifth day.* (More detailed information regarding identification requirements is discussed in Chapter 10.)
- *Replacement property information.* When the taxpayer knows the identity of the escrow/closing agent for the replacement property(ies), that information must be provided to the qualified intermediary to enable it to contact the escrow/closing office in order to complete the second phase of your exchange documentation. Simply identifying the replacement property without telling your qualified intermediary where the closing will take place is insufficient to allow the qualified intermediary to do its job.
- *Communication with the closing agent for the replacement property.* The qualified intermediary will communicate with the closing agent and obtain relevant documents for the replacement property, just as it did for the relinquished property. It will want to determine whether title is being taken in the same manner as title was relinquished to ensure that a valid exchange occurs, and that there are no other apparent problems that would cause the exchange to fail.
- *Exchange documents.* The qualified intermediary will draw up an assignment document as well as a Notice of the Assignment to the seller, which will need to be signed by the qualified intermediary, you, and the seller.

- *Exchange funds.* The closing agent will request funds from the qualified intermediary. The funds will be sent, usually by wire, according to the closing agent's instruction.
- *Final accounting.* Once all of the exchange money has been disbursed, the qualified intermediary will provide you with a statement of all funds received and disbursed.
- *Return of exchange funds.* Under the regulations, you will have very limited access to your exchange proceeds during the exchange (discussed in a later section). However, at the conclusion of the exchange, any funds remaining in the exchange account will be returned to you, and any such funds will be considered potentially taxable boot.

## Final Steps in the Exchange Process

- *Retain copies of documents for tax reporting purposes. Retain copies* of all exchange documents for *yourself,* your *lender,* and your *accountant,* Retention of copies of all exchange documents, as well as your other transaction documents and final closing statement and/or HUD–1s, will enable you and your accountant to prepare your tax returns accurately and without delay. (See Chapter 18 for a discussion of the tax reporting of the exchange.) These documents may also be required by lender(s) on your replacement property.

## Restrictions on Access to Exchange Funds

Once the exchange proceeds have been transferred to the qualified intermediary, your right to use them is severely restricted. The exchange agreement between the taxpayer and the qualified intermediary is required to limit your access to the exchange proceeds in accordance with Treasury Reg. 1.1031.(k)–1(g)(6). This states in pertinent part that a taxpayer is appropriately limited if "the taxpayer has no rights . . . to receive, pledge, borrow, or otherwise obtain the benefits of money or other property before the end of the exchange period."[6] The reason for the rule is to prevent you from being deemed in constructive receipt of the funds.

After the sale of the relinquished property closes and the proceeds are delivered to the qualified intermediary, but prior to the expiration of the 45-day identification period, the taxpayer may not access the exchange proceeds for any reason, *except*

- To acquire replacement property or
- To make an earnest money deposit or other payment related to the replacement property

Pledges of exchange proceeds are prohibited. If a bank has a lien on your relinquished property, and it is intended that the same lien be carried over to the replacement property, the exchange proceeds cannot be pledged to secure the loan during the interim period. This is a common request from SBA lenders, but it must be denied. Obviously, the intermediary cannot make a loan to the taxpayer, whether from the exchangor's funds or from its own funds.

After the expiration of the 45-day identification period, the rules on access to exchange proceeds change slightly. If you have not identified any replacement properties, or if you have rescinded any identification made prior to the forty-fifth day, your exchange has failed. At that point, you are entitled to receive the exchange proceeds (subject to any withholding tax requirements). If you have already acquired all the properties that were validly identified, then the exchange has been successfully completed. Since there is nothing more that the taxpayer can validly acquire, any remaining proceeds will be deemed to be boot and treated as described earlier.

The next situation, which can arise, is more complicated. Assume that you have identified three potential replacement properties in a timely manner and are unsure how many you will actually acquire. Assume further that we are now 100 days into the exchange period. You have already purchased one of the properties, but other identified properties that have not been acquired remain. The reason *why* they have not been acquired then becomes critical.

Reg. 1.1031(k)–1(g)(6), which we may from time to time refer to simply as the "(g)(6) rules," requires that there must have occurred a material and substantial contingency, which

- Relates to the deferred exchange
- Is provided for in writing
- Is beyond the control of the taxpayer

Some examples that do meet the foregoing test:

- Real property you have identified is destroyed, seized, requisitioned, or condemned, or
- A determination is made that the regulatory approval necessary for the transfer of the real property you identified cannot be obtained in time for it to be transferred to you before the end of the exchange period.

In that event, you are entitled to receive the balance of the exchange proceeds prior to the end of 180 days.

Here are some examples of situations that do not meet the (g)(6) criteria and therefore do not qualify for an early release of funds: (1) the buyer and seller cannot agree on a price, (2) the buyer is outbid, or (3) the buyer changes his mind and would rather acquire a property that was not identified or take a vacation to the South Pacific.

The taxpayer's property identification can affect when he or she can receive boot at the conclusion of the exchange. Consider the scenario in which the 1031 investor has identified three properties and bought only one. The qualified intermediary is still holding $100,000 of the proceeds, but the investor really does not intend to acquire any more properties. Unfortunately, the taxpayer does not qualify for any exception.[7] The exchangor should have clarified on his or her identification form that he or she would buy only one of the properties listed. Note, however, that if the taxpayer does use that approach, and does indicate that he or she will buy only one of several properties that have been identified, then once one of the properties is bought, the exchange is complete and the taxpayer *cannot* buy any more property. Any money remaining in the exchange account will then become boot.

## Selecting a Qualified Intermediary

Choose your qualified intermediary carefully. You will not be able to change or substitute a different qualified intermediary once the exchange has commenced without invalidating it. Some criteria to think about when choosing an intermediary are:

- How many years has the company been in business?
- What is the financial strength of the company?
- What kind of reputation does it have?

- Was it recommended by someone who has used it or someone whom you trust?
- Are you able to communicate freely with someone at the company?
- What are its fees and charges?
- Will you earn any interest while your funds are held?
- Is the company a member of the Federation of Exchange Accommodators?

Sometimes businesses get into financial trouble. Although this is exceedingly rare, it can also happen to qualified intermediaries.[8] Since the qualified intermediary you select will likely be in possession of a substantial amount of money belonging to you, you want to be sure you know who you are doing business with before you commit yourself to the arrangement.

## Communicating with Your Qualified Intermediary

It cannot be stressed too strongly how important it is for you to maintain contact with the qualified intermediary. Most large qualified intermediaries process a significant number of transactions every month. If you do not keep your qualified intermediary informed regarding the status of your sales or purchases, it is possible to have misunderstandings or miscommunications. Feel free to ask any questions relating to exchange requirements or procedures, and if there is any confusion as to the next step along the way, ask more questions. Let your qualified intermediary know such things as how many properties you intend to sell and buy. If your contact information (phone or address) changes during the exchange period, you should update the qualified intermediary. If you will be away on vacation during any part of the exchange period, your qualified intermediary should be made aware of this as well. The relationship should be a two-way street. You should communicate clearly with your qualified intermediary, and expect it to reciprocate.

## Changing Intermediaries during the Exchange

Please recall that, by definition, the qualified intermediary

> enters into a written agreement with the taxpayer (the "exchange agreement") and, as required by the exchange agreement, acquires the relinquished property from the taxpayer, transfers the relinquished property, acquires the replacement property, and transfers the replacement property to the taxpayer.[9]

These are statutory duties. Most commentators agree that an exchangor *cannot* substitute or change intermediaries in the middle of the exchange. If the intermediary were substituted, it could not fulfill its duty of acquiring and transferring the replacement property. Moreover, allowing the exchangor to substitute his or her qualified intermediary at will would make the independence of that intermediary open to question. The exchangor would be running the risk of having his or her exchange invalidated because the intermediary could be deemed his or her agent, and hence a disqualified person, or because the transfer of funds suggests control of exchange proceeds and hence would be likely to be deemed constructive receipt.

Selecting your qualified intermediary is a very important step in your exchange. Select one as soon as you are under contract to sell and know who will be handling your closing. Qualified intermediaries are diligent, and they want to do a good job for you. But they are not magicians. It takes time to process documents properly and accurately. If you don't call the intermediary in time to set up your exchange, you risk having your exchange fail before it even gets off the ground.

## Endnotes

1. Reg. 1.1031(k)–1(g)(2).
2. Reg. 1.1031(k)–1(g)(4)(iii)(B).
3. Reg. 1.1031(k)–1(g)(8) Ex. (5).
4. TAM 200130001.
5. Rev. Rul. 90–34, 1990–1 CB 154.
6. Reg. 1.1031(k)–1(g)(6).
7. Reg. 1.1031(k)–1(g)(6).
8. See *In re Nation-Wide Exchange Services, Inc.,* 91 AFTR 2nd 2003–1850 (Bkcy. MN 3/31/2003), which examined the claims of exchangors who lost their funds when their qualified intermediary filed for bankruptcy.
9. Reg. 1.1031(k)–1(g)(4)(iii)(B).

# PART 2

# 1031 EXCHANGES AND FINANCIAL MATTERS

# Exchanges Involving Related Parties

*Can I buy my property from or sell it to a relative? Are there any special rules or cautions that I should be aware of?*

The IRS is very strict about people exchanging with other family members. They allow it only subject to stringent rules.

## Related-Party Exchanges

It is not unusual to encounter an exchangor who wishes to sell to or buy from a "related party" in the course of a 1031 exchange. However, the Code, the Regs., and various court cases and rulings impose many restrictions on doing so. Exchanges between related parties are governed by IRC 1031(f).

As discussed earlier, *basis* is what the property originally cost to buy. Basis shifting is a way to reduce income taxes. The IRS, in imposing additional requirements on related-party exchanges, is seeking to prevent *basis shifting* between family members, which is explained below. The overall effect of basis shifting is to reduce the impact of total income taxes on a family unit. As with many other aspects of exchanges, whenever related parties are involved, it is always wise to discuss the matter with a tax advisor as well as with your qualified intermediary before proceeding.

Related parties are defined to include blood relatives, spouses, and siblings, but they do not include more attenuated relationships such as sisters-in-law or cousins.[1,2] Related parties also include entities controlled by the taxpayer, which means entities owned more than 50 percent by the taxpayer. So if a taxpayer has greater than a 50 percent interest in a corporation, LLC, or limited partnership, that entity will be considered a related party, and this can affect a contemplated exchange. It also affects trusts and fiduciaries established by the same grantor, or trusts and their beneficiaries.[5]

## Consequences of Selling to a Related Party—The Two-Year Rule

Sales to related parties are not prohibited and will not automatically disqualify an exchange transaction. The only hard and fast restriction on sales between related parties is the two-year holding rule, set forth in IRC Section 1031(f)(1)(C).[3,4] If a taxpayer sells her apartment or office building to her sister, the sister must continue to own the acquired property for at least two years after the acquisition. If the sister sells the property within the two-year time limit, the exchange will become invalid, and the taxpayer will have to pay the taxes that would have been due had the exchange never taken place, plus interest and penalties, if any. Generally it is wise to contractually obligate that party to the two-year holding period.

There are some exceptions to the two-year holding period.[6] For example, if the related party dies or there is an involuntary conversion such as a disaster loss or a governmental taking, the exchange will not be affected. But those exceptions are rare, and they tend to involve circumstances beyond the parties' control.

## Consequences of Buying from a Related Party

We just examined a sale to a related party. What if you are the buyer instead of the seller? This is much more difficult to achieve. The two-year holding period following the exchange still applies, but there are additional considerations.

Given the difficulty that can sometimes be encountered when attempting to identify replacement property, it is not unusual for a taxpayer to identify more than one potential property to buy. Perhaps the taxpayer has a relative who owns a property that she would be willing to sell, and the taxpayer lists that property as one of his choices. It may not be what the taxpayer really wants, but it serves as a backup or "sure thing" in the event that none of the other identified properties pan out for one reason or another.

Purchasing a replacement property from a related party is frowned upon by the IRS and will be allowed only in limited circumstances.[7] In essence, the relationship between the parties can taint the transaction and potentially invalidate the exchange. The IRS is auditing this issue. Form 8824, which is required to be filed with your tax return to report a 1031 exchange, now specifically asks if the exchange involved a related party.

The concern with related-party transactions is that family members or controlled business entities are in a good position to implement a basis-shifting scheme. Basis shifting involves transferring property with a higher adjusted tax basis to a taxpayer in a higher tax bracket (resulting in a lower capital gain), while transferring property with a lower adjusted tax basis to a taxpayer in a lower tax bracket (resulting in a higher gain, but perhaps a lower amount of tax). See Rev. Rul. 2002–83 cited in footnote 9.

For example, assume that Big John owns Yellow Rock, a parcel of improved real property that he acquired in 1970 for $100,000, and that has been depreciated so that it now has an adjusted basis of $50,000. Yellow Rock is now worth $1,500,000. If Big John were to sell it, he would have a long-term capital gain of $1,450,000 and a very substantial tax burden. Big John has a brother, Little Bill, who owns Red Rock, which also has a current fair market value of $1,500,000, but it has an adjusted tax basis of $1,200,000. So in order to minimize his tax, Big John does an exchange. He sells Yellow Rock to an unrelated third party for $1,500,000. He identifies as his replacement Little Bill's property Red Rock, which he acquires for $1,500,000. Little Bill realizes a gain of only $300,000 on the sale and has far less tax to pay than Big John would have owed. The family unit will reap a huge tax benefit, having avoided paying tax on $1,150,000 ($1,450,000 minus $300,000) of gain.

But wait! The IRS and the tax courts have determined that this is not acceptable, and that this transaction will not qualify as an exchange. A recent case from Hawaii concerned an exchange involving related entities that was not allowed to stand.[8] The taxpayer owned a highly appreciated property that had a low basis. It was sold to a third party in an exchange. The taxpayer, an entity, identified and acquired a replacement property from a related entity. (Because both entities were under common ownership and control, according to Section 267(b), they were related.) The related entity had a high basis in the replacement property, resulting in a lower tax being due. In actuality, although the second entity technically recognized a substantial taxable gain, it was actually able to avoid its tax liability because it also had an offsetting tax write-off as a result of an existing tax loss carryover. The Tax Court and the IRS concluded that this transaction would be treated no differently from the situation in which the taxpayer sells its relinquished property directly to the related party, who then disposes of it right away, instead of waiting for the requisite two-year holding period to elapse. That fact pattern—an insufficient holding period—would have caused the exchange to fail.

The IRS also disallowed an exchange between two related individuals involving the following facts: Mr. A owned low-basis Property 1, while related Mr. B owned high-basis Property 2.[9] Mr. A sold Property 1 to an unrelated third party through a qualified intermediary, and then acquired Property 2 from Mr. B as his replacement property. Mr. B recognized no gain on the sale because his high basis was equal to the fair market value of the property on the date of the exchange. The IRS ruled that this was a classic example of structuring a transaction to avoid gain recognition. The IRS further ruled that a taxpayer cannot insulate an exchange from the effects of IRC Section 1031(f)(1) by inserting a qualified intermediary into the transaction.

## Related Party also Doing an Exchange

It is permissible to buy property from a related party in cases where the related party will also be disposing of its property in a nonrecognition transaction (i.e., the related party also does an exchange). So, going back to our earlier example, assume that Little Bill, instead of pocketing his profit on Red Rock, chose to do his own 1031 exchange. His proceeds from Big John would go to his qualified intermediary. The funds would subsequently be invested in another replacement property, instead of going into his pocket. In that case, as long as Big John does not sell Red Rock within two years, both parties would have valid exchanges. The difference is that in this situation, neither related party "cashed out," but rather, both carried over their respective tax bases into replacement properties.

In a very recent ruling, the IRS said it would allow an exchange between related parties, despite the fact that one of the parties would actually be receiving some cash boot.[10] The IRS distinguished the transaction from the one in Rev. Rul. 2002–83, again acknowledging that here the parties were not seeking to cash out and avoid gain recognition. Each of the related parties was engaging in an exchange. The mere receipt of some amount of cash boot would not trigger an invalidation of the entire exchange.

## Endnotes

1. IRC Section 267(b).
2. IRC Section 707(b)(1).
3. PLR 200541037 (10/14/05). The exchange of timberland between related parties was approved; cutting of timber during the two-year holding period is not a disposition.
4. PLR 200440002 (10/1/04), in which related partnerships exchanging with one another is approved.
5. IRC Section 1031(f)(1).
6. IRC Section 1031(f)(2).
7. TAM 200126007 (7/2/2001).
8. *Teruya Brothers, Ltd. & Subsidiaries v. Commissioner,* 124 TC 45 (2/9/2005).
9. Rev. Rul. 2002–83, 2002–2 CB 927.
10. PLR 200616005, issued April 21, 2006.

# How Much Do I Need to Reinvest?— Exchange Value, Boot, and Boot Netting

*After you sell your relinquished property, how much do you need to reinvest in the purchase of the replacement property?*

There are two very common misconceptions about this issue: (1) that the taxpayer need reinvest only the cash proceeds from the sale of relinquished property, or (2) that the taxpayer need reinvest only the amount of profit resulting from the sale. *Both are wrong.*

## Exchange Value

As described by 1031 law, what needs to be rolled over is the total of (1) all mortgage indebtedness and (2) all net cash received. Succinctly stated, the *exchange value*, the amount that needs to be reinvested, is the net selling price of the relinquished property after deduction of costs of sale, such as sales commissions, closing costs, and recording costs. Basically, in order to defer capital gain taxes entirely, there is a two-pronged requirement:

**Table 8–1   Exchange Value**

| Relinquished Property | |
| --- | --- |
| 1. Sale price | $100,000 |
| 2. Commissions to real estate agent | 5,000 |
| 3. Other closing costs | 3,000 |
| 4. Exchange value—amount to be reinvested (Line 1 minus Lines 2 and 3) | **$92,000** |
| 5. Amount of encumbrances paid at closing | 20,000 |
| 6. Cash proceeds—cash to be reinvested | **$72,000** |

- The value of the replacement property must be equal to or greater than the net sale price of the relinquished property (gross sales price less deductible expenses of sale).
- All of the sales equity (cash proceeds from the sale) must be reinvested.

The example in Table 8–1 involves Karen, who sells her rental property for $100,000 subject to $5,000 for a Realtor's commission, $3,000 in closing costs, and a $20,000 mortgage. Assume that Karen's property has an adjusted basis of $45,000. In order to defer 100 percent of the tax liability, Karen must spend at least $92,000 on the replacement property (gross sale price less closing costs and brokerage commission). Also, the cash proceeds of $72,000 (the equity remaining after paying off the mortgage) must be reinvested in one or more replacement properties.

## Partial Exchanges

What if Karen is unable to satisfy these two requirements? Can Karen pocket some amount of her proceeds instead of reinvesting it? Yes, but this will result in a *partial exchange*. She may still complete a successful 1031 exchange, but any proceeds that are not reinvested or any shortfall in value of her replacement property below the exchange value creates a tax liability for Karen.

Therefore, to defer 100 percent of your capital gains tax liability, all of the net proceeds, in the form of cash or other consideration (such as carry-back notes—see Chapter 9), needs to be reinvested. Any money or nonqualifying property that you receive, actually or constructively, is considered boot, as described later in this chapter, and is subject to tax. Of course, you may always trade up. This means that you can always purchase a more expensive piece of property by adding additional cash to your exchange proceeds and/or increasing the debt on your replacement property.

## Boot

*Boot* is the term used to describe anything received by the taxpayer that is *not* like kind to the relinquished property. Boot is either cash *or* some other type of nonqualifying property received by the taxpayer.

## Cash Boot

Cash boot is not a difficult concept to explain. If the taxpayer is handed a check at the closing of the sale of the relinquished property, or if there is money left in the exchange account when the exchange is completed, that is taxable cash boot.

Boot remaining at the end of the exchange is always taxable. Remember that if the taxpayer has acquired all of his replacement properties and the qualified intermediary still has some part of the exchange proceeds remaining in the exchange account, this will most probably be taxable cash boot.

**Table 8–2  Partial Exchange with Cash Boot**

| | |
|---|---:|
| **Relinquished Property** | |
| 1. Sale price | $100,000 |
| 2. Commissions to real estate agent | 5,000 |
| 3. Other closing costs | 3,000 |
| 4. Exchange value—amount to be reinvested (Line 1 minus Lines 2 and 3) | **$92,000** |
| 5. Amount of encumbrances paid at closing | 20,000 |
| 6. Cash proceeds—cash to be reinvested | **$72,000** |
| **Replacement Property—Cash Boot** | |
| 7. Cash down payment | $62,000 |
| 8. New encumbrance | 20,000 |
| 9. Purchase price (Line 7 plus Line 8) | 82,000 |
| 10. Cash boot (Line 4 minus Line 9 | **$10,000** |

For an example of cash boot, see Table 8–2. In that case, the exchanger borrows enough to replace the entire $20,000 mortgage, but expends only $62,000 of the cash; as a result, the exchanger will have $10,000 of cash boot and a resulting tax liability.

## Boot—"Other Nonqualifying Property"

Examples of other nonqualifying property that would be considered boot in an exchange are seller financing in the form of carryback notes going directly to the exchanger (as further explained in Chapter 9) and personal property that may be included in a purchase of real property. This could include items such as washing machines and dryers included with an apartment building. If an exchange involves farmland, there may be farm equipment that is included in the purchase; this would be other nonqualifying property and therefore would be classified as boot.

## Mortgage Boot

Another type of boot is called *mortgage boot*. This type of boot arises when a taxpayer trades down in value, using all of his or her cash, but replacing the mortgage on the relinquished property with one of lesser amount. Mortgage boot can be demonstrated by the example in Table 8–3.

### Table 8–3   Partial Exchange with Mortgage Boot

| | |
|---|---:|
| **Relinquished Property** | |
| 1. Sale price | $100,000 |
| 2. Commissions to real estate agent | 5,000 |
| 3. Other closing costs | 3,000 |
| 4. Exchange value—amount to be reinvested (Line 1 minus Lines 2 and 3) | **$92,000** |
| 5. Amount of encumbrances paid at closing | 20,000 |
| 6. Cash proceeds—cash to be reinvested | **$72,000** |
| **Replacement Property—Mortgage Boot** | |
| 7. Cash down payment | $72,000 |
| 8. New encumbrance | 15,000 |
| 9. Purchase price (Line 7 plus Line 8) | $87,000 |
| 10. Mortgage boot (Line 4 minus Line 9 | **$5,000** |

The mortgage paid off upon sale is $20,000, and the net cash (what is left over after paying closing costs and the mortgage) is $72,000. Both of these values combined equal $92,000, or the exchange value. Both the amount of the mortgage and the net cash generated need to be rolled over into the replacement property. If the exchangor spends all $72,000 of the cash, but borrows only $15,000 (the amount of the new mortgage), giving a total of $87,000, then the IRS deems that $5,000 of mortgage boot resulted, and the exchangor is liable for tax on that amount.

Mortgage boot can arise inadvertently if exchangors are not careful in their planning. Mortgage boot was found to have been received in the following actual case: two partners dissolved two real estate partnerships and distributed the properties to themselves. They then exchanged those properties between themselves, resulting in relief from liability to one partner/taxpayer and gain recognition to him.[1]

## Substituting Cash for Debt

A taxpayer may substitute new cash for mortgage debt, but not vice versa.[2] In the previous examples, the taxpayer could buy the replacement property entirely for cash in the amount of $92,000 and incur no debt at all. The IRS views cash or equity as "real" money, while debt is viewed as something less than real. In our example, the $92,000 replacement property can be purchased with $10,000 of mortgage and $82,000 cash (substituting $10,000 cash for part of the mortgage), but increasing the amount of the mortgage to $32,000 and reinvesting only $60,000 cash creates cash boot of $12,000. The $12,000 represents the shortfall of equity that the IRS requires be reinvested. *A simple rule of thumb is: if the taxpayer retains any cash, it is always taxable.*

The total amount of boot in an exchange may consist of a combination of cash boot and mortgage boot, depending upon the circumstances.

## Timing for the Receipt of Boot

Boot received in a transaction is considered taxable income.[3] Receipt of boot *at the wrong time* can potentially *invalidate* an entire exchange.

It is not uncommon for a party that is selling property to want to take some amount of cash out of the transaction for some personal purpose. At the time the sale of the relinquished property closes, a taxpayer may take boot directly from the closing agent, prior to any funds coming to the qualified intermediary. If a taxpayer takes some boot at that time, then he or she is doing a *partial exchange*; it will not invalidate the exchange. Once the money reaches the qualified intermediary account, however, it cannot be accessed by the exchangor until the exchange is complete without invalidating the entire transaction.

### Effect of Receiving Boot on Carryover Basis

When a taxpayer receives both qualifying and nonqualifying property (boot), the provisions of Section 1031(b) are applicable. Basis is not allocated between the qualifying and nonqualifying property. Carryover basis is allocated first to the qualifying (replacement) property. Boot is taxed to the extent that the taxpayer has realized a gain in the transaction, but not in excess of the value of the nonqualifying property received. What this means is that the "first dollars out" are deemed to be taxable gain; the taxpayer cannot elect to treat those first dollars as basis, or return of capital. Put another way, a taxpayer cannot shelter just his or her capital gain by reinvesting only that amount and pocketing the amount of his or her initial investment. This is a fairly common misconception.

## Boot Netting

What happens in an exchange where the taxpayer receives cash and mortgage relief on his or her sale, and gives cash and undertakes a new mortgage on his or her purchase? The cash received and given is netted and the two mortgages are netted, meaning that one is offset against the other.[4]

The previous examples actually involve what is called *boot netting*. Mortgages in each leg of the exchange can be netted against each other.[5] In a delayed exchange transaction using a qualified intermediary, the IRS was asked to rule whether the mortgage paid off on the relinquished property could be offset by a new mortgage acquired to finance the replacement property.[6] There was no assumption of liabilities. The IRS ruled affirmatively and stated: "Under these facts, we rule that the consideration received by Taxpayers in the form of the liability relieved upon the retirement of the mortgage on Property, the relinquished property, may be netted against the liability incurred by Taxpayers to acquire Replacement Property." This will be true in most typical delayed exchanges, where old mortgages are not assumed, but rather new mortgages are created. The IRS has also analyzed the mortgage netting rule in the context of a partnership engaged in a 1031 exchange that straddled two tax years.[7]

In one case, the taxpayer was involved in a three-party exchange, and the escrow holder paid off the mortgage in such a way that the taxpayer never got control of the cash. In approving the exchange, the court stated:

> While a taxpayer who receives boot by surrendering mortgaged property can offset the boot by any boot given, including cash, a taxpayer who receives consideration in the form of cash *to compensate for a difference in net values in the properties (fair market value less mortgage)* cannot offset the cash boot by boot given by virtue of receiving mortgaged property.\*\*\*
>
> Thus, a taxpayer who *receives cash* consideration *to compensate for a difference in net values must recognize gain* realized to the extent of the sum of cash received and the net difference in favor of himself between the mortgage on the property transferred and the mortgage on the property received. \*\*\* 74 T.C. at 569. (Emphasis supplied in part, citations and footnote references omitted.)[8]

Reg. 1.1031(b)–1(c) explains the rule as follows:

> (c) Consideration received in the form of an assumption of liabilities (or a transfer subject to a liability) is to be treated as "other property or money" for the purposes of section 1031(b). Where, on an exchange described in section 1031(b), each party to the exchange either assumes a liability of the other party or acquires property subject to a liability, then, in determining the amount of "other property or money" for purposes of section 1031(b), consideration given in the form of an assumption of liabilities (or a receipt of property subject to a liability) shall be offset against consideration received in the form of an assumption of liabilities (or a transfer subject to a liability).[9]

*Authors' Note:* Like most aspects of exchanges, this is a complex topic. This discussion is intended only as an introduction. You should consult your accountant to address the specifics of your situation.

## Endnotes

1. *Miles H. Mason*, TC Memo 1988–273 (6/27/88).
2. Reg. 1.1031(d)–2, Ex.2(c); Rev. Rul. 79–44, 1979–1 CB 265.

3. IRC Section 1031(b).
4. *Coleman v. Commissioner*, 180 F2d 758 (8th Cir 1950); $14,000 of cash received by the taxpayer to equalize mortgages was considered taxable boot.
5. Reg. 1.1031(b)–1(c).
6. PLR 9853028 (1/04/1999).
7. Rev. Rul. 2003–56, 2003–1 CB 985 (5/9/2003).
8. *Barker v. Commissioner*, 74 TC 555 (1980).
9. See Reg. 1.1031(d)–2, examples (1) and (2).

# Seller Financing and Its Implications for an Exchange

*What happens if your buyer wants you to finance part of the purchase price and you want to do an exchange?*

You can do both!

## Seller Carrybacks Generally

In some transactions, a seller agrees to finance a portion of the sale price of the relinquished property. The buyer's obligation to make payments to the seller is generally evidenced by a promissory note (note). The note is the buyer's promise to pay the seller; it will contain the amount due, the date due, and the interest rate on the outstanding balance. The note is usually secured by the property by recording a mortgage or a deed of trust. The mortgage or deed of trust may be a primary encumbrance (a first) or a secondary or subordinate encumbrance (a second, or even a third).

When the seller is providing any portion of the buyer's financing, it represents a part of the purchase consideration. If, however, the seller is doing an exchange, and the exchangor is named as the beneficiary of the note, which represents exchange proceeds, the exchangor will be receiving nonqualifying property. That is because the note is not like kind to either relinquished real property or relinquished personal property.

## Section 453 *and* Section 1031

Normally, the receipt of nonqualifying property is immediately taxable to the seller/exchangor. However, another deferral exception (and opportunity) exists in this situation as a result of IRC Section 453. This is the section that deals with installment sales, where the consideration is paid over time, instead of all at once. The payments received on a note will normally be taxable on an installment basis, with the tax coming due only when the principal and interest are actually collected. A taxpayer may avail himself or herself of both Sections 453 and 1031 in the same transaction. However, there are special tax issues that arise in combining the application of these two sections. One is allocation of the basis of the relinquished property between the replacement property and the installment note.

IRC Section 453(f)(6) provides that basis is to be allocated *first* to the qualifying property received by the exchangor, and *second* to the installment note. The taxability of each installment payment is then computed accordingly. This can be easily seen in Table 9–1.

**Table 9–1   Partial Exchange with Seller Carryback Financing**

| | |
|---|---|
| **Relinquished Property** | |
| 1. Original purchase price | $650,000 |
| 2. Depreciation taken | 50,000 |
| 3. Adjusted basis (Line 1 minus Line 2) | **$600,000** |
| 4. Sale price | $1,000,000 |
| 5. Capital gain (Line 4 minus Line 3) | $400,000 |
| | |
| **Like-Kind Replacement Property** | |
| 6. Purchase price | $700,000 |
| 7. Carryover basis from relinquished property | $600,000 |
| | |
| **Non-Like-Kind Property Received—Taxable Boot** | |
| 8. New promissory note (Line 4 minus Line 6) | **$300,000*** |

* Tax will be due as the installments on the note are received.

For example, assume William contracts to exchange his apartment building, which has a fair market value of $1,000,000 and an adjusted basis of $600,000, with Tessa for a building that has a fair market value of $700,000 and a note for $300,000. William has a realized gain of $400,000. The recognized gain is $300,000, the difference between the $1,000,000 building given and the $700,000 like-kind property received. That $300,000 gain is then reported and taxed on the installment basis as the payments are collected. The entire $600,000 basis in the relinquished property is carried over into the replacement property.

As can readily be seen, combining the two Code sections will not invalidate the 1031 exchange. But it is less advantageous to the exchangor than if all of the sale proceeds are used for the acquisition of replacement property. Still, occasionally an exchangor may prefer to carry back a portion of the sale consideration, if he or she actually wishes to receive the installments and pay tax as the principal is received.

## Disposition of a Note through an Exchange

Sometimes an exchangor does not wish to finance the sale, but has no choice because other financing is not readily available, or because this is the best alternative to achieve the highest price. However, there are alternatives that you should consider if the only way you can close your sale is with some form of seller carryback financing.

If you want to avoid the tax consequences of an installment sale, the note must be drawn so that the qualified intermediary is the beneficiary/payee. Then the qualified intermediary, not you, will be receiving all of the exchange proceeds, and you will not have received any nonqualifying property. There are then several possible approaches for dealing with the note, which now technically belongs to the qualified intermediary, that you may wish to consider.

*Caveat:* There is little or no guidance from the IRS approving any of these techniques. An exchangor should always consult with his or her tax advisor when considering a carryback transaction. This is another gray area in the tax law.

### Option 1: Short-Term Note

Perhaps you are extending only short-term credit to the buyer, to give the buyer more time to procure suitable financing. Assume, for example, that the note is all due and payable within 90 days. In that case, since the note will be paid in full prior to the date when you must buy replacement property, there may be no problem at all. At maturity, the buyer will deliver the total amount due on the note to the qualified intermediary, its legal beneficiary. The qualified intermediary will deposit the note payoff proceeds into your exchange account, after which the funds will be available to complete your purchase. But there is always a risk to this approach. What if the buyer fails to obtain timely financing, or to pay the note in full by the time you need the use of the money? If that happens, Option 4, discussed later, may be your only choice.

## Option 2: The Note Is Assigned to the Seller of the Replacement Property

If the seller from whom you are acquiring replacement property is willing to accept an assignment of the note from the qualified intermediary as a portion of the consideration for the purchase of the replacement property, this is a straightforward way for the note to be included in the exchange. Again, all proceeds from the sale will have been used to acquire your replacement property, resulting in no boot to you. However, this is most likely to work in circumstances where you and the seller know each other, as most sellers will be reluctant to accept an assignment of such a note.

## Option 3: The Note May Be Sold to a Third Party

Here again, the note reflects the qualified intermediary as beneficiary/payee. You must then arrange for the qualified intermediary to sell the note to a third party, who will deposit the funds directly with the qualified intermediary. You will not have actual or constructive receipt of the note or the proceeds from the sale of the note. Once the third party deposits the funds in the exchange account, the note will be assigned to him or her. These additional funds (the note proceeds having now been converted to cash) may be used to purchase the replacement property. This is a good technique for an exchangor who wants to maximize the amount spent on the replacement property and minimize current tax liability. However, the tax result is unclear if the note is sold at a discount, as is often the case when this type of asset is sold.

## Option 4: You Buy the Note from the Qualified Intermediary

If you have sufficient funds, you can purchase the note yourself. You can replace the full value of the note by depositing cash into your exchange account. The note will be assigned to you by the qualified intermediary, and you can then collect the payments on the note. This will usually result in your having to pay taxes only on the interest received. Again, the results are unclear if the note is sold at a discount from its face value.

There is limited authority for this technique. The IRS has held that the sale of a taxpayer's accounts receivable generated from the sale of equipment in connection with a program of exchanges would not create boot to the taxpayer.[1] The taxpayer in that case was in the equipment leasing business; its parent company was the manufacturer of the equipment. The taxpayer sold and leased its equipment to dealers, which generated receivables to the taxpayer. The IRS ruled that sale of the receivables at face value by the taxpayer's qualified intermediary to the taxpayer's parent company would not violate the (g)(6) regulations, and the taxpayer would not be deemed to be in actual or constructive receipt of such funds.

## All-Inclusive Deeds of Trust ("AITDs")

An *All-Inclusive Deed of Trust,* or *AITD*, is very similar to a seller carry-back note. The basic difference is that there is already an underlying encumbrance (mortgage or deed of trust) on the relinquished property, which will not be paid off at the time you sell it. This type of transaction is also sometimes referred to as a *wrap*, because a new loan amount is "wrapped around" an existing encumbrance to create a much larger loan amount and/or an interest-rate differential. AITDs work similarly to a second mortgage or second trust deed, but they are even more disadvantageous for the exchangor, because the exchanger will have to replace a larger amount of money if he or she wishes to convert the AITD to cash to use in the exchange.

A comparison of an AITD to a carryback note is shown in Table 9–2.

In our example, the buyer purchases the property for $100,000 and has a cash down payment of $30,000. In the standard transaction, the buyer obtains bank financing for $50,000, and the exchangor "carries back" the remaining $20,000. But in the AITD version, the buyer acquires the property subject to

**Table 9–2   Comparison of Seller Carryback Financing and AITD**

|                            | Standard Carryback | All-Inclusive Deed of Trust |
| -------------------------- | ------------------ | --------------------------- |
| Sale price                 | $100,000           | $100,000                    |
| Down payment               | 30,000             | 30,000                      |
| New (or underlying) loan   | 50,000             | 50,000                      |
| Seller carryback amount    | 20,000*            | 70,000*                     |

\* This is the amount that will have to be replaced in order for the exchanger to avoid taxable boot.

the underlying existing loan of $50,000, and there is a wrap of $70,000, which includes the existing $50,000 loan.

In the standard carryback example, the exchangor would need to replace the $20,000 note with his or her own cash to avoid having boot. In the AITD example, the amount of the note and trust deed in favor of the seller will be *$70,000*, not $20,000, even though the exchangor may believe that he or she is technically advancing only $20,000 to the buyer, the same as in the first example. That is because the buyer is, in actuality, agreeing to pay the exchangor $70,000, and the exchangor will be obligated to continue making payments on the existing $50,000 loan. Obviously, this may be much harder for the exchangor to accomplish. Therefore, AITDs are usually to be discouraged in connection with exchanges.

## Seller-Financing Transactions Require Careful Planning

In all of these cases, the decision as to how to treat any carryback financing must be made *prior* to the closing of the relinquished property sale. It is important that the escrow/closing agent be made aware of what you intend to do in such situations, so that proper documents can be drawn. In the authors' experience, it is not at all uncommon for notes and security instruments (mortgages and trust deeds) to be drawn with the exchangor as payee/beneficiary, despite the fact that the exchange instructions direct that the qualified intermediary be so named. All parties should be alerted to exactly how the documents should appear, to avoid inadvertent constructive receipt. Remember that, at closing, the note or other instrument must be drawn with the qualified intermediary as the payee, so that when it is paid, the proceeds are added to the exchangor's other exchange funds. The note and/or other instrument can then be assigned by the qualified intermediary to the seller of the replacement property, a third party, or the exchangor, as appropriate, to conclude the transaction, depending upon which of the options discussed earlier is elected. This way, the exchangor maintains as much flexibility as possible.

Of course, if the exchangor is ultimately unable to find a way to convert the note to cash, it will remain in the exchange account at the conclusion of the transaction. In that case, it will be assigned to the exchangor, who will then be in the same position he would have been in had he taken the note in his own name in the beginning. It will be taxable boot. However, by putting the note in the name of the qualified intermediary, you keep your options open.

*Authors' Note:* As always, consultation with a tax advisor before deciding how to proceed is highly recommended.

## Endnote

1. Private Letter Ruling 200241016 (7/2/02).

# 10

# Identification of Replacement Property

*After you start your exchange, how do you identify what you want to buy?*

Timely identification of potential replacement properties is often the most problematic aspect of a real property exchange. When and how you accomplish your identification is very important. There are very specific rules with which you must comply. Failure to adhere to them will cause your exchange to fail.

## The Identification of Property

This discussion about the identification process is applicable to both real and personal property exchanges. However, exchangors of personal property do not encounter identification difficulties as frequently. Personal property of most kinds is readily available. The supply is not usually finite. The price of any item, whether it be machinery, equipment, vehicles, or livestock, tends to be relatively stable, or within a predictable range. However, the very nature of real property makes locating just the right parcel a much greater challenge. Therefore, the discussion in this chapter will focus principally on identification issues related to real property exchanges.

IRC Section 1031(a)(1)(A) specifies that the taxpayer has precisely 45 days within which to identify his or her potential replacement properties. This deadline is relatively short. It can fly past in no time at all. Depending upon the nature of the broader real estate market at the time and the geographic location where the replacement property is being sought, prices can be much higher than the taxpayer had planned to pay, and supply may be limited, or properties may be snatched up before they even hit the market.

Regardless of whether you are exchanging real or personal property, the identification rules are rigid and inflexible, and they require strict compliance. The identification must be accurately done, or the exchange may not qualify.

The 1031 Treasury Regulations are very specific about *when* and *how* potential replacement property is to be identified.[1] Only property that has been validly identified will qualify as replacement property.

There are three critical things to know about identification of replacement property:

1. Timing requirements (the "when")
2. Format of the identification (the "what")
3. Three alternative identification options (the "how")

## Timing (the "When")

When do you have to identify replacement property? The duration of the identification period is only 45 days.[2] By midnight of the forty-fifth day following the closing on your relinquished property, you must "identify" one or more potential properties that you expect to acquire. The position of the IRS is that it is *calendar days*, not business days, that are counted. The day following the closing date is counted as Day 1. Thus, if the relinquished property is closed on May 5, Day 1 will be May 6, and Day 45 will be June 19. If there are multiple exchangors in a single exchange (say, two brothers, each owning 50 percent of a relinquished property), each exchangor must submit his or her own identification.

Moreover, if the forty-fifth day is a Saturday, Sunday, or holiday, the Regulations do not provide for any additional days. There are no extensions to the 45 days except in very rare circumstances, such as natural catastrophes like major hurricanes (Florida, 2004; Gulf Coast, 2005) or wildfires (California, 2003). These exceptions must be declared by the IRS.

The Tax Court has ruled in two cases that when the last day to act falls on a Saturday or Sunday, the time can be extended to the next business day.[3] In these two cases, the Tax Court relied on Section 7503 for its authority to extend the time, but the IRS has never conceded that point. Prudent taxpayers should strive to comply with the 45-day deadline, rather than risk litigating the validity of their exchange in the Tax Court in reliance on Section 7503.

## Requirements for a Valid Identification (the "What")

What form must a valid identification take? A replacement property identification must be *in writing*, and it must be *signed* by the exchangor. There is no requirement that you actually be under contract to purchase any of the identified properties. This should be a consideration, however, because you want some assurance that you will be in a position to acquire what you have identified.

### To Whom Must the Identification Be Delivered?

Regulation 1.1031(k)–1(c)(2) specifies that the written identification must be delivered either (1) to the person who is obligated to transfer the replacement property to the exchangor (presumably this means the qualified intermediary) or (2) to any other person "involved" in the exchange other than the taxpayer or a disqualified person (this could include the seller of the replacement property or the closing agent).

### Disqualified Person

A disqualified person is an important concept in 1031 law. This term is actually defined in Reg. 1.1031(k)–1(k). Generally, an agent of the taxpayer, a relative of the taxpayer, or a person with a preexisting business relationship with the taxpayer will be deemed a disqualified person. Disqualified persons include the exchangor's attorney, CPA, and real estate agent, even though some of these people may be very involved in the exchangor's transaction, and blood relatives of the exchangor.

Therefore, you may make the written identification to the seller or to another party to the transaction, such as the escrow agent. However, the *best* procedure is to make the identification directly to your qualified intermediary, because this avoids any questions as to the timeliness of the identification, as well as any issues of whether it was delivered to a disqualified person.

## Delivery of Timely Identification

The identification must be received by the nondisqualified party no later than midnight of the forty-fifth day following the close of the relinquished property. It can be transmitted via fax, mail, or personal delivery. A timely postmark will satisfy this deadline requirement. Actual receipt of the replacement property (meaning that the property was actually purchased and closed during the 45-day identification period) will obviate the need to identify it.

## Specificity of Property Identification

Replacement properties may be located anywhere within the United States, Guam, or the U.S. Virgin Islands. However, the property identification must be specific and unambiguous. The properties must be identified by street address, legal description, or a distinguishable name. The street address must include city and state or, if the property is not in a city, then the county or parish and state. If a property has no street address, such as vacant land, you must use a unique property tax number or parcel number, or a legal description. For condominiums, a unit number is mandatory.

If you are purchasing a fractional interest in a property, you must indicate the specific percentage on your identification document. Purchase of a fractional interest is typical when purchasing from a TIC sponsor. (See Chapter 12 for more detailed information about tenancies in common.)

The Treasury Regulations provide that the exchangor can use a "distinguishable name" to identify the replacement property. In order to be distinguishable, it must be the only such property in that locale. For example, "Empire State Building, New York City, New York" is acceptable, but "Home Depot, Atlanta, Georgia" is not. And remember, regardless of what is identified, you must receive all replacement properties before the end of your exchange period. This means that all of your purchases must close on or before the 180th day following the close of the sale of your relinquished property.

## The Identification Document

There is no established format for identification prescribed by the IRS. The exchangor can send a letter or a list. It can be written by hand on personal stationery or in a typed formal business letter. Whatever format is ultimately used must include all of the relevant information, and must be *signed* by the exchangor. Most qualified intermediaries will provide a special form for your convenience. Amendments or revocations of the identification are allowed, so long as they are made within the 45-day identification period.

# Methods of Identification (the "How")

Three alternative methods of identification are allowed by the IRS. The exchangor may elect any one of these, but not more than one. As already noted, you may modify or revoke an identification that has already been made, if you do so within the 45-day identification period. Amending your identification may result in a change in the option being used.

## Option 1: The Three-Property Rule

The most commonly used option, and the easiest to implement, is the so-called three-property rule. You may identify any three properties, located anywhere within the United States, Guam, or the U.S. Virgin Islands. Property values are not restricted in any way. If you sold your relinquished property for $200,000, you could identify three properties with values of $1 million each and still use the three-property rule. You may acquire one, two, or all three of the properties you have identified. You should, but are not required to, specify how many of the identified properties you intend to purchase.

On occasion there is an issue about whether an identified "property" is really one property or two. This can be critical under the three-property rule. Consider, for example, an office tower on one parcel and a parking structure on an adjacent parcel. Contiguous parcels that are part of an integrated use or leasing scheme probably qualify as a single property; non-contiguous parcels that are separately managed or operated, or that have unrelated uses, probably do not. There is little IRS guidance on this issue; taxpayers should take a commonsense approach if faced with this situation

## Option 2: The 200 Percent Rule

Under the so-called 200 percent rule, you are allowed to identify more than three properties—in fact, you may identify as many properties as you wish. But, of course, there is a catch. There is a dollar limit on the total value of the identified properties. The exchangor must provide the fair market value of each of the properties identified. The aggregate value of all properties on the identification document cannot exceed 200 percent (that is, double) of the sale price of the relinquished property. You may acquire one, more than one, or all of the properties identified.

Obviously these limitations can be very restricting. If you sold one property for $500,000 and you want to identify four potential properties, the total fair market value of all four cannot exceed $1,000,000. Unless you intend to acquire multiple replacement properties of smaller value than what you sold, you will not find this option very useful.

## Option 3: The 95 Percent Rule

If you found the 200 percent rule a bit unusual, the so-called 95 percent rule is even more so. It is the most difficult rule to comply with, and the least frequently used. Under the 95 percent rule, exchangors may identify as many properties as they wish, and there is no dollar limitation at all. Again, the exchangor must provide the fair market value of the properties identified. However, under this rule, the exchangor *must actually purchase 95 percent of the aggregate value of what has been identified.* Usually that means that the exchangor must buy everything on the identification list.

For example, assume that the exchangor sold relinquished property for $1,000,000. If the list of identified properties consists of 10 properties, each valued at $1,000,000, for a total of $10,000,000, the exchanger falls outside of the 200 percent rule, and is left with no alternative but to comply with the 95 percent rule. Therefore, the exchangor must complete the exchange owning at least $9,500,000 worth of those properties—effectively all 10 of them. If the exchangor acquires only 9 of them, the exchange will fail. That is why this is a perilous rule to rely upon.

## Invalid Property Identification

Table 10–1 is an example of an invalid identification, exhibiting several frequently encountered difficulties. Note that it contains a list of four properties,

**Table 10–1   Example of an *Invalid* Identification**

Dear Friendly Accommodator Company:

The following are the properties I am considering as replacement property in my 1031 exchange.

1. 258 Happy Lane, San Francisco, California
2. Parcel #123–456–789
3. 6 acres on Route 66, Chicago, Illinois
4. McDonald's Restaurant, Columbus, Ohio

*Michael Q Taxpayer*                              *Marilyn Q. Taxpayer*

Michael Q. Taxpayer                              Marilyn Q. Taxpayer

but the fair market values are missing, so it is impossible to determine whether it falls within the 200 percent rule or the 95 percent rule.

The first property listed appears to be satisfactorily specified. The second property on the list has a parcel number, but no other information to reveal where in the United States it is located. The third property on the list, "6 acres on Route 66, Chicago," is too vague and ambiguous to be useful, and the fourth property could be applicable to several possible locations in Atlanta, Georgia. Finally, since the signature is illegible, the qualified intermediary may not even be able to determine whose identification this purports to be!

Sadly, every qualified intermediary has no doubt received identifications similar to this. Since the qualified intermediary is unable to even determine to whom the identification belongs, the taxpayer may not realize until it is too late that his exchange is jeopardized because the qualified intermediary is not even able to contact the person and urge her or him to try again.

That fact brings us to another cautionary note. Although identifications received by fax at 11:59 p.m. on your forty-fifth day are valid, if you wait until then to send your identification, no one at your qualified intermediary is likely to be in the office to receive it. When the qualified intermediary opens for work the following business day, if it finds anything that would render the identification invalid, it will be too late to let you know how to remedy any discrepancies.

## Valid Property Identifications

Table 10–2 provides a good example of a proper identification under the three-property rule. It is clear, and it is complete. Furthermore, the taxpayers affirmed that they intend to buy only one of the properties on the list, a prudent move.

**Table 10–2   Example of a *Valid* Identification—Three-Property Rule**

To:   Friendly Accommodator Company:

The following are the properties I am considering as replacement property in my 1031 exchange. I plan to acquire only one of these:

1. 123 Main Street, Columbus, Ohio
2. 857 Elm Street, Baltimore, Maryland
3. A 50% interest in the Rio Grand Apartments, SW corner of Peachtree Street and Brand Boulevard, Atlanta, Georgia.

*Michael Q Taxpayer*           *Marilyn Q. Taxpayer*
Michael Q. Taxpayer            Marilyn Q. Taxpayer

Table 10–3 represents a valid identification under the 200 percent rule. The taxpayers provided the value of each property and indicated, where applicable, the percentage interest that they proposed to acquire.

**Table 10–3   Example of a Valid Identification—200 Percent Rule**

To:   Friendly Accommodator Company:

The following are the properties we are considering as replacement properties in our 1031 exchange.

| Address | Fair Market Value* | |
|---|---|---|
| 1 123 Main Street, Columbus, Ohio | $500,000 | |
| 2 857 Elm Street, Baltimore, Maryland | $250,000 | (Value of 1/2 interest) |
| 3 A 50% interest in Rio Grande Apartments SW Corner of Peachtree and Peartree Streets Atlanta, GA | $340,000 | |
| 4 999 First Street, Parma, OH | $875,000 | |
| Total | $1,965,000 | (less than 200% of sale price) |

* Assume relinquished property sold for $1,000,000.

*Michael Q Taxpayer*           *Marilyn Q. Taxpayer*
Michael Q. Taxpayer            Marilyn Q. Taxpayer

In both Table 10–2 and Table 10–3, the taxpayers signed their identification lists, and also very sensibly printed their names so that their qualified intermediary would not have to guess to whom the lists might belong.

## Common Identification Issues, Questions, and Problems

Every experienced qualified intermediary has heard a multitude of reasons, excuses, complaints, suggestions, and demands from its clients regarding untimely identifications. When a taxpayer finds that he or she has missed the identification date or has been unable to locate an appropriate or suitable replacement property, the angst is appreciable. Taxpayers and their agents have been known to plead, beg, and even threaten their qualified intermediaries for relief. A professional qualified intermediary will not be swayed by such entreaties and, in fact, has no legal authority to extend the deadline.

### Identification Deadlines Are Fixed by Law

The replacement property must be identified within the 45-day period. Qualified intermediaries cannot be flexible about identification dates. To allow a taxpayer to backdate or otherwise falsify an identification is tax fraud—a federal crime. Taxpayers, their agents, and even their qualified intermediary could be convicted and sent to prison for that. Bear in mind that when you select a qualified intermediary, you will be entrusting that company with a substantial sum of your hard-earned money. You may want to think twice about whether you would want to use the services of a company that is willing to bend the rules and compromise its integrity.

In a 1999 case, the taxpayers claimed to have orally identified properties to one another, and then schemed to backdate a written identification.[4] The IRS held their exchange to be invalid. The court found their testimony about their property identification to be incredible. They were ordered to pay $1,030,663 in taxes and assessed a fraud penalty of $772,997.

### Be Mindful of Which Rule You Are Using

If you list three or fewer properties, you are usually quite safe. However, determining whether an identified property should be considered one or two properties is not always easy. If two properties are "operated as a single operating unit," they may qualify as one for identification purposes. The two properties usually should be contiguous, but they may not be—for example, if there is an office building with a parking lot on the next block.

## An Identification Form May Be Signed by Someone with a Power of Attorney

A property identification is required to be signed by the taxpayer. If the taxpayer is unavailable, it arguably may be signed on his or her behalf by someone who is authorized to do so—someone with a power of attorney. Nevertheless, it is always safer to have the exchangor sign it personally. This is another one of those "gray areas."

## Specify Fractional Interests

If you are identifying less than a 100 percent interest as a replacement property, this should be clearly shown on your property identification form. If you will be the only one taking title to a property, you are buying 100 percent of it. But if you are buying only a fractional share as a tenant in common with others, including in a sponsored TIC (see Chapter 12), you must specify the percentage that you intend to acquire on your identification form. Otherwise, what you ultimately acquire is inconsistent with what you identified (a 5 percent interest versus a 100 percent interest), causing the exchange to fail. Of course, if a taxpayer identifies a 65 percent interest and ultimately acquires a 67 percent interest, the different is *de minimus* and will probably have no effect in the event of an audit.

## You Must Buy One of the Identified Properties

You cannot buy something else (i.e. unidentified) after your forty-fifth day if you change your mind for any reason. Only a property that has been validly identified in a timely manner may be received as qualified replacement property to complete a valid exchange. Otherwise, all exchangors would simply identify "the Empire State Building, the White House, and the Golden Gate Bridge" and then buy whatever they wanted, rendering the concept of the 45-day identification period utterly meaningless.

## You May Modify, Amend, or Revoke Your List of Identified Properties

Such changes, however, must be made on or before midnight of the forty-fifth day. The revocation or amendment must be done with the same formality as the original identification, i.e., it must be in writing, signed, and timely delivered. It cannot be done after the deadline.

## There Is No Need to Identify if the Exchange Is Completed within 45 Days

If all replacement properties are received within the 45-day identification period, you need not identify them further. Once you have acquired all the properties you intend to acquire, your exchange is complete. It is not necessary to further identify anything. What greater evidence of intent and identity could be shown than to actually acquire the properties? However, if only some, but not all, purchase transactions are closed by the forty-fifth day, then written identification is required.

If you close on three properties within 45 days and you want to buy a fourth, you should submit an identification list reflecting all four properties. You must then adhere to either the 200 percent rule or the 95 percent rule.

## Substitutes for Formal Identification

A sales contract signed within the 45-day window *may* qualify as an identification made to the seller. Still, it is a better practice to identify the property to your qualified intermediary. Furthermore, if you have already identified three other properties and this is a fourth property, you will have to qualify under the 200 percent rule or the 95 percent rule in order to include this property in the exchange.

## Precise Identification Is Important

If you identify the property in a timely fashion, but it is identified in a manner that is slightly different from the actual property you receive, this can be problematic. This can happen if the property is on a corner lot and has both a legal address and a commonly used address that is different from the legal one. Perhaps the property was identified by parcel number, but there was a subsequent lot split or other change in the legal lot number. You will need to document exactly what happened. Sometimes human error intervenes and people make transcription errors. The exchangor must be prepared to explain such discrepancies to the IRS if audited.

## An Identification Cannot Be Ambiguous

If your identification turns out to be vague or ambiguous, this can invalidate an exchange. Consider the case where you identify "123 Main Street,

Seattle, Washington," which appears on its face to be clear and complete. But the building turns out to be a condominium project, and you are actually buying a property accurately described as 123 Main Street, *Unit 102*, Seattle, Washington. This could present difficulties in the event of an audit by the IRS.

### Verify the Property Information

If you rely on an address provided by your real estate agent and it turns out to be erroneous, this may not survive IRS scrutiny. In fact, you may find that you cannot complete the exchange, because your agent told you that the property was 456 Green Street, but the correct address was 756 Green Street. To be prudent, be very careful about verifying the addresses, parcel numbers, or legal descriptions on your identification form.

Historically, the Tax Court has been more sympathetic to taxpayer error on these issues than has the IRS. However, it is best not to rely on the Tax Court to get you out of a jam with the IRS. You could use up all your 1031 exchange tax savings in attorney's fees.

## Endnotes

1. Reg. 1.1031(k)–1(c).
2. Reg. 1.1031(k)–1(b)(2).
3. *E-B Grain Co. v. Commissioner*, 81 TC 70 (1983); *Snyder v. Commissioner*, TC Memo 1981–216 (relying on Section 7503).
4. *Dobrich v. Commissioner,* 188 F3d 512 (9th Cir 1999).
5. Reg. 1.1031(k)–1(c)(5)

# 11

# Treatment of Early Release Money, Earnest Money Deposits, and Prorations

*What do you do if your buyer wants to give you money before the deal closes to "tie up" the purchase? What do you do if you need money for a deposit to buy your replacement property?*

Once your sale closes, your qualified intermediary will be holding all of your exchange proceeds. You cannot touch those funds; they must be used to acquire replacement property. Notwithstanding this general rule, the funds may be used to make a deposit on a property. Likewise, sometimes a buyer may wish to give you money to bind a deal. You will probably want your qualified intermediary to hold that money for you while the transaction is pending.

## Early Release Money

In a real estate transaction, it is not unusual for money deposited by a buyer to be released to the seller prior to the closing. The term *early release money*, as used in this book, describes money that is either

- Released to an exchangor by the buyer of the relinquished property prior to the closing (such as a nonrefundable deposit)
- Disbursed by the qualified intermediary to the seller of the replacement property (but never to the exchangor/taxpayer), usually in the form of an earnest money deposit, prior to the closing

Sometimes the terms of the exchangor's contract for sale of a relinquished property provides that the buyer's deposit is to be released prior to the closing. But if the money goes to you, as the exchangor, it will be taxable as boot. That is because the amount received will, more likely than not, appear as a credit toward the purchase price on the final closing statement, and it will be in your pocket, not in your exchange account. To avoid this, a way must be found to keep that money in the exchange account.

So long as the closing has not occurred, the early release money should not go to you directly. The best option is for your closing agent to forward those funds to your qualified intermediary. The money will remain with your qualified intermediary until it is needed to complete your purchase of replacement property.

It is preferable that your qualified intermediary prepare the exchange documents prior to receipt of the early release funds, if at all possible. At a minimum, you should agree in writing to engage the qualified intermediary and assign your rights under the contract for sale to the qualified intermediary. The qualified intermediary will probably also enter into a written agreement with your closing agent that provides that in the event the transaction fails to close, then the closing agent will accept a return of the money advanced.

The reason for this last precaution is that the qualified intermediary does not usually wish to be the arbiter of your contract with your buyer if your sale falls through, nor does it want to become involved in a lawsuit between you and your buyer about who is in breach of contract or who keeps the deposit.

## Earnest Money Deposits

Earnest money deposits are usually a necessary part of any purchase transaction. The best practice is to use exchange proceeds for the earnest money deposit, provided that the relinquished property has already closed or there has been an early release to you from your buyer. This is one of the few ways in which you may access exchange proceeds prior to closing on replacement property. But if you don't have that option, you may need to advance your own funds.

### Use of Exchange Funds

Once your relinquished property has closed, or if there has been an early release of funds from the buyer, exchange funds are available and may be applied toward a deposit on your replacement property. It is not unusual, in the authors' experience, for exchangors to attempt to initiate a deposit by making a telephone call. But no competent qualified intermediary will send any of your money to anyone in the absence of a written request, signed by you. Fortunately, a written request for an earnest money deposit may also serve as your replacement property identification, as long as it is submitted to the qualified intermediary prior to the forty-fifth day (your identification date), and as long as it contains the essential elements—the property address or parcel identification and your signature.

If a request for an earnest money deposit is submitted after the identification date, the qualified intermediary will want to verify that the property was properly identified before sending out the funds. Each qualified intermediary may have its own procedures for accomplishing that. The earnest money deposit will subsequently be reflected on the final closing statement, or HUD–1, as a part of the exchange consideration, as well as in the accounting provided by the qualified intermediary to the exchangor at the conclusion of the exchange.

If the purchase falls through and does not close, the closing officer will probably be directed to return the funds to the qualified intermediary, not directly to you. If the money were to go to you, not only would it be deemed boot, but it would probably prevent you from completing your exchange altogether by acquiring subsequent property. That is because once you have actual or constructive receipt of any portion of the exchange funds, you are precluded from acquiring any other replacement properties. Your exchange is over.

## Use of Nonexchange Funds

If you need a deposit before the relinquished property closes, and you have not obtained an early release from the buyer of your relinquished property, you may be required to advance your own funds. If you intend to contribute additional cash in order to complete your purchase, then the earnest money deposit will merely be applied toward that amount, which would otherwise be due later anyway.

However, if you will not be adding any funds and are planning to use only exchange proceeds for your acquisition, you and your qualified intermediary must be careful. You should alert the closing officer that the amount of the earnest money deposit you have made from your own funds will be replaced at the closing by money coming from the qualified intermediary. For example, say you were required to remit $15,000 as your deposit. In that case, when your closing officer eventually calls for funds from the qualified intermediary, the request can include an extra $15,000, which will create an excess balance in the closing agent's account. Then the $15,000 you deposited can be returned to you, and more of your exchange proceeds will be applied toward your purchase.

**Table 11–1   Replacement of Earnest Money Deposit Made by Exchangor**

| | |
|---|---|
| **Relinquished Property—Closing Date April 1** | |
| 1. Sale price | $300,000 |
| 2. Commissions to real estate agent | 15,000 |
| 3. Other closing costs | 5,000 |
| 4. Exchange value—amount to be reinvested (Line 1 minus Lines 2 and 3) | **$280,000** |
| 5. Amount of encumbrances paid at closing | 150,000 |
| 6. Exchange proceeds—cash to be reinvested | **$130,000** |
| **Replacement Property—Mortgage Boot—Closing Date May 20** | |
| 7. Purchase price | $295,000 |
| 8. New encumbrance | 165,000 |
| 9. Down payment needed (Line 7 minus Line 8) | 130,000 |
| 10. Earnest money deposit—paid by exchangor March 1 | $30,000 |
| 11. Cash down payment from exchange proceeds | 130,000 |
| 12. Total down payment received (Line 10 plus Line 11) | **$160,000** |
| 13. Refund deposit received from exchangor (line 10) | **$30,000*** |

* This amount was not exchange proceeds, so it is not boot.

In Table 11–1, our exchangor, Zoe, deposited $30,000 with the closing agent upon entering into a contract to purchase replacement property on March 1. Zoe's relinquished property did not close until April 1, at which time $130,000 of exchange proceeds were deposited with the qualified intermediary. On May 20, her closing agent needed an additional $100,000 to complete a total down payment of $130,000.

However, Zoe had consulted with her tax advisor and her qualified intermediary, and she understood that if the closing agent called for only $100,000, there would be a balance remaining in the exchange account of $30,000, resulting in cash boot in that amount. So she advised her closing agent to call for the full $130,000. Consequently, the closing agent had an excess $30,000 remaining upon closing, which amount could be refunded to Zoe and reflected as a separate line item on the closing statement, or HUD–1, as a reimbursement to exchangor of her deposit. This meant that none of the exchange proceeds ended up in Zoe's hands, and all of the exchange proceeds were applied to the purchase. The refund to Zoe of her own earnest money deposit should not be deemed to be boot.

## Prorations and Security Deposits

Just as a deposit from an exchangor must be treated with care so as not to create unexpected boot, so must certain other items that typically appear on a closing statement. These items appear as credits and debits and adjust the final amount due to or from the seller and buyer. Some examples of these are real property taxes, security deposits, and prorations of rents. None of these items are allowable expenses of an exchange, but each of them must be dealt with to avoid problems. (See Chapter 18 for a more detailed discussion of this topic.)

### Tenant Security Deposits

The landlord usually holds security deposits from tenants of an apartment or office building. They are similar to an unsecured debt on the property. When the tenant vacates, all or part of the security deposit is returned, depending on the condition of the premises and whether or not the tenant owes the landlord any money.

Therefore, when a building is sold, the old landlord must deliver these security deposits to the buyer, who, as the new landlord, will then be accountable to the tenants upon the termination or expiration of their tenancies. So at the closing, the security deposits usually appear as a debit against the seller and a credit in favor of the buyer.

### Rental Payments and Other Prorations

Likewise, if all rents are paid on the first of the month and the closing occurs on the fifteenth of the month, the buyer will be entitled to a credit for half of the rents. Again, this will usually create a debit against the seller and a credit to the buyer. If there are homeowner association dues that have been or must be paid for the month, the same will apply. The same may also be true for insurance or other miscellaneous fees that recur and are related to property ownership.

### Property Taxes

Finally, any property taxes due and unpaid as of the date of the closing will be prorated and debited against the seller, with a credit to the buyer. Or, if the property taxes for the full year have already been paid, they will be a debit to the buyer for the prorated amount and a credit to the seller.

## Review of the Settlement Statement

All of this may sound a little confusing, but closing agents are experts at sorting it all out. As an investor, you just want to make sure you review the estimated settlement statement, which is usually provided for your approval, before it is finalized.

If there is no exchange involved, the closing agent most likely will determine the amounts due to or from the parties based in part upon the rents, taxes, and security deposit adjustments. However, if one or both parties are doing an exchange, they may wish to review their estimated settlement statements beforehand with an eye toward ensuring that they do not create unexpected and unwanted tax liabilities. Any exchange proceeds used for those items would be boot. Therefore, if you are the seller, you may elect to deliver the security deposits, rents, and tax prorations at the closing or to write a check directly to your buyer, to avoid having the closing agent debit your exchange proceeds to account for those amounts. This is because any exchange proceeds used for a purpose other than the acquisition of replacement property would be boot. Please refer to Table 11–2.

**Table 11–2    Security Deposits and Tax and Rental Prorations—Relinquished Property**

| | |
|---|---|
| 1. Sale price | $500,000 |
| 2. Commissions to real estate agent | 25,000 |
| 3. Other closing costs | 5,000 |
| 4. Exchange value—amount to be reinvested (Line 1 minus Lines 2 and 3) | **$470,000** |
| 5. Amount of encumbrances paid at closing | 225,000 |
| 6. Exchange proceeds—cash to be reinvested | **$245,000** |
| **Possible Adjustments from Exchange Proceeds** | |
| 7. Security deposits to be transferred to buyer | $10,000 |
| 8. Rental prorations to be transferred to buyer | 5,000 |
| 9. Property tax prorations to be transferred to buyer | 7,500 |
| 10. Total adjustments due to buyer | **$22,500*** |

* If the exchange proceeds are debited to deliver these amounts to the buyer, it will create boot in the amount of $22,500, which is taxable to the seller. If the seller delivers this amount separately to the buyer, instead of taking a credit against the exchange proceeds, it will not be taxable.

Likewise, if you are the buyer, you may prefer to receive such amounts in cash to cover anything due to you for taxes, security deposits, or rental prorations, rather than as a credit, which would reduce the amount of exchange proceeds necessary to close. That way you can avoid possibly having leftover exchange funds, which would be boot. Of course, if you will need to put more money into the deal to close it anyway, this may not make any difference. Please refer to Table 11–3.

The foregoing is only a cursory discussion of these topics. Consultation with a knowledgeable tax advisor who reviews your settlement statement prior to closing is good insurance against possible surprises at tax time.

Of course, as most investors are aware, the items we are concerned with here, such as taxes, are deductible expenses on your tax return. However, these are not deductible as part of your 1031 exchange. These expenses will most likely be written off in a different part of your tax return. Your accountant can also advise you about that. Remember that it is very important to retain your closing statement and provide a copy to your tax preparer at tax time.

**Table 11–3   Security Deposits and Tax and Rental Prorations—Replacement Property**

| | |
|---|---|
| 1. Purchase price | $ 500,000 |
| 2. Closing costs | 5,000 |
| 3. Exchange value—amount to be reinvested (Line 1 plus Lines 2 and 3) | **$505,000** |
| 5. New encumbrances | 265,000 |
| 6. Exchange proceeds—cash to be reinvested | **$240,000** |
| **Possible Adjustments from Exchange Proceeds** | |
| 7. Security deposits to be transferred to exchangor | $10,000 |
| 8. Rental prorations to be transferred to exchangor | 5,000 |
| 9. Property tax prorations to be transferred to exchangor | 7,500 |
| 10. Total adjustments due to buyer | **$22,500*** |

*If this amount is credited against the cash needed to close, there may be boot created, because there will be excess exchange proceeds that are not used to acquire the replacement property.

# PART 3

# COMPLEX ISSUES IN 1031 EXCHANGES

# 12

# Tenancies in Common; Delaware Statutory Trusts; and Oil, Gas, and Mineral Rights

*What is a tenancy-in-common investment? Is this something I should be interested in?*

Within the last few years, a new market has been created to serve 1031 taxpayers looking for replacement properties. Sponsors acquire large investment-quality properties and then sell fractional interests to investors. These types of investments have become very popular because they do not require any management time or create headaches for the investors.

## Overview of Tenancies in Common

At first blush, this chapter may seem to have an odd grouping of subjects. In a way it does. The reason these subjects appear together in one chapter has to do with the current popularity of investing in TIC deals. TIC stands for tenancy in common, which has long been a typical way for two or more people to hold title to property. However, a *TIC deal* (as discussed in this chapter) involves purchasing a fractional interest in a large-dollar, "institutional-quality" property. Each of the subjects discussed in this chapter usually falls into the category of a TIC deal.

The IRS issued guidance on structuring TIC deals in 2002.[1] Before that time, most advisors cautioned investors against *pooling* their funds with other investors to buy property together because they were likely to be deemed partners. Recall that in a 1031 exchange, a taxpayer who sells as an individual must purchase a direct interest in qualifying property and may not purchase an interest in a partnership. Conversely, if they are deemed partners, investors who are pooling funds cannot do individual exchanges. To better understand the current state of the law, we think it is important to provide some background. This explanation is also important in the event that a particular deal does not meet all of the IRS qualifications.[2]

Are investors who pool their funds considered to be individual co-owners, or are they joint venturers who are taxed like a partnership? Partnership Reg. 301.7701–2(a) provides that a joint venture or other contractual arrangement may create a separate taxable entity (like a partnership) if the participants carry on a trade or business together. Contrast this with Reg. 301.7701–1(a)(2), which states that the mere co-ownership of property that is maintained and rented or leased does not constitute a separate entity for federal tax purposes.

Several earlier cases had held that a co-ownership arrangement was a partnership for federal tax purposes. The Ninth Circuit Court of Appeals held that a computer equipment leasing deal with 78 investors was a partnership. The Appellate Court stated:

> The Tax Court found that the economic benefits to the individual participants were not derivative of their co-ownership of the computer equipment, but rather came from their joint relationship toward a common goal.[3]

The Seventh Circuit Court of Appeals held that an unincorporated joint venture between three utility companies was a partnership. The court examined the degree of business activity engaged in by the venture and held that it met the statutory definition of a partnership.[4]

By contrast, the IRS had stated that when the two owners of an apartment building employed an agent to manage the building, collect the rents, pay the bills, and otherwise provide customary tenant services, the co-ownership was not a partnership for federal tax purposes.[5] Historically, real estate syndications had almost always involved the use of limited partnerships. Those, however, were unsuitable for individual investors who wished to pool their money in 1031 transactions. This uncertain state of the law is what existed prior to 2002.

## Tenancy-in-Common (TIC) Ownership

Tenancies-in-Common ("TICs") are the current hot topic in real estate investing. They are not for everyone. However, for those investors who are interested in owning a small piece of a larger property, along with other similarly situated investors, a TIC may be just the thing. TIC investors are interested in receiving monthly checks for their ownership interests and not dealing with what is frequently referred to in the industry as the "three Ts"—tenants, trash, and toilets. On the other hand, if you prefer a more hands-on approach to real estate investing, or if you wish to control your own destiny, these types of investments may not be for you.

TIC ownership, as it relates to 1031 exchanges, has taken on a new importance since 2002. In March 2002, the IRS issued Rev. Proc. 2002–22 (see Appendix C). It is not a ruling; instead, it sets forth criteria for receiving a ruling from the IRS on a proposed TIC structure. It establishes 15 conditions that, if complied with, effectively create a safe harbor TIC structure. (The details of these 15 conditions are beyond the scope of this book.) The purpose of this revenue procedure was to clear up the potential tax issue of TIC-owned property being classified as a partnership for tax purposes.

Since March 2002, when the IRS issued Rev. Proc. 2002–22, an entire industry has developed to market and sell fractional interests in larger real estate investments to 1031 investors. The IRS sanctioned the use of a more formal TIC structure by setting forth those 15 requirements, which, if they are all met, will qualify the TIC ownership for valid 1031 tax treatment. There is a limit of 35 investors in any one property, although lenders normally want to have fewer than that. There are also limits on payments to TIC sponsors.

The properties in TIC deals may be multitenant office buildings, industrial complexes, or retail centers. They may also include large credit tenants, such as single-user buildings (Wal-Mart, Walgreens, and so on). In any event, a co-ownership agreement is always signed by all the buyers; it designates a manager/management company and contains other provisions that satisfy, or do not violate, the requirements of Rev. Proc. 2002–22. The sponsors are sophisticated in real estate and able to undertake all the due diligence required to evaluate a property, and they can usually obtain more favorable loan terms than an individual investor could get.

## Vesting in a TIC

Because of lender requirements, each of the parties is usually required to take title in the name of an LLC. The lenders also usually require that each LLC be a *single-purpose entity* (SPE), meaning that the LLC cannot own any other assets. As we discussed in Chapter 5, "Vesting Issues and Entity Structures That May Affect Exchanges," LLCs are owned by their members and may be managed by their members or by a designated manager. To satisfy 1031 requirements, multiple single-member LLCs (SMLLCs) are set up.

As you already know, each 1031 investor acquiring an interest in the TIC property must do so in the same manner in which he or she sold a previous property. Therefore, all the TIC investors in one property cannot be members of the same LLC unless they all originally sold their relinquished properties in that LLC. Since that is not likely, if they all now joined into one LLC, that would constitute a partnership interest (nonqualifying personal property). For example, if 10 people each acquired a 10 percent interest in one entity, but had each sold different properties to begin with, none of them would have a valid exchange. Thus, each investor has to take his or her portion of the new property in his or her very own separate single-member LLC.

## Identification in a TIC Transaction

Another special issue that arises when 1031 investors purchase an interest in a TIC has to do with *identifying* the replacement property. As you will recall, a taxpayer must identify what he or she intends to purchase "with specificity." If you want to buy an interest in a TIC property, you *must* indicate the percentage of the real property that you intend to acquire on your identification document. It is insufficient to identify "the Empire State Building, New York City." You absolutely must identify "a 3 percent interest in the Empire State Building, New York City."

## Is It Real Estate or Is It a Security?

Another issue affecting TIC deals has to do with how they are sold. As of this writing, there is a question as to whether TIC deals should be treated as securities. If so, they should be qualified under federal and state securities laws and sold accordingly. In that case, there would be much more regulation and much more protection for potential buyers in terms of the documentation required to be made available. If these deals are not securities, then they are simply real estate transactions, which can be sold by real estate agents. Currently they are being sold both ways. In either case, both the investor and her or his advisor should carefully review all of the offering materials so that they have a clear understanding of what they are investing in, what the costs are anticipated to be, and what the risks are.

An interesting point arises concerning the implications of TIC deals being classified as securities. If these deals are securities for purposes of compliance with the securities laws, then one would question whether they qualify under Section 1031, given that the language of Section 1031(a)(2) prohibits exchanges of "stocks, bonds, or notes (or) other securities." Notwithstanding this language, the term *securities* used in the statute has historical reference to debt securities. In any case, at the present time, it appears that what may be a security for securities law purposes is not necessarily a security for tax law purposes.

## Delaware Statutory Trusts

A Delaware statutory trust (DST) is a trust established under the laws of the state of Delaware to hold title to property. A person who has an interest in a DST is a "beneficiary." The elements are one or more trustees to administer the trust, one or more beneficiaries who own the financial interests in the trust, and a corpus, or real estate investment. Delaware statutory trusts are similar to tenancies in common and limited liability companies, but they are not identical. This is a trust structure that some TIC sponsors are using in place of the more familiar TIC (individual) ownership. Title is held by one entity instead of multiple entities. Like a normal trust, a trustee manages it. The extent of the trustee's powers is an issue.

Prior to 2004, it was generally believed that a DST was unsuited for an exchange. However, Revenue Ruling 2004–86 (see Appendix E) addressed the suitability of a DST for holding title to replacement property in 1031 exchanges, and found that the specific DST described in that ruling would qualify. The IRS also ruled that by acquiring the beneficial interest in the DST, the taxpayer would be treated as acquiring the underlying real estate that the DST owned. The IRS further ruled that the taxpayer would not be treated as having received a certificate of trust or beneficial interest prohibited in Section 1031(a)(2)(E). Note, however, that the DST in this ruling had only a single owner and was not particularly typical of what is usually done in TIC-sponsored DST ownership structures. It is an open question whether DSTs *with multiple owners* will be acceptable to the IRS. It will definitely depend on the actual trust terms and the operating agreement among the owners and the designated trustee.

Inasmuch as this is a very new area of 1031 law, the future use of DST structures in 1031 transactions is very much up in the air. It is suggested that taxpayers and their advisors attempt to stay up to date if they are contemplating an investment in a TIC using one of these DST structures.

As is the case with a normal TIC purchase, if a 1031 investor elects to purchase a replacement property with a TIC sponsor using a DST structure, he or she *must* indicate the percentage of the DST being acquired on the identification document.

## Oil and Gas Investments; Mineral and Timber Rights

Oil, gas, and mineral interests are common in Texas, Colorado, and some other western states. These interests come in many shapes and sizes. Some qualify as real property interests; some do not. Some interests will qualify for 1031 exchanges; some will not. Other natural resources, such as timber rights and water rights, have similar characterization issues. Investments in oil, gas, and mineral rights have been common for many years. Recently, oil and gas drilling sponsors have "discovered" 1031 investors as a potential source of investment dollars. By its own terms, Rev. Proc. 2002–22 (tenancy in common), discussed earlier, does *not* apply to mineral rights deals, but only to rental real estate investments.

Generally, oil, gas, and other mineral rights are part of the real property to which they are connected (they are literally "in the ground"), but the rights can be severed and sold separately. Timber and timber rights have a similar treatment under Section 1031.

The owner of the mineral rights cannot use the land where the minerals are located, but may be entitled to an "easement" or "right" to extract the underground or above-ground assets. Where the mineral or timber rights are "unlimited" by time or amount, they have generally been held to be like kind to other real property interests. Where these various interests are deemed interests in real property, they can be exchanged not only for each other, but also for all other types of real property interests. (Review the discussion of qualifying property in Chapter 4 for more detailed information.)[6–8]

## Identification of Oil, Gas, and Mineral Rights

One of the problems with exchanges involving this type of property is that it may be difficult to determine whether the sale or purchase should be deemed to involve a single property or multiple properties. When TIC sponsors are offering oil and gas interests, these interests often involve multiple noncontiguous properties in different counties and possibly even different states. This fact creates potential identification issues for 1031 investors. When these interests are used as replacement properties, they probably need to be identified using the 200 percent rule rather than the three-property rule. (You may wish to review Chapter 10, "Identification of Replacement Property," if you are interested in this type of replacement property

## Real Estate Investment Trusts (REITs)

Real estate investment trusts (REITs) are entities created under the Internal Revenue Code to own and manage real estate activities.[9] They are so-called pass-through entities, which means that there is no tax at the entity level; instead, income is flowed through to the owners and taxed at the shareholder level. REITs can own underlying real estate (equity REITs) or hold mortgages on real estate (mortgage REITs). REITs, as entities, can and do often engage in 1031 exchanges.

Most REITs are large public companies. Their shares are usually traded on a stock exchange. A direct interest in real estate cannot be exchanged for an interest in a REIT. Ownership of REIT shares is an *indirect* way of owning real estate; the shares will not qualify as like-kind property.

## Some Final Thoughts on TICs

If you are considering investing in a TIC with any of the several types of ownership structures we have mentioned, be sure to check the credentials of the sponsor you are dealing with, the sponsor's track record, and the sponsor's familiarity with Section 1031. Some are excellent, and they can be a valuable resource for the right investor.

The TIC industry has a separate trade organization, called TICA (Tenant in Common Association), and TIC sponsors have become big players in the real estate industry. Some of the sponsors have been in business for a long time and are extremely professional. Usually TIC sponsors market "institutional-quality" properties to individuals who do not know one another and who are seeking to avoid personal management of their property.

One final factor to consider with respect to TIC deals is your ability to sell the TIC if you want or need to do so. If you own a 3 percent interest in a large property, it may not be as readily marketable as a 100 percent interest in a property. Since the TIC industry remains relative new, more investors have gone into these deals than have attempted to sell them. The sponsors generally advise that they will work with you on this should the issue arise, but it would be prudent to inquire about this before you make a decision to proceed.

*Authors' Note:* We are not expressing an opinion on this, but merely alerting you to a potential issue that should be considered when you are evaluating whether a TIC deal is right for you.

## Endnotes

1. Rev. Proc. 2002–22, 2002–1 CB 733.
2. Rev. Proc. 2002–22.
3. *Bergford v. Commissioner,* 12 F3d 166 (9th Cir 1993).
4. *Madison Gas & Electric v. Commissioner,* 633 F2d 512 (7th Cir 1980).
5. Rev. Rul. 75–374, 1975–2CB 261.
6. *Commissioner of Internal Revenue v. Crichton* 122 F2d 181 (5th Cir 1941). Under a predecessor statute to 1031, applying Louisiana law, the court approved an exchange of a city lot for unimproved country land containing "oil, gas and other minerals."
7. See also Rev. Rul. 68–331, 1968–1 CB 352, in which the exchange of oil leases for a fee interest in an improved ranch was approved
8. See also Rev. Rul. 72–117, in which, under Section 1033, the sale of unimproved real estate under threat of condemnation and purchase of overriding oil and gas royalties with the proceeds was approved.
9. IRC Section 856 et seq.

# 13

# Personal Residences— Combining Sections 121 and 1031

*Can I do a 1031 exchange with my personal residence? Can I buy a property as part of a 1031 exchange and convert it into my residence?*

Section 1031, by definition, involves investment property. A personal residence is not considered investment property. Some property, however, may qualify as both personal and investment property at the same time. Consider, for example, a duplex where you live in one of the units. Other situations to consider involve a residence that has been converted to a rental property, and vice versa.

## The Importance of Section 121

IRC Section 121 governs the tax liability arising from the sale of a primary residence. Most owners of real estate are familiar with the special exemption from capital gains taxes that arise from the sale of their personal residence that Section 121 affords. Although Congress has changed the law from time to time over the years, it has consistently provided homeowners with a special kind of tax benefit when they sell their homes. Previously this subject was dealt with in Internal Revenue Code Section 1034, which was a rollover provision similar to its companion sections, 1031 and 1033.

The current law, IRC Section 121, allows an individual homeowner to shelter the first $250,000 of capital gains on the sale of his or her principal residence; a husband and wife can shelter $500,000 of gain if they file a joint tax return. The primary requisite is that the homeowner must have lived in the residence for two of the prior five years, and it must be his or her principal residence. This exemption is not available for a vacation home or second home, but only for one's primary residence.

Property that is eligible for the Section 121 exemption, however, will usually be ineligible for an exchange, because personal residences are not considered qualifying property under Section 1031. However, there are some specific fact patterns in which taxpayers will be permitted to utilize both IRC Sections 121 and 1031 to their advantage. There are four types of property for which this could be so.

## Primary Residence Converted to a Rental

Assume that Dale and Julia acquired a residence, Homestead 1, in 1990 for $100,000 and lived in it for several years. In June 2003, Dale and Julia moved to Homestead 2, their new primary residence, and began to rent Homestead 1 to tenants. If Homestead 1 is then sold in March 2006 for $700,000, they have a gain of $600,000 (for the sake of this example, we will ignore any depreciation). Since Dale and Julia resided in Homestead 1 for at least two of the prior five years, they will qualify for exemption of the first $500,000 of gain under Section 121. However, they still have an additional gain of $100,000, which could be subject to capital gains tax.

Fortunately, pursuant to Rev. Proc. 2005–14, Dale and Julia can use Section 1031 to shelter the remaining gain. Since Homestead 1 has been used as a rental property for nearly three years, it is also eligible for an exchange. Dale and Julia may do as they wish with the $500,000, which comes to them exempt from any tax. If they have set up an exchange transaction and complied with Section 1031, they may also now acquire a qualified replacement property; if they reinvest at least the $100,000 of cash equity at the time of purchase, they will fully defer all taxes.

The effect on the carryover basis related to a 1031 exchange cannot be overlooked. According to Rev. Proc. 2005–14, the basis in the replacement property will be "increased by any gain attributable to the relinquished business property that is excluded under Section 121." What this means is that you get a big benefit. You get either $250,000 or $500,000 tax free, and you get to include it in the basis of your replacement property.

## Property Used both as a Primary Residence and for Business or Investment

As an alternative, what if Dale and Julia own a four-unit apartment building, where they occupy one unit as their primary residence, and the other three units are rented out to tenants? Similarly, consider a property where Dale and Julia live upstairs and run a business, such as a day care center or a bakery, in the downstairs area. In either of these situations, Dale and Julia can allocate a portion of the property for a 1031 exchange and a portion for tax treatment under Section 121. In one case, the court approved an allocation made based upon the square footage of the respective areas,[1–3] but other allocations, such as rental value, may also be appropriate, depending upon the circumstances. Your tax advisor can assist you if this is your situation.

## Property Used as a Primary Residence, with a Portion Used for Business

The most obvious example of this would be a home with a room or suite of rooms set aside as a home office or other area used exclusively for a trade or business purpose. Code Section 280A limits the deductions available to homeowners who use a portion of their home for business purposes.

*Authors' Note:* A further discussion of Section 280A is beyond the scope of this book, but investors who are in this situation should be aware of the provisions of this section.)

*Caveat*: Section 121 cannot be used to offset the gain resulting from depreciation deductions taken on the investment portion of the property. If Dale and Julia, during the time they were renting out Homestead 1, took a depreciation deduction of $20,000 on their tax return, that depreciation cannot be taken under Section 121, but it can be included in the deferred gain under Section 1031.[4]

## Conversion to a Primary Residence

Assume that on January 15, 2002, Dale and Julia acquired a replacement property in a 1031 exchange and rented it out to tenants. Further assume that they bought the property for $500,000, but that it had a carryover basis of $200,000 because of the earlier exchange. In June 2004, they moved into the property and converted it to their personal residence. If they sell it in July 2006 for $700,000, after residing there for over two years, can they claim the $500,000 exemption for a married couple filing a joint tax return, and thus avoid owing any taxes?

Regrettably, they cannot. Under the American Jobs Creation Act of 2004, signed into law by President Bush on October 22, 2004, in order to take advantage of the benefits of Section 121 with respect to property acquired in a 1031 exchange, the taxpayer is required to have owned the property for at least five years before disposing of it. Since Dale and Julia owned the property for only $4^{1}/_{2}$ years, they cannot rely on Section 121.

Alternatively, if Dale and Julia were to sell the property as described in this scenario, but not before January 15, 2007, they could take advantage of both Sections 1031 and 121. At that point, they would have owned the property for a full five years and would have resided in it for at least $2^{1}/_{2}$ years.

The confluence of Sections 121 and 1031 may offer opportunities for great benefits to taxpayers in some circumstances, if they plan carefully. Although it is not the typical exchange, in certain cases it can be a terrific way to shelter your gains from taxes.

## Endnotes

1. *Poague v. United States*, 66 AFTR2d (RIA) 5825 (E.D. Va. 1990), aff'd., 947 F2d 942 (4th Cir 1991).
2. See also Rev. Proc. 2005–14, Example 2.
3. See PLR 8051054 (9/23/80) (a Section 1033 case) for further examples of how this can be used.
4. See Rev. Proc. 2005–14, Example 3.

# 14

# Refinancing Exchange Property

*Can you refinance your property, pull out some equity, and then do an exchange?*

As a general rule, no. The IRS treats this as if you received boot at the closing of the sale/exchange.

## Refinancing as an Alternative to Section 1031

As a general proposition, refinancing your property is a nontaxable event. That means that you do not incur any tax liability when you borrow money. Refinancing property is one way to access some of the equity in your property without a sale. This chapter examines when you can refinance property involved in an exchange.

Refinancing may in fact be used as an alternative to doing a 1031 exchange. You can refinance an existing property, and then use the cash obtained from the new loan to purchase additional property. In deciding whether to refinance or to sell (exchange) a particular property, the owner needs to analyze the potential for continued appreciation and balance it against whatever better alternative investments are available. Refinancing to increase cash flow is common when interest rates are falling, or in a low-interest-rate environment. But things can get more complicated if the refinancing is done in contemplation of an exchange.

## Refinancings before or after an Exchange

The IRS distinguishes between refinancing your relinquished property prior to a sale and refinancing your replacement property following its acquisition. The IRS views the former as a method for "cashing out" or partially cashing out in anticipation of an exchange. Apparently, the IRS does not find the latter quite as problematic as the former.

For example, if Patty has an investment property with a fair market value of $500,000 that is encumbered by a loan of $100,000, then Patty has $400,000 of equity to be reinvested if she does an exchange. If Patty buys a replacement property for her full exchange value of $500,000, but uses only $200,000 as a down payment, the remaining $200,000 that she keeps in her pocket will be cash boot.

However, consider the difference if she refinanced her property prior to the sale and replaced the existing encumbrance with a new loan of $300,000. At that point, Patty would immediately pocket $200,000, with no tax consequences at all. She would then have only $200,000 of equity remaining in the property. If Patty then did an exchange, she could buy replacement property for $500,000 and use the $200,000 as a down payment, leaving her in what seems to be the same circumstances as in the former example.

However, this type of refinancing can put Patty at risk of having her exchange invalidated, or at least of having the IRS decide that the refinancing was really done to skirt the 1031 requirement that all the equity be reinvested, and she may have to pay tax on the $200,000 anyway. Patty's timing and intent become very critical in this situation. Therefore, if you are contemplating a refinancing, to be followed by an exchange, you should definitely consult with your tax advisor before proceeding.

### Limited Tax Authority Available

There is limited authority on this subject. In a 1984 Private Letter Ruling, the IRS held that refinancing the relinquished property just prior to closing on the sale would constitute taxable boot. In making this ruling, the IRS applied a tax doctrine called the *step-transaction doctrine*.[1] This is an IRS principle that allows it to connect two or more seemingly unrelated, sequential steps and treat them as if they occurred together (as one transaction). Under this doctrine, the IRS held that if a taxpayer refinances and draws out cash, and immediately thereafter does an exchange, it is the equivalent of the taxpayer's receiving cash boot at the closing, because this is a way for the taxpayer to accomplish exactly what Section 1031 does not allow.

The opposite result was reached in a 1994 Tax Court case.[2] In that case, the taxpayer refinanced his property one week after entering into an agreement to sell it. The court held that the refinancing was unrelated to the exchange, and thus the loan proceeds were not taxable boot. The court focused on the fact that the taxpayer's existing loan was almost due and that he had been attempting to refinance for some time prior to the sale.

The IRS also ruled that a partnership refinancing of its property approximately eight months prior to a sale did not result in taxable boot to the partners. The partnership represented to the IRS that the refinancing was arranged to take advantage of lower interest rates, at a time when no sale was contemplated.[3]

In another case, the Tax Court raised questions about a debt incurred just prior to the consummation of an exchange, which debt was taken out in order to equalize liabilities between the parties.[4] The court held that substance must prevail over form (another widely used tax doctrine), and ruled that the agreement to equalize debt was to be disregarded. This case is also a good example of when mortgage boot arises. Here the taxpayers were relieved of an amount of mortgage debt in excess of what they assumed in their purchase, and thus were deemed to have received mortgage boot.

In yet another Tax Court case, the exchange agreement required the seller of the replacement property to increase the indebtedness on that property as a condition of the transaction in order to balance equities.[5] The taxpayer assumed the new encumbrance as part of his acquisition of the replacement property. The IRS's argument against the taxpayer was that the increase in the mortgage should be considered taxable boot to the taxpayer. But the Tax Court took note of the fact that this was an encumbrance placed by the seller on his own property, and that taxpayer Garcia did not get any cash. Based on this fact, the court held that there was "economic substance" for the new indebtedness, and approved the transaction.

In another example of boot received, the taxpayer exchanged four old trucks with International Harvester for four new trucks. He also gave International Harvester a purchase money note for a portion of the purchase price.[6] The taxpayer received $22,000 cash in the transaction, and the money went for use in his business operations. The court held that the taxpayer received taxable boot. In an interesting side note, the court further stated that if the $22,000 had come from a third-party lender rather than from the seller, it would not have been taxable.

The IRS has ruled that replacement hotel properties acquired in an exchange can be refinanced after the conclusion of the exchange without triggering taxable boot.[7] The IRS also stated that the properties could be transferred into single-asset limited liability companies in order to satisfy the lenders' requirements.

Ultimately, each situation in which a refinancing is contemplated should be evaluated on its own merits. This is definitely another of those gray areas of Section 1031 where one must proceed with caution. For other decisions and rulings related to this issue, the reader is referred to additional citations set forth at the end of this chapter.

## Endnotes

1. PLR 8434015.
2. *Fred L. Fredericks*, TC Memo 1994–27.
3. PLR 200019014 (2/10/00).
4. *Long v. Commissioner*, 77 TC 1045 (10/29/81).
5. *Phillip M. Garcia* 80 TC 491 (1983), acq. 1984–2 CB 1.
6. *Frederick W. Behrens*, TC Memo 1985–195, aff'd. 786 F2d 1170 (8th Cir 1986).
7. PLR 200131014 (5/2/01).

# "Construction" ("Build to Suit") Exchanges

*Can you ever use your exchange proceeds to make improvements or repairs to exchange property?*

Yes; however, you cannot use the money to make improvements to property that is not involved in the exchange.

## Construction Exchanges, Generally

A *construction exchange* involves using a portion of the exchange proceeds to construct improvements on replacement real estate that is purchased as part of your exchange. A construction exchange is also referred to as an *improvement* or a *build-to-suit exchange*. For convenience, these will be collectively referred to here simply as a construction exchange. These types of transactions are more complex, and more expensive, than a typical delayed exchange. Generally, this issue of construction will not apply to personal property exchanges, so the discussion here will be limited to real property transactions only.

## Engage a Knowledgeable Qualified Intermediary

Achieving a successful result with a construction exchange requires careful planning and clear communication with your qualified intermediary. There are special procedures for identification of replacement property. You must utilize an experienced qualified intermediary who is willing to facilitate the transaction and knows how to do so. Not all qualified intermediaries can or will process construction exchanges. Thus, if your intent is to engage in construction on your replacement property, be sure to ask in advance if your qualified intermediary can handle your transaction. Once your qualified intermediary is holding your exchange funds, it is too late to change intermediaries. (Review Chapter 6 for an explanation.)

## "Parking Transaction"

In most exchanges, the documentation serves to create the "legal fiction" that the qualified intermediary is the seller of the relinquished property and the buyer of the replacement property. Title to the property never actually goes in the name of the qualified intermediary. However, a distinguishing feature of a construction exchange is that the exchangor cannot take title to the replacement property until the improvements are completed. Therefore, the qualified intermediary, usually acting through an entity it controls called an exchange accommodation titleholder (EAT), will actually take title to the replacement property for some period of time during the 180-day exchange period before delivering that property to the exchangor. This is often referred to as a *parking transaction*, because the property that the exchangor wishes to acquire is temporarily "parked" with the qualified intermediary. (The concepts of parking, as well as the use of an EAT, also arise in connection with reverse exchanges. These topics are discussed in more detail in Chapter 16.)

## Improvements Must Be Completed during the Exchange Period

Because the time available to complete an exchange is only 180 days to stay within the safe harbor of Section 1031, the extent of the improvements that an exchangor can make is necessarily going to be limited. It is important to understand that the exchange value of any replacement property is determined as of the time you receive that property. Receipt is established by the date on which the benefits and burdens of ownership change from seller to buyer.[1] If you have the intention to acquire a replacement property to which construction and/or improvements will be added, that will have a significant bearing on how the transaction must be structured. In other words, to be included in the exchange, all improvements must be completed during the exchange period. In practical terms, that means that in order for the costs of any improvements to be included as part of the exchange value, the work must be completed prior to the date when title is transferred to you.

## Identification—Again!

Another important concern regarding construction exchanges is identification of the replacement property. With a construction exchange, the replacement property you will ultimately acquire after the improvements are made may not actually exist at the time it is necessary to identify it. That is because the improvements are not yet a part of that property. You must do your best to describe the contemplated construction (e.g., a new roof, a new driveway, or a new barn). See Table 15–1 for an example description.

You must supply as much detail as is practicable regarding the intended improvements in order to describe not what exists presently, but what will exist as of the date of transfer to you.[2]

**Table 15–1    Valid Identification—Construction Exchange**

To:    Friendly Accommodator Company:

The following are the properties we are considering as replacement properties in our 1031 exchange. We plan to acquire only one of the properties listed.

**1. 987 Arcadia Street, Milwaukee, WI**
    To be improved with addition of a new roof and copper plumbing.

**2. Vacant Lot, Corner of Second and Locust Street, Boise, Idaho**
    To be improved with a duplex, approximately 3,000 square feet, consisting of two 1,500-square-foot, 3-bedroom units.

*Michael Q. Taxpayer*                          *Marilyn Q. Taxpayer*
Michael Q. Taxpayer                            Marilyn Q. Taxpayer

## "Like-Kind" Issue—Real versus Personal Property

To better comprehend a construction exchange, you need to have a clear understanding of the difference between real and personal property. As we discussed in Chapter 4, real property generally includes the land and any appurtenances (structures or improvements) affixed to it. Buildings, walls, outbuildings, and the fixtures attached to them will therefore be deemed real property. For example, when you buy a house, an apartment building, or an office building, the plumbing fixtures, built-in appliances, attached window coverings, and the like are considered part of the structure, and they enhance the actual value of the real property. They are not valued separately from the property. These appurtenances are a part of the underlying physical structure of the replacement property, and are therefore deemed like kind to the relinquished property.

### Appurtenances versus Incidental Property

Appurtenances are different from *incidental property*.[3] Incidental property is personal property of relatively minor value that does not require separate identification in an exchange transaction. A good example would be a 12-unit apartment building with a courtyard garden area that contains some patio furniture for use by the residents. The patio furniture—a few tables and chairs, perhaps a chaise lounge, and some umbrellas—is incidental property. Its monetary value is minuscule compared to the value of the entire complex, so it can, for all intents and purposes, be essentially disregarded in the exchange.

However, if there is a significant amount of furniture, equipment, or other items that are not affixed to the property, this may need to be valued separately. These might include items such as lawn mowers, free-standing appliances, beds, desks, tables and chairs, and office equipment. For example, if the real property were a motel, these could have a significant value relative to the value of the asset being sold. They are not like kind to real property, and they cannot be included in the value of the replacement property for exchange purposes.

---

### Example 1

The exchangor, Ima Trader, sells her relinquished property, a six-unit apartment building, for $1,000,000 on March 1. Assume that after deducting commissions and other allowable costs, the net exchange value that must be replaced is $950,000. All sales proceeds are sent to the designated qualified intermediary. Ms. Trader's 45th day is April 15, and her 180th day is August 28. Assume further that on or before April 15, Ms. Trader identifies to her qualified intermediary a 10-unit apartment building that can be acquired for $900,000, but that requires $50,000 in repairs. The necessary repairs consist of a new roof ($25,000), new copper piping ($15,000), and paint ($10,000).

If Ms. Trader acquires the property on May 15, prior to any of these repairs being done, her replacement property has a value of only $900,000. Even if the repairs are completed by July 30, well before the end of the 180th day of the exchange period of August 28, the roof, plumbing, and paint were not done until after Ms. Trader has already acquired ownership. Therefore, the additional $50,000 is not being spent on like-kind real property. It is being spent on shingles, pipes, paint and labor,. Those items are *services and personal property*. Ms. Trader will have to pay tax on the $50,000, which is boot.

## Example 2

Assume the same initial fact pattern as in Example 1. However, instead of Ms. Trader's taking title to the replacement property on May 15, title is taken in the name of an exchange accommodation titleholder (EAT) controlled by the qualified intermediary. Ms. Trader arranges for the roof repair, new piping, and painting. The repairs to the roof, copper piping, and paint are then undertaken and completed prior to July 30. The work is paid for using the exchange proceeds remaining with the qualified intermediary, or, if those funds have been exhausted, Ms. Trader pays for them directly. After July 30, but prior to the end of the exchange period, the replacement property is deeded from the EAT to Ms. Trader. It now has a value of $950,000. The exchange is completed, and Ms. Trader has no taxable boot. *Note:* If Ima Trader had used all of her cash to acquire the replacement property and borrowed money for the improvements (completed before she took title), the value of the improvements would still count toward the value of the replacement property received.

---

**Example 3**

Again, assume the same facts as in Example 2, with one difference. Title is again taken in the name of the EAT on May 15. The roof work and copper piping are completed. But the painting was not even begun, because of a very prolonged rainy season that prevented the painters from working. August 28 is approaching. Ms. Trader takes title to the replacement property on August 25, three days before her 180-day exchange period expires, in order to ensure that she has a valid exchange. At that point, the value of the real property received is $940,000. The exchange is successful, but Ms. Trader will owe tax on the boot of $10,000.

---

## Can Ima Trader Pay for Improvements in Advance of the Work Being Done?

In Example 3, could Ms. Trader have paid the painter $10,000 before the work was done, but prior to her taking title, and then have the work done afterward? Under that scenario, all of the exchange funds would have been spent prior to her acquiring ownership.

Nice try, but unfortunately, the answer is *no*. The value of the replacement property at the time it is received (i.e., when title is taken) is determinative. Work done afterward, even if paid for in advance, does not count toward the value of the exchange. The taxpayer must literally "snap a picture" of the replacement property as it exists on the date of receipt. What the camera sees is what Ima gets (credit for).

---

**Example 4**

Consider a situation, again, where Ima Trader sells her relinquished property for $1,000,000, with costs and commissions of $50,000. But this time, assume that she decides to acquire a large parcel of vacant land in a resort area for $510,000, and then to install four modular homes on that parcel and rent them out to vacationers. Each modular home will cost $110,000, resulting in a total investment of $950,000.

The land and the modular homes are purchased using the exchange proceeds. Title to the land and the modular housing must be taken in the name of the EAT. As described, this transaction should qualify as a construction exchange. Mobile homes, manufactured homes, and modular housing may all be similarly treated as construction.

Yet it is not sufficient that the modular homes are simply delivered to the location of the land prior to Ms. Trader's taking title. To be considered part of the real property, mobile homes cannot truly be mobile, because if they are, they will be classified as personal property and thus are not like kind to real property. They will be considered real property only after Ima has them affixed or permanently attached to the ground or bolted to a foundation. It is this act of permanently affixing the home to the land that converts it from personal property to real property. If that is done prior to Ms. Trader's exchange deadline of August 28, and title is then transferred from the EAT to Ms. Trader, the exchange will be complete, and all the tax will be deferred. However, if the modular homes are not yet attached when she takes title, there will be $440,000 of taxable boot.

## Minor Improvements versus True Construction

A variation on the idea of a construction exchange can arise when you wish to make some relatively minor repairs to your replacement property, which may require only a few days to complete. In that case, you can often avoid the complexity and expense of a parking transaction if you can obtain the cooperation of the seller of the replacement property.

By way of example, assume that Angela needs to spend $750,000 on her replacement property to fully defer all of her capital gains tax. Angela locates a suitable property, a fourplex, which will cost her $730,000 to acquire. But the property needs new carpeting and upgraded built-in appliances. The cost of those items will be $20,000. The carpet can be laid and the appliances installed in two days. If the seller will cooperate, Angela may be able to arrange for the work to be done just before closing, and to have the invoices submitted to the closing officer for payment directly to the vendors and reflected on the final settlement statement.

## Lease with Option to Buy

Another approach to doing improvements on the replacement property before closing might be for Angela to obtain a *lease with option to buy* from the seller. The lease must permit her to undertake the needed modifications to the replacement property. Angela can cause the improvements to be completed, using exchange funds controlled by the qualified intermediary. These funds are disbursed directly to the vendors and workers by the qualified intermediary. After the work is complete, the replacement property purchase transaction can actually close, and Angela will acquire the completed property.

Alternatively, Angela might amend the contract with the seller, obligating the seller to do the work and increasing the purchase price accordingly. Again, the closing agent can pay the costs of the repairs/improvements, using exchange proceeds, and include them on the closing statement. Thus, those costs will be reflected in the increased purchase price of the property.

Of course, there is an element of risk to Angela in using these last two methods, because she is improving property that belongs to someone else. What if the seller likes the improvements and decides not to complete the sale to Angela? Her exchange will be in peril. So this may not be appropriate in all circumstances. Angela must feel comfortable that her seller will perform. But in some instances, it is a good way to ensure that as much exchange value as possible is incorporated into the new property before the date of closing, at minimal expense to the taxpayer.

## A Construction Exchange on Property Currently Owned Is Prohibited

A question that inevitably arises is whether an exchangor can use exchange proceeds to make improvements to property that the exchangor already owns. Given the prior discussion, it should be obvious that he or she cannot do so. First, this would violate the exchange rule, which requires that the taxpayer relinquish one property and replace it with a new property. If you already own the subject property, by definition it cannot be a *replacement* property. Second, since the taxpayer already owns the property, the like-kind requirement would not be met, because the taxpayer would be using exchange proceeds for labor and materials (services and personal property), not for real property.

## Mechanics of a Construction Exchange

The sale of a relinquished property in a construction exchange will generally be the same as a sale in any delayed or forward exchange, as described in Chapter 6. But the replacement property paperwork will differ significantly because of the additional documentation and processing requirements.[4]

The following procedures involving the replacement property are likely to be included:

- *Assignment of the purchase contract.* The qualified intermediary will substitute into the transaction as the buyer (just as it would in a delayed exchange).

- *Title transferred to EAT.* The closing agent must be made aware that this is a construction exchange. Title to the replacement property must be conveyed to the nominee of the qualified intermediary, an exchange accommodation titleholder, which is typically an LLC controlled by the qualified intermediary.

- *Lease.* A lease agreement will be created between you and the EAT, and this may require you to pay a nominal monthly rent to the EAT during the period when you are the "tenant" and the EAT is your "landlord." It will be a "triple net" lease, meaning that you will be required to pay all taxes, insurance, and repairs and maintenance on the property during the tenancy. Unlike a typical rental agreement, the lease will provide that you are free to make alterations or improvements to the property without the consent of the landlord.

- *Insurance.* You will be required to provide evidence of insurance covering the EAT for all types of liability of a property owner, prior to the closing.

- *Replacement property funding.* At the closing, exchange proceeds will be transmitted from the qualified intermediary to fund the purchase.

- *Deed recorded.* A deed vesting title in the name of the EAT will be recorded.

- *Exchangor takes possession, makes improvements.* Following the closing, you will take possession of the property. You may proceed to undertake any construction or improvements that you require, and you may call for exchange proceeds to be paid to vendors to fund the work, to the extent that such money is available. You may also add additional funds, if necessary, to complete the work.

- *Replacement property conveyed to exchangor.* When the improvements are completed, but no later than the 180th day of the exchange period, the EAT will convey the replacement property to you. This will conclude your exchange, because you now own the replacement property.

## Document the Exchange Value

In a construction exchange, it is your responsibility to document the value of the replacement property as of the date you take title. This can be done in either of two ways. The soundest and easiest is to base the value on the actual amounts invested in the property, including the initial price paid for the land plus the actual cost of improvements. Therefore, you should keep careful track of all of the costs of acquisition and improvements. However, if you believe that the property value exceeds the amount you have invested, you may engage an appraiser to provide a written valuation of the property as of the date of acquisition. If you choose to do this, it is wise to consult a tax advisor about exactly how you should document the value.

It is not necessary to have a certificate of occupancy to complete a construction exchange. It is not even necessary that all of the construction be complete. Whatever is completed as of the date of receipt will be valued and may be included in the exchange.

## Example

Consider Sophia's situation. She sold her relinquished property for $500,000. Her intent is to improve a parcel of vacant land, Blackacre, with a 2,000-square-foot rental house. The vacant land cost $350,000. Her contractor is working more slowly than she expected. At the time she receives title, on the 179th day, the land and the architectural drawings are paid for, the grading is done, and the foundation is poured. However, the house is still not even framed. If the value of Blackacre, including the plans, grading, and foundation, are equal to $500,000, Sophia may have a fully taxdeferred exchange, despite the need for additional investment after her EAT deeds the replacement property over to her.

On the other hand, if the work done as of the date Sophia takes title, plus the value of the land, is equal to only $450,000, Sophia may have taxable boot of $50,000. Still, she has a valid exchange.

*Authors' Note:* As you can see, a construction exchange differs significantly from a typical forward exchange. It cannot be done successfully without effective preliminary planning and conversation with your qualified intermediary. It may also be possible to do a construction exchange outside 180-day safe harbor limitations, but that is very complex and beyond the scope of this book.

## Endnotes

1. *Keith v. Commissioner*, 115 TC 605, 611 (2000); sale occurs when the benefits and burdens of ownership transfer from seller to buyer.
2. Reg. 1.1031(k)–1(e).
3. Reg. 1.1031(k)–1(c)(5).
4. A good analysis of a construction exchange is found in PLR 200329021 (7/18/03); see especially footnote 2 for additional authority.

# 16

# Reverse Exchanges— Parking Transactions

*Can you buy a new property before you sell your old property and still qualify for an exchange?*

The answer is *yes*.

## Reverse Exchanges, Generally

Reverse exchanges are often difficult to understand, as by their very nature they are both complex and expensive, require a great deal of prior planning, and take additional time to set up. They should never be undertaken without consulting with very knowledgeable tax advisors. The discussion here will focus on real property reverse exchanges, although the basic structure described could theoretically apply to a personal property exchange as well.

A guiding principle of any exchange is that the taxpayer cannot hold title to both the relinquished property and the replacement property simultaneously. In the majority of cases, this presents no problems: the taxpayer sells a relinquished property and then locates a replacement property to trade into. The two may close on the same day (*concurrent exchange*), or there may be days, weeks, or months (not to exceed 180 days, of course) between the two closings (a *delayed exchange*). For purposes of this chapter, from time to time we will refer to both concurrent and delayed exchanges as *forward exchanges.* So long as the cash equity from the relinquished property is disbursed in time to acquire the replacement property in a forward exchange, the basic principle will not be violated.

If both properties are under contract at the same time, it is usually possible for the taxpayer to defer the closing of the replacement property until the relinquished property has been conveyed and the cash proceeds are disbursed.

A *reverse exchange*, as its name implies, is a vehicle to consider when the taxpayer finds that a forward exchange just won't work. Occasionally a taxpayer locates a very desirable replacement property that may be too good to pass up, but the property that he or she already owns has not been sold. If the taxpayer is unable to obtain the seller's agreement to extend the closing, he or she may have no choice but to have the the replacement property conveyed before selling the relinquished property.

Until relatively recently, the IRS had never actually indicated whether it would consider a transaction in which the taxpayer bought first and sold later to be valid. There is no specific provision for a reverse exchange in the Code. Reverse exchanges were undertaken by taxpayers and qualified intermediaries at their own risk. But, see an excellent analysis of reverse exchanges in PLR 200111025.

In September 2000, the IRS issued Rev. Proc. 2000–37, 2000–2 CB 308. Rev. Proc. 2000–37 providing the first solid IRS guidance concerning the procedures that would be sanctioned in order for a transaction to be deemed within the "safe harbor" for a reverse-order 1031 exchange. Rev. Proc. 2000–37 was made applicable to all reverse exchanges initiated on or after September 15, 2000.

Even if a transaction is not structured according to Rev. Proc. 2000–37, it may still be successful because this revenue procedure does not entirely rule out other schemes for creating a valid reverse exchange. However, the IRS may examine any non-safe harbor transaction and determine that it did not meet all the criteria to qualify for tax deferral. In that event, the taxpayer would have to pay the capital gains tax anyway. The discussion in this chapter will focus solely on the requirements under the safe harbor created by Rev. Proc. 2000–37.

Keep in mind that the requirements for *qualifying property* and *qualifying use* in a reverse exchange are no different from those in a forward exchange. Likewise, the independence of the intermediary, the necessity to properly identify property within 45 days, and the 180-day time limitations remain in place. The main difference is in the sequence in which the conveyances of the relinquished and replacement properties occur.

## What Is an EAT?

One overarching feature that distinguishes a reverse exchange from a forward exchange is that, instead of the qualified intermediary holding the taxpayer's money, it holds the taxpayer's property—the asset being exchanged. Thus, these transactions are often referred to as *parking transactions*, because the taxpayer will "park" one of the properties involved in the exchange with the assistance of the qualified intermediary.

Although there is no prohibition to prevent the qualified intermediary from taking title to the taxpayer's property directly, this would be undesirable from the standpoint of both the qualified intermediary and the taxpayer. It would not be a good business practice to have the qualified intermediary, who may also hold large amounts of cash, hold title to real property. The seemingly "deep pockets" of the qualified intermediary could be too great a temptation for the filing of lawsuits against properties owned by the qualified intermediary. Such "nuisance" lawsuits could tie up exchange funds that the qualified intermediary holds for other exchangors.

Therefore, the transaction is generally accomplished through a separate entity designated in Rev. Proc. 2000–37 as an *exchange accommodation titleholder*, commonly referred to in the exchange industry as an *EAT*. Usually, the EAT will be an LLC that is controlled by the qualified intermediary.

The best practice is for the qualified intermediary to set up a separate *single-purpose entity* (SPE) for each reverse exchange, to act as the EAT for that exchange transaction only. In this way, the taxpayer will be protected from claims of taxes, liens, or other liabilities of any other individuals, and the lender, if any, will be satisfied that the risk of claims or bankruptcy are minimized. The EAT is a separate taxpaying entity that must maintain books and records separate from those of both the taxpayer and the qualified intermediary. Because of these factors, and because of the more intense involvement required by the qualified intermediary to ensure that all aspects of the transaction are properly set up and documented, not all qualified intermediaries are able or willing to process this type of transaction.

(Note the number of parties involved in a reverse exchange: the taxpayer, the qualified intermediary, the EAT, maybe a lender, at least one buyer and at least one seller, and maybe some new entities created by all of the foregoing. No wonder these transactions are confusing!)

The involvement of an EAT means, of course, that a reverse exchange has certain features in common with a construction exchange, discussed in the previous chapter. Indeed, it is not unusual for a taxpayer to elect to combine the two types of transactions. But a reverse exchange is even more complex than a construction exchange.

One of the principal deterrents to doing a reverse exchange is finding the cash needed to buy the property. Financing the purchase of the replacement property can be difficult, unless the taxpayer has substantial resources above and beyond the equity expected (but not yet available) from the sale of the relinquished property. Only if the taxpayer does not need to rely on that equity to purchase the replacement property should a reverse exchange be attempted. Moreover, in contemplating a reverse exchange, it is imperative that the taxpayer involve his or her attorney, CPA, accountant, and/or other competent tax and financial advisors.

## Reverse Exchange Fees Are High

Another major factor that distinguishes a reverse exchange from a forward exchange is the fee. It is likely to range from an approximate minimum of $4,000 or $5,000 to considerably higher. Compare this to a typical forward exchange, which can usually be accomplished for a fee in the $400 to $1,000 range.

The reasons for this are many. As discussed earlier, the documentation required for a reverse exchange is extensive. The information and processing requirements of the transaction are complicated and necessitate much greater interaction with the qualified intermediary. The risks to the qualified intermediary and the EAT are much higher when they are holding title to property than when they hold only cash proceeds, because there is much more potential liability arising from ownership of real property. The qualified intermediary has the expense of setting up the EAT/SPE, keeping separate records, filing additional tax returns, and possibly dissolving the SPE at the conclusion of the transaction. If the taxpayer's goal is to defer the payment of a large amount of capital gains tax, the extra fee may be inconsequential. Still, a reverse exchange is probably not well suited to a small transaction. Again, sound tax advice and planning is a must.

## Two Possible Structures for a Reverse Exchange

A reverse exchange can be set up in either of two formats, each of which has unique advantages and disadvantages.

### Exchange Last

With the *exchange last* format, the qualified intermediary, through the EAT it designates, takes title to the replacement property—the *replacement* property is parked with the EAT. After the relinquished property is sold, the EAT transfers the replacement property to the taxpayer. This is a little easier to do, and may minimize the likelihood of inadvertently having boot.

### Advantages

The taxpayer does not need to identify the relinquished property immediately. If the taxpayer has more than one property that can be sold to complete the reverse exchange, he or she may delay making a decision for up to 45 days to evaluate which of his properties will be sold at the appropriate time.

If the value of the replacement property is insufficient to cover the entire value of the relinquished property, the time limits for finding a second replacement property to satisfy the entire amount will not start to run until the relinquished property is actually sold. For example, if the replacement property is acquired for $100,000 on March 1 and the relinquished property is eventually sold for $200,000 on June 1, the taxpayer's 45th and 180th days for acquiring an additional property in a possible forward exchange will be measured from June 1 provided the parties set up the transaction carefully. This will give the taxpayer more time to locate a subsequent property to buy.

This is the only option available if construction on the replacement property will be involved.

### Disadvantages

Financing can be a problem. If the taxpayer can pay all cash for the replacement property and has cash for any planned improvements, then the process is fairly easy. But if there will be a lender involved, the process may be difficult, because title will be temporarily vested in the EAT. Lenders usually will not loan money to someone who is not the property owner. Often banks and other licensed lenders must comply with regulations, which may prohibit them from loaning money under such circumstances. However, some sophisticated lenders do understand reverse exchanges and are willing to participate.

---

**Example 1—Exchange Last**

Ina expects to sell her relinquished property for approximately $1,000,000. Assume that after deducting commissions and other allowable costs, the net exchange value that Ina must replace is $950,000. Ina has a loan of $500,000 on the relinquished property, so the net proceeds will be approximately $450,000.

Ina finds a replacement property to buy for $1,000,000. She has $1,000,000 in cash available, and she pays for the property without any loan. Title is parked in the name of the EAT when the replacement property closes on March 1.

Ina and the EAT enter into a lease, giving Ina possession and management during the time that the EAT holds the title. Ina collects rents and pays all expenses of operation and management.

Ina has 45 days to identify which relinquished property she will sell, which is not a problem—her identification date is met in a timely manner. She sells the relinquished property on June 1. Shortly after that, the EAT deeds the replacement property to her. Ina thus never owns both properties at the same time.

Ina may thereafter elect to put a loan of $500,000 on the property, representing the same amount as the debt she had before. She will then still have equity of $450,000, which was the amount of the cash that came from the relinquished property.

---

## Exchange First

With the *exchange first* format, the qualified intermediary, through the EAT it designates, takes title to the relinquished property—the *relinquished* property is parked with the EAT. The EAT holds title to the relinquished property until it is sold, on terms determined by the taxpayer. The EAT executes a deed to the buyer for recording at the closing of the relinquished property.

## Advantages

This structure allows the taxpayer to acquire the replacement property with standard financing, because title to the replacement property will be vested directly in the taxpayer. Also, if the documents are already drawn up showing the taxpayer as the buyer, it is sometimes difficult to change that if the exchange is initiated just before closing.

## Disadvantages

More often than not, the relinquished property is encumbered with a promissory note, secured by a mortgage or deed of trust. There is probably a due on sale clause in the loan documents that may be triggered by the conveyance to the EAT. *Due on sale* provisions require that the loan be paid off immediately when a property is conveyed to a different owner. But in an exchange first transaction, the loan is not going to be paid off when the property is transferred to the EAT. Technically, this is a breach of the borrower's loan obligation, which could result in a foreclosure.

In practical terms, the risk may be minimal in most jurisdictions, because there will be some delay before a lender will be alerted to the conveyance, and there are further legal time limits before a foreclosure for breach of the due on sale provision could actually occur.

Of course, the authors are not encouraging readers to breach legal obligations to their lenders. If the taxpayer is planning on using this format, it may be prudent to advise the lender of the reason for the transfer, and to assure the lender that the property in question is on the market or is already under contract to be sold, and that the lender will be paid in full when the sale closes. The likelihood that a foreclosure would actually threaten the transaction prior to the legal time limits running is remote unless the property is particularly difficult to sell for some reason unrelated to the exchange. The authors have never actually seen this problem threaten any transaction. However, consultation with a real estate attorney about this possibility is recommended before any action is taken.

The issue of boot can be problematic. Remember that in any exchange, the amount of cash proceeds resulting from the sale of a relinquished property is the amount of cash that the client must invest in the replacement property. An insufficient down payment could result in unexpected tax consequences.

---

**Example 2—Exchange First**

In this scenario, Ina again expects to sell her relinquished property for approximately $1,000,000, and after deducting commissions and other allowable costs, the net exchange value that must be replaced is $950,000. Again, she has a loan on the relinquished property of $500,000, so the net proceeds will be approximately $450,000.

Ina finds replacement property to buy for $1,000,000. She will be putting a loan on the replacement property, so the EAT cannot take title to it. Assume that Ina has $500,000 in cash available, and she buys the property with a loan of $500,000. Title will go in Ina's name at the closing.

One day before she takes title to the replacement property, Ina parks the relinquished property in the name of the EAT. She never owns both properties at one time.

Ina and the EAT enter into a lease, giving her possession and management of the property during the time the EAT holds the title. She collects rents and pays all expenses of operation and management.

Again, Ina has 45 days to identify what she will sell, but because she has deeded her relinquished property to the EAT, it is already identified. No further identification will be required. When the relinquished property closes, it is deeded directly from the EAT to the buyer.

---

## Problem

What if Ina doesn't have $500,000 in cash to put down on the replacement property? What if she puts only $400,000 down and gets a $600,000 loan? This is likely to result in $50,000 of boot, since the down payment is less than the total of $450,000 equity that must be reinvested.

## Identification

Unlike the situation in a delayed exchange, where identifying replacement property in a tight real estate market can be nerve-wracking and challenging, in a reverse exchange, the identification is the easy part. The taxpayer knows what he owns and what he plans to sell. Generally only the three-property rule will apply, as neither the 200 percent rule nor the 95 percent rule would be applicable.

## Mechanics and Documentation

The paperwork and mechanics for a reverse exchange are extensive and complex.

- *Agreement.* An agreement to exchange is entered into between the qualified intermediary and the taxpayer, evidencing the intent to undertake a 1031 exchange and setting forth the duties and obligations of each party.
- *Designated titleholder.* The concept of an exchange accommodation titleholder arises from Rev. Proc. 2000–37. The qualified intermediary, or its designee, must take title to one of the properties. The EAT, which will own the property during the exchange period, is either a corporation or an LLC controlled by the qualified intermediary.
- *Transfer of title.* If the transaction is exchange last, title to the replacement property will be conveyed to the EAT at the closing of the replacement property. If the transaction is exchange first, title to the relinquished property must be conveyed to the EAT before the replacement property closes, to ensure that the client doesn't have title to both at once.
- *Qualified exchange accommodation agreement.* A qualified exchange accommodation agreement (QEAA) is executed between the qualified intermediary, the exchangor, and the EAT. This sets forth the terms of the agreement and the obligations of the respective parties regarding ownership rights in the parked property.
- *Assignment of purchase contract.* The qualified intermediary substitutes for the buyer in the replacement property transaction, but directs that title be put in the name of the EAT if it is an exchange last transaction. If it is an exchange first transaction, title goes directly to the taxpayer at the time of the closing.
- *Lease.* There is a lease between the EAT and the taxpayer covering the parked property. It allows the taxpayer to be in possession of the property and requires the taxpayer to manage the property and pay all taxes, insurance, and maintenance during the term of the lease. It allows alterations or improvements. The lease may provide a nominal rent. The rent does not have to be at market value.

- *Promissory note.* There is typically a promissory note given to the taxpayer by the EAT. The amount of the promissory note will be the equity value of the parked property.
- *Insurance.* The client must insure the EAT for property owner liability, as well as provide any other coverage that the EAT and/or the qualified intermediary may require.
- *Closing.* Closing funds are delivered to the qualified intermediary and wired to the closing agent upon request.
- *Fees.* The client is usually required to pay all fees up front.
- *Sale of relinquished property.* On or before the 180th day, the relinquished property must be sold. Documentation will be prepared whereby the role of the qualified intermediary will be specified in the contract for sale. If this is an exchange last transaction, the closing agent will be instructed to have the property conveyed directly to the ultimate buyer. If it is an exchange first transaction, the parked property, then vested in the name of the EAT, is deeded by the EAT to the ultimate buyer.
- *Sale proceeds.* Cash proceeds at the closing go to the qualified intermediary.
- *Disbursement of proceeds.* The qualified intermediary uses the cash proceeds received from the relinquished property to pay off the promissory note. Any variation in the amount of the note that results from a greater or lesser sale price of the property than was initially anticipated is adjusted, as provided in the terms of the promissory note and permitted by the provisions of Rev. Proc. 2000–37.
- *Closing the exchange and disposition of the replacement property.* In an exchange first format, the replacement property is already vested in the name of the taxpayer. If the transaction is using the exchange last format, the qualified intermediary, pursuant to the terms of the exchange agreement, the QEAA, and the promissory note, conveys the parked replacement property to the taxpayer. Any shortage in the total amount of proceeds from the relinquished property is made up for by the additional equity the taxpayer is getting in the replacement property.

## Potential Problems and Miscellaneous Issues

If you plan to undertake a reverse exchange, you want to keep the following factors in mind.

## Financing

To use the exchange last format, the taxpayer must either pay all cash or find a cooperative lender. If a lender will be involved, careful coordination and planning are necessary to ensure that the lender understands the transaction and is willing to work with the parties to achieve a successful exchange.

Sophisticated lenders are able to arrange to loan the purchase money to the EAT, provided that the taxpayer is otherwise qualified according to their underwriting standards. They then usually require that the taxpayer be the guarantor of the loan, which is permissible under Rev. Proc. 2000–37. When title goes into the name of the taxpayer at the conclusion of the exchange, the lender agrees in writing that it will release the EAT from further responsibility on the loan. It would be difficult to induce an EAT to act in the capacity of the titleholder in the absence of such nonrecourse terms.

Further, if they take this route, the parties want to ensure that the loan does not have a due on sale clause, which would require that the loan be repaid when title is transferred.

## Title Insurance

Again, if the transaction is structured as exchange last, there will be an initial conveyance to the EAT, followed by a conveyance to the exchangor. Title insurance will most likely have been obtained at the beginning of the transaction. The exchangor will want to obtain assurance from the title insurer, usually in the form of an endorsement, that the exchangor will be covered by the policy after the title is transferred.

## Boot

Regardless of which format is used, the taxpayer must be sure to put a sufficient cash down payment on the replacement property to equal the estimated equity coming from the relinquished property, and it must be paid as of the date that title to the replacement property is vested in the taxpayer's name. There may be unexpected boot in the transaction if there is not enough available cash to equal the equity in the relinquished property at the time the replacement property is acquired by the taxpayer. For example, what if exchange proceeds are used for unqualified items? (See Chapter 18 regarding deductible and nondeductible exchange expenses.)

Once funds are received by the qualified intermediary, it may need to review the closing statements on the replacement and relinquished properties to determine if there may be boot.

## Examples

If the cash down payment on the replacement property was $500,000 on a $1 million purchase, but the net proceeds from the relinquished property were $600,000, there would appear to be at least $100,000 in boot.

If the price of the replacement property is $1,000,000 and the relinquished property sold for $1,200,000, there may be at least $200,000 in boot, even if the equity in the relinquished property is equal to the equity in the replacement property.

If funds were used in either property transaction to pay taxes, prorations or rents, security deposits, insurance, loan fees, or any other obviously nondeductible expenses, there may be more boot.

Furthermore, depending upon the state in which the relinquished property was located, the qualified intermediary may have an obligation to remit some portion of the estimated boot to the local taxing authority. For example, in California, the remittance would be $3^{1}/_{3}$ percent of the apparent cash boot.

## Potential Double Transfer Tax

Transfer taxes are a cost related to the recording of deeds in real estate transactions. They are an expense of closing in most jurisdictions. Typically, transfer taxes bear some relationship to the value of the property being conveyed. Depending upon the jurisdiction and the value of the property, this item may be inconsequential, or it may be substantial.

### Example

In California, all counties are authorized to, and most do, impose a transfer tax equal to $1.10 per $1,000, calculated on the value of the property that is being conveyed. On a property being sold for $1,000,000, that amounts to $1,100.00. However, under California law, individual cities may impose their own *additional* transfer taxes, which will be assessed separately. In the City of San Francisco, the additional amount is $7.50 per $1,000 of value. So the total transfer tax will be increased by $7,500.00, for a total of $8,600.00.

Because a reverse exchange usually requires the recording of one extra deed at the conclusion of the exchange, this documentary transfer tax can significantly increase the cost of the exchange. Consider the exchange last format, where the replacement property was initially vested in the name of the EAT at the closing, pending the successful sale of the relinquished property by the taxpayer. A transfer tax was most likely paid at that time. Once the relinquished property has been sold, the qualified intermediary will instruct the EAT to convey the replacement property to the taxpayer. The local recording office expects the transfer tax to be paid for most, if not all, recordings. Unless a waiver can be obtained, that tax will be due once again. In our San Francisco example of a $1,000,000 property, the extra $8,600.00 substantially increases the cost of the reverse exchange.

## Possible Solution

One approach is to attempt to convince the recording office that no true change in ownership is occurring, and that the second deed being recorded is a mere formality, required solely as a result of the 1031 exchange. Sometimes this works. Sometimes it doesn't.

Another approach that has been used successfully is for the property to have been acquired by the EAT under an SPE, usually an LLC, owned wholly by the qualified intermediary, as described earlier. Instead of conveying the property to the taxpayer at the end of the transaction and dissolving the SPE, the qualified intermediary conveys the ownership interest of the SPE to the taxpayer. This effectively eliminates the need for a new deed to be recorded, because the property remains vested in the name of the same SPE at all times. Title is unchanged. So long as the taxpayer was a single entity or an individual initially, this should not be a problem. (See the discussion in Chapter 5 regarding single-member LLCs.) Only the ownership of the SPE is changed. Of course, the local taxing authorities may still determine that this was a change of ownership.

## Producing and Recording of Deeds

Most parties rely on their attorney or their escrow or title company for the preparation of deeds conveying real property. In a reverse exchange, there will be a deed conveying property either to the EAT (exchange first) or from the EAT (exchange last) that will not be a part of the real estate closing in the normal course of events. Occasionally the closing agent handling the original transaction is willing to assist with this, as a professional courtesy. But that is not always the case. Therefore, independent arrangements must often be made to draw up the deed and cause it to be recorded, along with any related items such as change of ownership documents specific to the relevant jurisdiction, and to pay any required fees. The best approach is to consult a real estate attorney for assistance with this. Alternatively, there are companies that will draw up documents and deliver them for recording at the instruction of the taxpayer.

## Multiple Properties

Just as in any exchange, there can be multiple sales or purchases in a reverse exchange. A knowledgeable qualified intermediary will be able to work with this according to the needs of the parties and of the exchange. But it is critical that the qualified intermediary be advised well in advance of any closings of additional properties involved. Additional properties will no doubt entail additional fees.

## Partial Reverse–Partial Delayed Exchanges

Exchanges in which there are multiple relinquished and/or replacement properties can sometimes be structured so that they involve both a reverse and a forward exchange at the same time. These transactions are even more complex than a basic reverse exchange. They require a great deal of expertise to be processed properly. We include this discussion because this is a situation that does arise with some frequency.

### Example

Andrea owns two properties, Greenacre and Whiteacre, that she wants to exchange for one larger property, Redacre. Assume in this example that both properties are owned free and clear of any encumbrances, and that, because of the demands or requirements of the other parties involved, the transactions must close on the dates given.

Andrea contracts to sell Greenacre for $1,000,000, with a closing set for June 1. She is under contract to sell Whiteacre for $2,000,000, but the buyer for Whiteacre, Les, cannot possibly close until December 15. Redacre is available for purchase at a price of $3,000,000, so it is an ideal trade for Greenacre and Whiteacre. But Justin, the seller of Redacre, refuses to wait until December. Justin insists that he needs to close no later than August 1, because he is retiring and moving to Tahiti. So Andrea consults with her attorney and her CPA and decides to do a *partial reverse exchange*.

The sale of Greenacre will be a forward exchange. Upon closing on June 1, Andrea's qualified intermediary will receive the proceeds. The *purchase* of Redacre will be processed partly as a forward exchange and partly as a reverse exchange. Because of the relative values of the properties, one-third of Redacre will be acquired with the proceeds of the forward exchange involving Greenacre, and two-thirds will be acquired with an outside source of funds to be reimbursed with the proceeds from the reverse exchange involving Whiteacre.

This example is simplistic, but it shows how the basic concept can be applied. Because there was no debt on any of the properties in this hypothetical example, it was not difficult to make the allocation between the reverse and forward exchanges. However, if there had been debt on any of the properties, or if a lender was involved, the transaction could have been considerably more complicated. Andrea's CPA or attorney would have had to assist her in the allocation of equity and debt between the two relinquished properties to minimize the possibility of boot on one or the other.

Only an experienced qualified intermediary should be engaged for this type of exchange. The taxpayer should obtain legal and tax advice well in advance to ensure that the process goes smoothly and to give his or her qualified intermediary sufficient notice for setting it up. Again, additional fees will be involved. The taxpayer needs to weigh the increased cost against the increased benefit of a reverse exchange.

# 17

# Personal Property Exchanges

*Can I do an exchange with other kinds of property? What else qualifies for this type of tax deferral?*

So far, we have focused mostly on real property exchanges. However, you can also exchange personal property. Farmers, truckers, and others who own and use valuable equipment or livestock in their businesses will find this chapter very useful.

## Personal Property Exchanges Are Widely Used

Personal property exchanges are widely used in various industries. Airlines use them when they exchange old 747s for new 777s. Rental car companies use them to trade old automobiles for newer models. Farmers use them when they exchange an old John Deere tractor for a new one. There is a whole series of private letter rulings that cover this subject.[1-4] A complete and detailed explanation of personal property exchanges is outside the scope of this book for the most part. This chapter is intended only to introduce you to the concepts and provide some highlights.

## The Concept of Like Kind Relating to Personal Property

As we have stated many times, all 1031 exchanges require that the replacement property be like kind to the relinquished property, and personal property is never like kind to real property. Personal property exchanges are separate and distinct from real property exchanges. Sometimes an exchange can involve both types of property (consider, for example, a restaurant, a hotel, or a manufacturing plant). Exchanges involving both real and personal property require a segregation of assets into separate *exchange groups*.[5]

The IRS has provided guidelines for determining which personal property is like kind to other personal property.[6] (Oh, no, some more "tax talk"!) Like-kind personal property must be of the same kind or class.[7] The Treasury Regulations distinguish between depreciable tangible personal property, which can be exchanged for either "like-class" or "like-kind" property,[8] and other types of personal property, which can be exchanged only for "like-kind" property.[9]

The system of classification used in the United States is called *NAICS*, which stands for North American Industrial Classification System. It was developed in the late 1990s to standardize products and services for the purpose of evaluating business activity in the United States, Canada, and Mexico. In connection with 1031 exchanges, NAICS provides guidelines for determining whether various types of personal property will be considered like kind to one another.

For example, items falling within the asset class that includes office furniture, fixtures, and equipment will not be like kind to items falling within the asset class that includes information systems (computers and peripheral equipment). Neither of those groups is like kind to the asset class for data-handling equipment, which does not include computers. Likewise, items falling within the asset class for automobiles and taxis are not like kind to items in the asset class that includes buses. Heavy-duty general-purpose trucks are not like kind to lighter general-purpose trucks.

*Authors' Note:* You can see that a personal property exchange requires consultation with a CPA or other expert who can advise you. It is essential to get professional advice to ensure that the types of property being exchanged will qualify, and will satisfy the IRS.

## Sale of a Business

A sale of a business will typically be considered a sale of multiple personal property assets. This means that if you want to exchange your motel business for another motel, including the real property on which it is located, there would be a real property exchange for the land and the structures thereon, and a personal property exchange involving the beds, chairs, tables, kitchen appliances, computers, cash registers, vending machines, and the like. A 1031 exchange can be especially valuable if the owner of a franchise business is considering trading one location for a different one.

Certain items that are typically valued as part of the sale of a business may not be exchanged at all. For example, the goodwill or going concern value of the business, which may be a substantial portion of the value of a motel, liquor store, or restaurant, cannot be exchanged.[10] Nor can a covenant not to compete be exchanged. Consequently, taxpayers often find that it is difficult to use a 1031 exchange successfully in some transactions, or that it may be impossible to avoid paying some tax on those items that are not included. However, in Private Letter Ruling 8453034, involving the exchange of two motels, the IRS decided that the motel names could be exchanged pursuant to Section 1031 because they did not come under the prohibited category of "choses in action," which we mentioned in Chapter 4 and which cannot be exchanged. Again, a knowledgeable tax advisor is essential to navigate through these issues. It is suggested that the foregoing asset classification issues be discussed with counsel before a sale agreement is even drafted.

## Animals and Livestock

Under IRC Section 1031(e), "livestock of different sexes are not property of a like kind" to one another, and cannot be exchanged.[11] Thus, male pigs must be exchanged for male pigs, and cows (by definition female) for cows.[12,13] If you are exchanging racehorses, mares and fillies are not like kind to colts and stallions!

## Identification

You still have the same 45 days to identify your replacement property(ies). Timing, as we noted at the beginning of Chapter 10, is not as big a problem with personal property exchanges as it is with real property exchanges. However, other identification issues with respect to personal property are just as important. You cannot merely identify "a truck." Instead, you should identify more particularly "a 2004 heavy general-purpose truck, manufactured by XYZ Company, model number 123456789," to ensure that the IRS will not question the validity of an identification after the fact.

If you are considering an exchange involving personal property, discuss your transaction and your concerns with your tax advisor. Have him or her do a basic tax projection before you make a decision on whether or not the exchange is right for you. He or she may want to review the adjusted basis of the assets you are considering exchanging, to determine if they are good candidates for an exchange.

## Endnotes

1. PLR 200240049 (vehicle leasing business).
2. PLR 200241013 (vehicle leasing business).
3. PLR 200241016 (equipment leasing business).
4. PLR 200242009 (vehicle leasing business).
5. Reg. 1.1031(j)–1.
6. Reg. 1.1031(a)–2
7. Reg. 1.1031(a)–1(b).
8. Reg. 1.1031(a)2-(b).
9. Reg. 1.1031(a)2-(c).
10. Reg. 1.1031(a)–1(c).
11. Reg. 1.1031(e)–1.
12. Rev. Rul. 82–96, in which an exchange of gold bullion for Canadian Maple Leaf gold coins by an investor was upheld.
13. Reg. 1031(a)–1(c)(3); in Ex. 1, an exchange of a copyright on a novel for a copyright on a different novel was okay; but in Ex. 2, a copyright on a novel was not like kind to a copyright on a song.

# PART 4

# MISCELLANEOUS 1031 EXCHANGE ISSUES

# 18

# Reporting Your Exchange to the IRS and Related Matters

*Now that you are the proud owner of your replacement property, are you done?*

Not quite. Section 1031 is, after all, a federal tax statute, so it should come as no surprise that sooner or later you will have to report your transaction to the IRS. A 1031 exchange is reported to the IRS on Form 8824.

## Federal Tax Reporting Requirements

Once you have completed a successful exchange, you will need to let the IRS know about it in order to reap the tax deferral benefits. Reporting is done in connection with the filing of your annual tax return. It is imperative that you collect and retain the transaction information in order to file your return accurately.

At the closing for the sale of the relinquished property and the closing for the purchase of the replacement property, the closing agent will typically prepare and distribute a closing statement, also known as a HUD–1. This document will reflect the gross sale price, itemized sale expenses (commissions, title charges, escrow fees, and so on), proration items (property taxes, interest, rent, and so on), and any other matters pertinent to the sale transaction. This is a very critical document, and you need to retain it with your other important tax documents.

Whenever you sell any real property, the closing agent is required, in accordance with federal tax law, to report the transaction to the IRS on a Form 1099-S. That is how the IRS knows that your sale has occurred. The Form 1099-S will reflect the gross proceeds of the sale. When you file a tax return for the tax year in which the sale occurred, you append a Form 8824 to your tax return, setting forth the fact that you did an exchange and the details of the transaction. You or your tax preparer will need the HUD–1 information for both the relinquished property and the replacement property in order to prepare this form.

Form 8824 requires that you provide the specifics of the transaction, among which are the following:

• The date your relinquished property was acquired
• The date your relinquished property was sold
• The date your replacement property was identified
• The date your replacement property was acquired
• Whether there were any related parties involved in the transaction
• If there were any related parties, confirmation that there were no transfers of property in violation of the two-year holding period required in related-party exchanges
• The financial details of your exchange, including cash, basis, adjusted basis, realized and recognized gain and/or loss, and new basis in the replacement property

Keep in mind that misrepresentation on Form 8824 can result in a conviction for tax fraud. Tax fraud is a felony, which may be punished by fines, penalties, and imprisonment. So if you are undertaking an exchange, it is wise to have a tax advisor oversee the transaction early on, to avoid possible unexpected pitfalls.

## Deductible Expenses

One of the issues that will come up in preparing your tax return and Form 8824 is the deductibility of expenses that arise out of the exchange

**Table 18–1   Common Deductible Expenses**

---

Brokerage commissions
Finder's fees
Escrow fees
Title insurance premiums
Transfer taxes
Recording and notary fees
Legal fees related to the exchange
Exchange fees charged by the qualified intermediary
Inspection and testing fees*

---

* Some of these may vary depending upon whether they are an expense related to the relinquished property or the replacement property, as well as the reason for the expense.

transaction. Therefore, it is important that you have a basic understanding of how these will be treated. Table 18–1 is helpful here.

As you are no doubt aware, some costs associated with owning an asset, whether real or personal property, are *deductible* as operating expenses, and some expenses must be *capitalized*. Such items as repairs to roofs or leaky toilets, janitorial expenses, gardening expenses, and general maintenance costs fall into the first category. The amount of the operating expenses are usually reported in full on the annual tax return and reduce the taxable income of the taxpayer by the amount of the deductible expenses.

Capitalized expenses are deductible over their useful life, rather than all at once.[1] Examples of these would be a roof or driveway replacement, or adding additional units to an apartment building. Capitalized expenses usually result in an upward adjustment in your basis in the asset, and they may subsequently be depreciated over time. Capitalized expenses will also reduce income taxes due, but over a period of years, instead of all in one year. Different types of assets (roof, driveway, and so on) have different useful lives and therefore different allowable depreciation schedules, which are prescribed by the IRS.

The Internal Revenue Code addresses the deductibility of expenses directly. IRC Section 162 states in pertinent part: "There shall be allowed as a deduction all the ordinary and necessary expenses paid or incurred during the taxable year in carrying on any trade or business." Similarly, Sections 163 and 164 deal, respectively, with the deductibility of interest and property taxes. These Code sections govern what *operating* expenses are deductible from rental income generated from owning and managing investment real estate.

However, *operating* costs must be distinguished from the deductible expenses incurred in selling investment real estate. Transaction expenses that are incurred in connection with the disposition of the property are not recurring expenses like operating expenses. Examples of transaction expenses are brokerage commissions, title expenses, legal fees, and escrow charges. Upon sale of the relinquished property, each of these expenses is subtracted from the gross sale proceeds before computing the net amount realized.[2] The gain on sale is then the difference between the net amount realized and the adjusted basis.[3] The net amount realized establishes the amount that you must reinvest (the exchange value) in order to have a fully deferred exchange.[4] The amount of the mortgage is *not* subtracted in arriving at the exchange value, nor are any of the operating costs.

Table 18–1 gives a brief list of the most common deductible exchange expenses.

Use of the exchange funds is strictly circumscribed by Reg. 1.1031(k)–1(g)(6), which states in pertinent part: "The taxpayer has no rights . . . to receive, pledge, borrow, or otherwise obtain the benefits of money or other property before the end of the exchange period." There is a specific exception provided in the following section of the Regulations relating to "transactional items," which are typically found on closing statements under local standards. However, the tax effect is different when you are purchasing rather than selling. At the closing of the relinquished property, you may direct that these types of transaction expenses be paid out of the exchange proceeds before the balance is sent to the qualified intermediary, without jeopardizing the exchange. Naturally, you may also wish to utilize a portion of the 1031 proceeds being held by the qualified intermediary to pay some of the expenses that arise in connection with the purchase of replacement property. You should be aware that there is a difference between the use of 1031 proceeds to pay certain acquisition expenses and their actual tax treatment. Some of the foregoing items must be capitalized as part of the basis of the replacement property, while others are merely current-year deductions.

But there are also items in a typical real estate transaction that cannot be capitalized, nor can you use any of the 1031 proceeds to pay them. See Table 18–2 for a listing of some common expenses that are not allowable deductions.

**Table 18–2    Common Nondeductible Expenses**

---

Rents, including prorations
Property taxes, including prorations
Utilities
Security deposits
Repairs to the property
Property insurance premiums
Loan fees
Points
Loan application fees
Mortgage insurance
Lender's title insurance
Assumption fees
Homeowner's association dues

---

# Exchanges by Foreign Persons

People who live outside of the United States can also do exchanges. Many people who live outside of the United States want to own property that is located here. We have a stable political system, a respected legal system, and attractive investment opportunities. As a result, more and more foreign persons have been learning about and engaging in exchanges. A *foreign person* is defined as a nonresident alien, a foreign partnership, a foreign corporation, or a foreign trust.[5] If this does not apply to you, you may wish to skip this part.

## The Foreign Investment in Real Property Tax Act

Special treatment is prescribed for foreign persons selling real estate in the United States. In 1980, Congress enacted the Foreign Investment in Real Property Tax Act (commonly known as FIRPTA). The act is codified in IRC Section 897 and related sections. The purpose of this law is to ensure the collection of income tax from foreign persons upon the sale of a "United States real property interest" (both are defined terms in the Code and Regulations.). A *United States real property interest* is defined as any interest in real estate located in the United States or the U.S. Virgin Islands, including any personal property associated therewith.[6]

A full discussion of FIRPTA is beyond the scope of this book; we will instead narrow our focus to the use of Section 1031 by foreign persons. Foreign persons can take advantage of Section 1031 to exchange U.S. property. There are special requirements imposed, since people in this class are not normally U.S. taxpayers.

Relevant law is split between several Code sections and applicable Regulations. Section 897 governs the disposition of real estate by foreign persons. Section 1445 governs withholding tax requirements. Foreign persons are specifically authorized to utilize the nonrecognition provisions of the Code, i.e., Section 1031, as set forth in Section 897(e) and Reg. 1.897–6T.

## Withholding Taxes

Code Section 1445(a) sets forth the general withholding requirement as follows:

> Except as otherwise provided in this section, in the case of any disposition of a United States real property interest (as defined in Section 897(c)) by a foreign person, *the transferee shall be required to deduct and withhold a tax equal to 10 percent of the amount realized* on the disposition" (emphasis added).

Thus, the buyer (but usually the closing agent on behalf of the buyer) must withhold 10 percent of the amount realized out of the seller's proceeds. If you are a foreign person engaging in a 1031 exchange, there are additional steps. There are different procedures depending on whether you are doing a simultaneous exchange or a delayed exchange.[7]

## Withholding Certificates

In the case of a delayed exchange, the transferee/buyer cannot know at the time of the sale of the relinquished property whether you will be able to complete your exchange successfully. That fact will be known only after your receipt of the replacement property. Therefore, the Treasury Department adopted Reg. 1.1445–2(d)(2)(iv), which sets forth the procedural steps in a delayed exchange. This regulation directs that an application for a withholding certificate be made pursuant to Reg. 1.1445–3(b)(6), which states:

(6) *Special rule for like-kind exchanges under Section 1031.* A withholding certificate may be requested with respect to a like-kind exchange under section 1031 as a transaction subject to a nonrecognition provision under paragraph (c)(2)(ii) of this section. The application must include information substantiating the requirements of section 1031. The IRS may require additional information during the course of the application process to determine that the requirements of section 1031 are satisfied. In the case of a deferred like-kind exchange, the withholding agent is excused from reporting and paying the withholding tax to the IRS within 20 days after the transfer only if an application for a withholding certificate is submitted prior to or on the date of transfer. See §1.1445–1(c)(2) for rules concerning delayed reporting and payment where an application for a withholding certificate has been submitted to the IRS prior to or on the date of transfer.

## Form 8288-B, Application for Withholding Certificate

The actual form, which must be filed with the IRS, is Form 8288-B, entitled "Application for Withholding Certificate for Dispositions of Foreign Persons of US Real Property Interests." Rev. Proc. 2000–35, 2000 I.R.B. 211, provides guidance for issuance of a withholding certificate to reduce or eliminate the need for income tax withholding. It sets forth specific procedures and requirements for foreign persons doing a 1031 exchange. One important requirement is the necessity that the applicant provide his or her Taxpayer Identification Number (TIN). Rev. Proc. 2000–35 states in pertinent part:

.05. If a withholding certificate is sought on the basis of a claim that the transaction is entitled to nonrecognition treatment or is exempt from U.S. taxation, provide the following:
1. A brief description of the transfer;
2. A brief summary of the law and facts supporting the claim of nonrecognition or exemption;
3. Evidence that the transferor has no unsatisfied withholding liability, as described in section 4.06(3); and
4. The contract price (if any), or if no contract price is available, the most recent assessed value, for state or local property tax purposes, of the U.S. real property interest to be transferred, or, if such assessed value is not available, then the good faith estimate of its fair market value (no supporting evidence concerning the value of the property need be supplied).

## Submission of Application to IRS

Your Application for Withholding Certificate must be submitted to the IRS prior to or on the date of the transfer of the relinquished property. As a foreign transferor/seller, you must provide the transferee/buyer with notice that you have submitted the application in a timely manner. The transferee must still withhold from your proceeds, but it may then delay remitting the tax to the IRS until you have had an opportunity to complete the exchange by receiving the replacement property. This necessarily means that 10 percent of your proceeds will be unavailable to use for the purchase consideration, unless you either obtain a withholding certificate prior to receipt of the replacement property or provide the transferee with an alternative form of security for the payment of tax to the IRS. In any case, the transferee must report the transaction and pay any withheld money by the twentieth day following a final IRS determination on the application if no certificate is received.

*Authors' Note:* Readers to whom this law may apply are urged to seek competent tax counsel, as we have only touched on tax reporting requirements here. If you have questions as you are moving ahead with your exchange, your accountant or attorney should be able to assist you.

## Endnotes

1. IRC Section 263(a).
2. See Rev. Rul. 72–456, 1972–2CB 468, which states that brokerage commissions are deductible in calculating the amount realized.
3. IRC Section 1001(a).
4. Reg. 1.1031(d)–1.
5. Reg. 1.897–9T(c).
6. Reg. 1.897–1(c).
7. See Reg. 1.1445–2(d)(2)(iii) for a special notice procedure for a simultaneous exchange.

# 19

# Involuntary Conveyances—IRC Section 1033 Issues

*What happens if your property is destroyed by a hurricane or taken by the government? Can you use Section 1031?*

Casualty losses and condemnations are governed by Section 1033. In many ways, this section operates very similarly to Section 1031. Over the years, the authors have received many questions about Section 1033 from their 1031 clients; hence, this discussion is included.

## Sections 1031 and 1033 Compared

Section 1031 deals with *voluntary* sales by taxpayers seeking to reinvest in like-kind replacement property. Section 1033 is a companion nonrecognition section. It is entitled "Involuntary Conversions," and it deals with sales that are not made voluntarily. This is another topic that is not necessarily of general interest, so you may wish to skip it. But if you find yourself in the right circumstances, it may be useful to know about.

Section 1033 is somewhat similar in function to Section 1031, and that is why we have included a brief chapter here. Section 1033 deals with what happens when a taxpayer suffers a casualty loss (fire, flood, or theft), or when property is taken by a governmental authority (through condemnation or eminent domain).

When evaluating the types of reinvestment that may be appropriate under Section 1033 in the event of a casualty loss, the applicable language refers to replacement property that is "similar or related in service or use." This is a narrower definition than we use for a 1031 exchange. Thus, if, for example, your home is destroyed in a hurricane, flood, or fire, you must replace the lost personal residence with a new personal residence. Property that is stock in trade or held primarily for resale, which does not qualify under Section 1031, can qualify for nonrecognition treatment under Section 1033(a).[1]

There is a broader rule in Section 1033(g) for real estate taken by condemnation, which adopts the like-kind standard of Section 1031.[2] In order to make this chapter relevant to the topic of real estate exchanges, we shall limit our discussion to Section 1033(g), entitled "Condemnation of Real Property Held for Productive Use in Trade or Business or for Investment." Note that this is the same definition used for qualifying property in Section 1031(a)(1).

There is no requirement that the property actually be condemned; it may be voluntarily sold to the condemning agency while "under threat or imminence of condemnation." This is a complex and technical area of the law, and the taxpayer faced with a condemnation threat will be well advised to seek competent legal and tax advice.

Another difference between Sections 1031 and 1033 is that apparently under Section 1033, but not under Section 1031, a taxpayer can make improvements to land he already owns.[3–5]

## Longer Replacement Period

As under Section 1031, under Section 1033 you must acquire qualifying replacement property within a specified time period. However, the replacement time period under Section 1033 is much longer. Pursuant to Reg. 1.1033(a)(2)(B), as modified by Reg. 1.1033(g)(4), the taxpayer has a period that begins with the date of disposition of the converted property or the earliest date of threat or imminence of condemnation, whichever is earlier, and ends three years after the close of the first taxable year in which any of the conversion proceeds is received. There is also provision in the Regulations to make application for an extension of time upon a showing of reasonable cause.

## No Need for a Qualified Intermediary; No Identification Period

There is no requirement that the condemnation proceeds be held by a qualified intermediary or other third party.[6] There is no identification requirement, as there is with Section 1031. There is a prohibition against acquiring property from a related person, but there is also a $100,000 exception for replacement property acquired by an individual taxpayer from a related party.[7]

As with Section 1031, if the proceeds are not reinvested in qualifying replacement property, gain is recognized to the extent that the amount realized exceeds the cost of the replacement property. No gain is recognized if all of the proceeds are reinvested as required. Sometimes a portion of the condemnation award are designated as compensation for legal fees, interest, or severance damages.

There is also basis carryover from the condemned property to the replacement property. The basis carried over into the replacement property is the cost of that replacement property, reduced by the amount of any unrecognized gain.[8]

Again, this chapter is intended only as a very rudimentary introduction to this subject. The authors do not purport to be experts in this area. If you want to know more about Section 1033, you are urged to consult competent legal counsel.

## Endnotes

1. *Westchester Development Co.,* 63 TC 198 (1974); property acquired for development and resale that was taken under threat of condemnation by a school district could be replaced with similar-use property.
2. Reg. 1.1033(g)-(1)(a).
3. *Davis v. United States*, 411 FSupp. 964, aff'd. 589 F2d 446 (9th Cir 1979).
4. Rev. Rul. 67–255, 1967–2, Cum. Bull. 270.
5. PLR 8307007.

6.  Reg. 1.1033(a)–2(c).
7.  IRC Section 1033(i)(2)(C).
8.  Reg. 1.1033(b)(1).

# Miscellaneous Exchange Issues

This chapter is intended to address some topics that are not covered elsewhere in this book, but that may be of concern to you as you contemplate doing a 1031 exchange.

## Treatment of Interest

You can earn interest on your exchange proceeds while they are being held by your qualified intermediary. When delayed exchanges first became popular after the decision in the *Starker* case,[1] prudent accommodators did not pay their clients any interest. (There were not any qualified intermediaries yet because the final 1031 Regulations were not published until 1991.) This no-interest policy was undertaken out of fear that the client might be deemed to be in constructive receipt of the exchange funds because he or she was receiving the "benefit" of the money. Reg. 1.1031(k)–1(g)(5) created a safe harbor for the payment of "any interest or growth factor." The payment of interest is subject to the other safe harbor (g)(6) restrictions. Specifically, under (g)(6), no interest may be paid or received until the conclusion of the exchange period.

Upon the closing of the sale of the relinquished property, the closing agent sends your exchange proceeds to the qualified intermediary you have selected. Presumably the intermediary will deposit the funds in some sort of interest–bearing account or similar investment. Whether or not interest is payable to the exchangor is subject to the contractual arrangement negotiated between the parties. In many cases, the qualified intermediary will retain part of the interest and pay part of the interest to you.

The Treasury Department has recently proposed a change in the way interest earned on exchange balances is to be reported. Proposed Reg. 1.468B–6 is complicated and is not yet final (as of this writing). In essence, what it says is that notwithstanding any agreement between the parties regarding the splitting of interest income, all interest income earned on exchange balances will be treated as if it were earned solely by the exchangor/taxpayer.

Prior to selecting a qualified intermediary, the exchangor should have a clear understanding of what the intermediary is going to do with the exchange proceeds, where the proceeds are going to be deposited, whether any interest will be earned by the taxpayer, and how much interest income will be taxable to the taxpayer. (Review Chapter 6, "Role of the Qualified Intermediary.")

## Pledging Property Held by the Qualified Intermediary

Recall that the (g)(6) Regulations require that the agreement between the exchangor and the qualified intermediary limit the taxpayer's access to the exchange proceeds. The agreement must provide in substance that the taxpayer

> has no rights, except as provided in paragraphs (g)(6)(ii) and (g)(6)(iii) of this section, to receive, pledge, borrow, or otherwise obtain the benefits of money or other property before the end of the exchange period.

First, you cannot request and *receive* any money from the qualified intermediary until the exchange has been completed. Second, you cannot pledge (offer as a guaranty or as security) any funds to a lender or other party. Third, you cannot borrow money from the intermediary, even if it comes from a separate fund. Finally, you cannot otherwise obtain any benefit from the exchange proceeds. This means that you cannot receive any interest or income earned from the fund until the conclusion of the exchange. The foregoing restrictions are a very important part of the 1031 process.

## Installment Sale Election for Failed Exchange

Sometimes you commence a 1031 exchange in good faith, but for any number of reasons are unable to acquire a suitable replacement property.

As a result, your exchange fails. What happens if you commenced your exchange in Year 1, but the inability to complete it occurs in Year 2? Do you report the gain in your tax return for Year 1 or for Year 2?

The answer is provided in Reg. 1.1031(k)–1(j)(2), which states that a failed exchange overlapping two tax years is to be treated as an *installment sale* under IRC Section 453. (Please review Chapter 9 regarding Section 453 and the seller carryback.) This means that under these circumstances the sale will be reported in the tax return for Year 2.

Reg. 1.1031(k)–1(j)(2)(iv) also requires the taxpayer to have entered into the exchange with a bona fide intent to complete it. Basically, that means that you are not supposed to set up an exchange when you have no intent to actually acquire replacement property, just because you are selling your property in December 2006 and you don't want to have to pay the capital gains tax until you file a tax return for 2007. The regulation then goes on to set forth several examples of the operation of this rule.[2]

## Short Sale

A *short sale* occurs when the debt on your relinquished property exceeds the price that you can sell the property for. This can come about either because you refinanced sometime along the way and took out some of your equity, or because the property has dropped in value. Even in this situation, where there will be no cash proceeds at all, you could still have a taxable gain that you may wish to defer. Theoretically, a 1031 exchange is possible even where there are no cash proceeds.

---

### Example

Matt purchased his relinquished property for $50,000 in 1995. It has appreciated significantly. Matt refinanced his property and encumbered it for $95,000. Subsequently, he sold the relinquished property for $100,000. Matt must pay his Realtor commissions of $5,000 and closing costs of $3,000. However, the debt on the property is $95,000. So, in order to close, even though Matt is the seller, either he has to *add* money ($3,000) to the transaction to pay off the loan or the lender has to accept less than the face value of its note. No cash proceeds will be received. (See Table 20–1.)

**Table 20–1    Short Sale**

| Relinquished Property | |
| --- | --- |
| 1. Sale price | $100,000 |
| 2. Commissions to real estate agent | 5,000 |
| 3. Other closing costs | 3,000 |
| 4. Exchange value—amount to be reinvested (Line 1 minus Lines 2 and 3) | **$92,000** |
| 5. Amount of encumbrances paid at closing (taxpayer will need to add $3,000 to close) | 95,000 |
| 6. Cash proceeds—cash to be reinvested | $0 |
| 7. Assume an adjusted basis in property | $50,000 |
| 8. Capital gain (Line 4 minus Line 7) | **$42,000*** |

* Although there are no proceeds, taxpayer must still reinvest this amount, or there will be tax due on the $42,000 capital gain from this transaction. If the taxpayer does a 1031 exchange, the tax can still be deferred.

An exchange is still possible, and may be necessary if Matt is to avoid paying capital gains tax. (In this example, assume that the property is vacant land and has not been depreciated.) Since the property was originally acquired for $50,000, his basis remains $50,000, his costs of sale are $8,000, and his taxable gain is $42,000 ( $92,000 − $50,000), even though he later refinanced the property and borrowed an additional $45,000, and therefore is receiving absolutely *no cash* from the sale. Remember, Matt already took the cash out earlier, when he refinanced. If he does not do an exchange, he will owe federal and state taxes on this gain.

Matt certainly can do an exchange here. He must still spend $92,000 on qualifying replacement property to have a fully deferred exchange. But if he can find a suitable replacement property requiring little or no cash in the deal, or if he has cash available from some other source, the exchange will still work.

## Endnotes

1. See the discussion of *T. J. Starker v. United States*, 602 F2d 1341 (9th Cir 1979), in Chapter 1.
2. In *D. G. Smalley et ux v. Commissioner*, 116 TC 450 (6/14/01), there is an excellent analysis and discussion of this topic where taxpayers had a failed exchange involving timber rights.

# Final Thoughts

In this book, we have attempted to cover the major issues that most commonly arise in connection with 1031 exchanges. We hope you will take from it, at a minimum, the following basic ideas:

- A 1031 exchange is a fantastic tool for building wealth and deferring payment of capital gains taxes.
- A 1031 exchange is a highly technical type of transaction that is driven entirely by federal statutes and regulations. Each "i" must be dotted and each "t" must be crossed if you want to have a successful exchange.
- There are several *necessary elements*, all of which must be present for an exchange under Section 1031.
  - The properties involved must *qualify*.
  - An *exchange* must occur—there must be a reciprocal and inter-dependent transfer of those qualifying properties, rather than a sale followed by a purchase.
  - The *same taxpayer* must be involved at the beginning and at the end of the transaction.
  - The taxpayer must have no actual or constructive receipt of the sales proceeds.
- If you believe that an exchange may benefit you, consult with your tax advisors to determine whether a 1031 would truly work to your advantage. Make sure your advisor is familiar with 1031 exchanges. Explore with him or her the amount of gain you can expect from the sale of your asset, the amount of tax you would have to pay if you sold without doing an exchange, and whether you may have offsetting losses. Consider whether or not you will need to use the sales proceeds for some purpose that would preclude your immediate reinvestment in a new property.

- Once you have decided that a 1031 exchange is the right course for you to take, seek out an experienced and knowledgeable qualified intermediary to process your transaction. Do not be embarrassed to express your concerns—most first-time exchangors are slightly intimidated by the process and need reassurance. Do not hesitate to ask every question you can think of in order to broaden your knowledge and fill in the gaps that will inevitably have been left by this book. If your questions are not being answered, or if you don't feel comfortable with that qualified intermediary, maybe you should select a different one who suits you better. Remember, it is not necessarily important that the company you select be located right in your community. Most qualified intermediaries are able to process transactions throughout the United States, regardless of where their headquarters are located.
- Once you select your qualified intermediary, you should take advantage of the intermediary's expertise to assist you in complying with the law.
- Consult with your own real estate agents, tax advisors, and/or attorneys, all of whom are valuable resources who can assist you to have a successful exchange.

We believe Section 1031 is one of the most powerful and taxpayer-friendly provisions in the entire Internal Revenue Code. We trust you have found this book to be instructive and enlightening. Take advantage of the information in this book and continue to use it as a reference. Use the insights given here to structure your own exchanges and build wealth for yourself and your family.

A P P E N D I X

This is the Internal Revenue Code section that is the focus of this book. Section 1031 allows for the deferral of gain or loss on the sale of investment assets provided that replacement property is acquired within certain specified time limits. There are extensive Treasury regulations that explain and elaborate the provisions of this section. References to Section 1031 are found throughout this book.

# Section 1031 Exchange of Property Held for Productive Use or Investment

**(a) Nonrecognition of gain or loss from exchanges solely in kind.**

**(1) In general.**

No gain or loss shall be recognized on the exchange of property held for productive use in a trade or business or for investment if such property is exchanged solely for property of like kind which is to be held either for productive use in a trade or business or for investment.

**(2) Exception.**
This subsection shall not apply to any exchange of—

(A) stock in trade or other property held primarily for sale,
(B) stocks, bonds, or notes,
(C) other securities or evidences of indebtedness or interest,
(D) interests in a partnership,
(E) certificates of trust or beneficial interests, or
(F) choses in action.

For purposes of this section, an interest in a partnership which has in effect a valid election under section 761(a) to be excluded from the application of all of subchapter K shall be treated as an interest in each of the assets of such partnership and not as an interest in a partnership.

**(3) Requirement that property be identified and that exchange be completed not more than 180 days after transfer of exchanged property.**
For purposes of this subsection, any property received by the taxpayer shall be treated as property which is not like-kind property if—

(A) such property is not identified as property to be received in the exchange on or before the day which is 45 days after the date on which the taxpayer transfers the property relinquished in the exchange, or
(B) such property is received after the earlier of—
 (i) the day which is 180 days after the date on which the taxpayer transfers the property relinquished in the exchange, or
 (ii) the due date (determined with regard to extension) for the transferor's return of the tax imposed by this chapter for the taxable year in which the transfer of the relinquished property occurs.

**(b) Gain from exchanges not solely in kind.**
If an exchange would be within the provisions of subsection (a), of section 1035(a), of section 1036(a), or of section 1037(a), if it were not for the fact that the property received in exchange consists not

only of property permitted by such provisions to be received without the recognition of gain, but also of other property or money, then the gain, if any, to the recipient shall be recognized, but in an amount not in excess of the sum of such money and the fair market value of such other property.

**(c) Loss from exchanges not solely in kind.**

If an exchange would be within the provisions of subsection (a), of section 1035(a), of section 1036(a), or of section 1037(a), if it were not for the fact that the property received in exchange consists not only of property permitted by such provisions to be received without the recognition of gain or loss, but also of other property or money, then no loss from the exchange shall be recognized.

**(d) Basis.**

If property was acquired on an exchange described in this section, section 1035(a), section 1036(a), or section 1037(a), then the basis shall be the same as that of the property exchanged, decreased in the amount of any money received by the taxpayer and increased in the amount of gain or decreased in the amount of loss to the taxpayer that was recognized on such exchange. If the property so acquired consisted in part of the type of property permitted by this section, section 1035(a), section 1036(a), or section 1037(a), to be received without the recognition of gain or loss, and in part of other property, the basis provided in this subsection shall be allocated between the properties (other than money) received, and for the purpose of the allocation there shall be assigned to such other property an amount equivalent to its fair market value at the date of the exchange. For purposes of this section, section 1035(a), and section 1036(a), where as part of the consideration to the taxpayer another party to the exchange assumed (as determined under section 357(d)) a liability of the taxpayer, such assumption shall be considered as money received by the taxpayer on the exchange.

**(e) Exchanges of livestock of different sexes.**

For purposes of this section, livestock of different sexes are not property of a like kind.

**(f) Special rules for exchanges between related persons.**

**(1) In general.**

If—

(A) a taxpayer exchanges property with a related person,

(B) there is nonrecognition of gain or loss to the taxpayer under this section with respect to the exchange of such property (determined without regard to this subsection), and

(C) before the date 2 years after the date of the last transfer which was part of such exchange—

    (i) the related person disposes of such property, or

    (ii) the taxpayer disposes of the property received in the exchange from the related person which was of like kind to the property transferred by the taxpayer,

there shall be no nonrecognition of gain or loss under this section to the taxpayer with respect to such exchange; except that any gain or loss recognized by the taxpayer by reason of this subsection shall be taken into account as of the date on which the disposition referred to in subparagraph (C) occurs.

**(2) Certain dispositions not taken into account.**

For purposes of paragraph (1)(C), there shall not be taken into account any disposition—

(A) after the earlier of the death of the taxpayer or the death of the related person,

(B) in a compulsory or involuntary conversion (within the meaning of section 1033) if the exchange occurred before the threat or imminence of such conversion, or

(C) with respect to which it is established to the satisfaction of the Secretary that neither the exchange nor such disposition had as one of its principal purposes the avoidance of Federal income tax.

**(3) Related person.**

For purposes of this subsection, the term "related person" means any person bearing a relationship to the taxpayer described in section 267(b) or 707(b)(1).

(4) **Treatment of certain transactions.**

This section shall not apply to any exchange which is part of a transaction (or series of transactions) structured to avoid the purposes of this subsection.

**(g) Special rule where substantial diminution of risk.**

(1) **In general.**

If paragraph (2) applies to any property for any period, the running of the period set forth in subsection (f)(1)(C) with respect to such property shall be suspended during such period.

(2) **Property to which subsection applies.**

This paragraph shall apply to any property for any period during which the holder's risk of loss with respect to the property is substantially diminished by—

(A) the holding of a put with respect to such property,
(B) the holding by another person of a right to acquire such property, or
(C) a short sale or any other transaction.

**(h) Special rules for foreign real and personal property.**

For purposes of this section—

(1) **Real property.**

Real property located in the United States and real property located outside the United States are not property of a like kind.

(2) **Personal property.**

(A) In general. Personal property used predominantly within the United States and personal property used predominantly outside the United States are not property of a like kind.
(B) Predominant use. Except as provided in subparagraphs (C) and (D), the predominant use of any property shall be determined based on—
(i)  in the case of the property relinquished in the exchange, the 2-year period ending on the date of such relinquishment, and

(ii) in the case of the property acquired in the exchange, the 2-year period beginning on the date of such acquisition.

(C) Property held for less than 2 years. Except in the case of an exchange which is part of a transaction (or series of transactions) structured to avoid the purposes of this subsection —
   (i) only the periods the property was held by the person relinquishing the property (or any related person) shall be taken into account under subparagraph (B)(i), and
   (ii) only the periods the property was held by the person acquiring the property (or any related person) shall be taken into account under subparagraph (B)(ii).

(D) Special rule for certain property. Property described in any subparagraph of section 168(g)(4) shall be treated as used predominantly in the United States.

This revenue procedure authorizes safe harbor reverse exchanges. In a reverse exchange, the replacement property is acquired before the relinquished property is sold. Prior to the issuance of this rev. proc., it was unclear how the IRS was going to treat exchanges done in reverse order. It is a subject that is not covered by the 1031 Treasury regulations. Reverse exchanges are discussed in Chapter 16.

# Rev. Proc. 2000–37, 2000–2 CB 308, 9/18/2000, IRC Sec(s). 1031

### Exchange of Property Held for Productive Use or Investment— Treatment of Deferred Exchanges—"Qualified Exchange Accommodation Arrangement"

IRS won't challenge qualification of property as either "replacement property" or "relinquished property" for purposes of applying non-recognition rules of Code Sec. 1031, or treatment of accommodation party as property owner, if property is held in qualified exchange accommodation arrangement (QEAA). Regs issued in 1991 didn't apply to exchanges where replacement property is acquired before relinquished property is transferred. Since regs were published, taxpayers engaged in various transactions to facilitate reverse like-kind exchanges, and IRS believed establishment of "safe harbor" would enable taxpayers who had genuine intent to accomplish like-kind exchange to qualify. Requirements are specified for QEAAs, and permissible agreements, regardless of whether their terms result from arms' length bargaining, were also provided. Safe harbor applies to QEAAs entered into by qualified exchange accommodation titleholder on or after 9/15/2000.

*Reference(s):* ¶ 10,315.03(30); Code Sec. 1031

## 1. Purpose

This revenue procedure provides a safe harbor under which the Internal Revenue Service will not challenge (a) the qualification of property as either "replacement property" or "relinquished property" (as defined in section 1.1031(k)–1(a) of the Income Tax Regulations) for purposes of section 1031 of the Internal Revenue Code and the regulations thereunder or (b) the treatment of the "exchange accommodation titleholder" as the beneficial owner of such property for federal income tax purposes, if the property is held in a "qualified exchange accommodation arrangement" (QEAA), as defined in section 4.02 of this revenue procedure.

## 2. Background

.01. Section 1031(a)(1) provides that no gain or loss is recognized on the exchange of property held for productive use in a trade or business or for investment if the property is exchanged solely for property of like kind that is to be held either for productive use in a trade or business or for investment.

.02. Section 1031(a)(3) provides that property received by the taxpayer is not treated as like-kind property if it: (a) is not identified as property to be received in the exchange on or before the day that is 45 days after the date on which the taxpayer transfers the relinquished property; or (b) is received after the earlier of the date that is 180 days after the date on which the taxpayer transfers the relinquished property, or the due date (determined with regard to extension) for the transferor's federal income tax return for the year in which the transfer of the relinquished property occurs.

.03. Determining the owner of property for federal income tax purposes requires an analysis of all of the facts and circumstances. As a general rule, the party that bears the economic burdens and benefits of ownership will be considered the owner of property for federal income tax purposes. See Rev. Rul. 82–144, 1982–2 C.B. 34.

.04. On April 25, 1991, the Treasury Department and the Service promulgated final regulations under section 1.1031(k)–1 providing rules for deferred like-kind exchanges under section 1031(a)(3). The preamble to the final regulations states that the deferred exchange rules under section 1031(a)(3) do not apply to reverse-Starker exchanges (i.e., exchanges where the replacement property is acquired before the relinquished property is transferred) and consequently that the final regulations do not apply to such exchanges. T.D. 8346, 1991–1 C.B. 150, 151; see Starker v. United States, 602 F.2d 1341 (9th Cir. 1979). However, the preamble indicates that Treasury and the Service will continue to study the applicability of the general rule of section 1031(a)(1) to these transactions. T.D. 8346, 1991–1 C.B. 150, 151.

.05. Since the promulgation of the final regulations under section 1.1031(k)–1, taxpayers have engaged in a wide variety of transactions, including so-called "parking" transactions, to facilitate reverse like-kind exchanges. Parking transactions typically are designed to "park" the desired replacement property with an accommodation party until such time as the taxpayer arranges for the transfer of the relinquished property to the ultimate transferee in a simultaneous or deferred exchange. Once such a transfer is arranged, the taxpayer transfers the relinquished property to the accommodation party in exchange for the replacement property, and the accommodation party then transfers the relinquished property to the ultimate transferee. In other situations, an accommodation party may acquire the desired replacement property on behalf of the taxpayer and immediately exchange such property with the taxpayer for the relinquished property, thereafter holding the relinquished property until the taxpayer arranges for a transfer of such property to the ultimate transferee. In the parking arrangements, taxpayers attempt to arrange the transaction so that the accommodation party has enough of the benefits and burdens relating to the property so that the accommodation party will be treated as the owner for federal income tax purposes.

.06. Treasury and the Service have determined that it is in the best interest of sound tax administration to provide taxpayers with a workable means of qualifying their transactions under section 1031 in situations where the taxpayer has a genuine intent to accomplish a like-kind exchange at the time that it arranges for the acquisition of the replacement property and actually accomplishes the exchange within a short time thereafter. Accordingly, this revenue procedure provides a safe harbor that allows a taxpayer to treat the accommodation party as the owner of the property for federal income tax purposes, thereby enabling the taxpayer to accomplish a qualifying like-kind exchange.

## 3. Scope

### EXCLUSIVITY

.01. This revenue procedure provides a safe harbor for the qualification under section 1031 of certain arrangements between taxpayers and exchange accommodation titleholders and provides for the treatment of the exchange accommodation titleholder as the beneficial owner of the property for federal income tax purposes. These provisions apply only in the limited context described in this revenue procedure. The principles set forth in this revenue procedure have no application to any federal income tax determinations other than determinations that involve arrangements qualifying for the safe harbor.

### NO INFERENCE

.02. No inference is intended with respect to the federal income tax treatment of arrangements similar to those described in this revenue procedure that were entered into prior to the effective date of this revenue procedure. Further, the Service recognizes that "parking" transactions can be accomplished outside of the safe harbor provided in this revenue procedure. Accordingly, no inference is intended with respect to the federal income tax treatment of "parking" transactions that do not satisfy the terms of the safe harbor provided in this revenue procedure, whether entered into prior to or after the effective date of this revenue procedure.

## OTHER ISSUES

.03. Services for the taxpayer in connection with a person's role as the exchange accommodation titleholder in a QEAA shall not be taken into account in determining whether that person or a related person is a disqualified person (as defined in section 1.1031(k)–1(k)). Even though property will not fail to be treated as being held in a QEAA as a result of one or more arrangements described in section 4.03 of this revenue procedure, the Service still may recast an amount paid pursuant to such an arrangement as a fee paid to the exchange accommodation titleholder for acting as an exchange accommodation titleholder to the extent necessary to reflect the true economic substance of the arrangement. Other federal income tax issues implicated, but not addressed, in this revenue procedure include the treatment, for federal income tax purposes, of payments described in section 4.03(7) and whether an exchange accommodation titleholder may be precluded from claiming depreciation deductions (e.g., as a dealer) with respect to the relinquished property or the replacement property.

## EFFECT OF NONCOMPLIANCE

.04. If the requirements of this revenue procedure are not satisfied (for example, the property subject to a QEAA is not transferred within the time period provided), then this revenue procedure does not apply. Accordingly, the determination of whether the taxpayer or the exchange accommodation titleholder is the owner of the property for federal income tax purposes, and the proper treatment of any transactions entered into by or between the parties, will be made without regard to the provisions of this revenue procedure.

## 4. Qualified Exchange Accommodation Arrangements

### GENERALLY

.01. The Service will not challenge the qualification of property as either "replacement property" or "relinquished property" (as defined in section 1.1031(k)–1(a)) for purposes of section 1031 and the regulations thereunder, or the treatment of the exchange accommodation titleholder as the beneficial owner of such property for federal income tax purposes, if the property is held in a QEAA.

## QUALIFIED EXCHANGE ACCOMMODATION ARRANGEMENTS.

.02. For purposes of this revenue procedure, property is held in a QEAA if all of the following requirements are met:

(1) Qualified indicia of ownership of the property is held by a person (the "exchange accommodation titleholder") who is not the taxpayer or a disqualified person and either such person is subject to federal income tax or, if such person is treated as a partnership or S corporation for federal income tax purposes, more than 90 percent of its interests or stock are owned by partners or shareholders who are subject to federal income tax. Such qualified indicia of ownership must be held by the exchange accommodation titleholder at all times from the date of acquisition by the exchange accommodation titleholder until the property is transferred as described in section 4.02(5) of this revenue procedure. For this purpose, "qualified indicia of ownership" means legal title to the property, other indicia of ownership of the property that are treated as beneficial ownership of the property under applicable principles of commercial law (e.g., a contract for deed), or interests in an entity that is disregarded as an entity separate from its owner for federal income tax purposes (e.g., a single member limited liability company) and that holds either legal title to the property or such other indicia of ownership;

(2) At the time the qualified indicia of ownership of the property is transferred to the exchange accommodation titleholder, it is the taxpayer's bona fide intent that the property held by the exchange accommodation titleholder represent either replacement property or relinquished property in an exchange that is intended to qualify for nonrecognition of gain (in whole or in part) or loss under section 1031;

(3) No later than five business days after the transfer of qualified indicia of ownership of the property to the exchange accommodation titleholder, the taxpayer and the exchange accommodation titleholder enter into a written agreement (the "qualified exchange accommodation agreement")

that provides that the exchange accommodation titleholder is holding the property for the benefit of the taxpayer in order to facilitate an exchange under section 1031 and this revenue procedure and that the taxpayer and the exchange accommodation titleholder agree to report the acquisition, holding, and disposition of the property as provided in this revenue procedure. The agreement must specify that the exchange accommodation titleholder will be treated as the beneficial owner of the property for all federal income tax purposes. Both parties must report the federal income tax attributes of the property on their federal income tax returns in a manner consistent with this agreement;

(4) No later than 45 days after the transfer of qualified indicia of ownership of the replacement property to the exchange accommodation titleholder, the relinquished property is properly identified. Identification must be made in a manner consistent with the principles described in section 1.1031(k)–1(c). For purposes of this section, the taxpayer may properly identify alternative and multiple properties, as described in section 1.1031(k)–1(c)(4);

(5) No later than 180 days after the transfer of qualified indicia of ownership of the property to the exchange accommodation titleholder, (a) the property is transferred (either directly or indirectly through a qualified intermediary (as defined in section 1.1031(k)–1(g)(4))) to the taxpayer as replacement property; or (b) the property is transferred to a person who is not the taxpayer or a disqualified person as relinquished property; and

(6) The combined time period that the relinquished property and the replacement property are held in a QEAA does not exceed 180 days.

## PERMISSIBLE AGREEMENTS

.03. Property will not fail to be treated as being held in a QEAA as a result of any one or more of the following legal or contractual arrangements, regardless of whether such arrangements contain terms that typically would result from arm's length bargaining between unrelated parties with respect to such arrangements:

(1) An exchange accommodation titleholder that satisfies the requirements of the qualified intermediary safe harbor set forth in section

1.1031(k)–1(g)(4) may enter into an exchange agreement with the taxpayer to serve as the qualified intermediary in a simultaneous or deferred exchange of the property under section 1031;

(2) The taxpayer or a disqualified person guarantees some or all of the obligations of the exchange accommodation titleholder, including secured or unsecured debt incurred to acquire the property, or indemnifies the exchange accommodation titleholder against costs and expenses;

(3) The taxpayer or a disqualified person loans or advances funds to the exchange accommodation titleholder or guarantees a loan or advance to the exchange accommodation titleholder;

(4) The property is leased by the exchange accommodation titleholder to the taxpayer or a disqualified person;

(5) The taxpayer or a disqualified person manages the property, supervises improvement of the property, acts as a contractor, or otherwise provides services to the exchange accommodation titleholder with respect to the property;

(6) The taxpayer and the exchange accommodation titleholder enter into agreements or arrangements relating to the purchase or sale of the property, including puts and calls at fixed or formula prices, effective for a period not in excess of 185 days from the date the property is acquired by the exchange accommodation titleholder; and

(7) The taxpayer and the exchange accommodation titleholder enter into agreements or arrangements providing that any variation in the value of a relinquished property from the estimated value on the date of the exchange accommodation titleholder's receipt of the property be taken into account upon the exchange accommodation titleholder's disposition of the relinquished property through the taxpayer's advance of funds to, or receipt of funds from, the exchange accommodation titleholder.

## PERMISSIBLE TREATMENT

.04. Property will not fail to be treated as being held in a QEAA merely because the accounting, regulatory, or state, local, or foreign tax treatment of the arrangement between the taxpayer and the exchange accommodation titleholder is different from the treatment required by section 4.02(3) of this revenue procedure.

## 5. Effective Date

This revenue procedure is effective for QEAAs entered into with respect to an exchange accommodation titleholder that acquires qualified indicia of ownership of property on or after September 15, 2000.

## 6. Paperwork Reduction Act

The collections of information contained in this revenue procedure have been reviewed and approved by the Office of Management and Budget in accordance with the Paperwork Reduction Act (44 U.S.C. 3507) under control number 1545–1701. An agency may not conduct or sponsor, and a person is not required to respond to, a collection of information unless the collection of information displays a valid control number.

The collections of information are contained in section 4.02 of this revenue procedure, which requires taxpayers and exchange accommodation titleholders to enter into a written agreement that the exchange accommodation titleholder will be treated as the beneficial owner of the property for all federal income tax purposes. This information is required to ensure that both parties to a QEAA treat the transaction consistently for federal tax purposes. The likely respondents are businesses and other for-profit institutions, and individuals.

The estimated average annual burden to prepare the agreement and certification is two hours. The estimated number of respondents is 1,600, and the estimated total annual reporting burden is 3,200 hours.

The estimated annual frequency of responses is on occasion.

Books and records relating to a collection of information must be retained as long as their contents may become material in the administration of any internal revenue law. Generally, tax returns and tax return information are confidential, as required by 26 U.S.C. 6103.

## Drafting Information

The principal author of this revenue procedure is J. Peter Baumgarten of the Office of Associate Chief Counsel (Income Tax and Accounting). For further information regarding this revenue procedure, contact Mr. Baumgarten on (202) 622–4950 (not a toll-free call).

A  P  P  E  N  D  I  X

This revenue procedure sets forth the method of structuring a tenancy in common (TIC) investment so that it qualifies under Section 1031. Prior to the issuance of this rev. proc., there was a concern that a TIC structure would be taxed as a partnership. If it were taxed as a partnership, the ownership in the underlying real estate would be considered indirect, and hence, it would not qualify under Section 1031. See further discussion in Chapter 12.

# Rev. Proc. 2002–22, 2002–1 CB 733, 03/19/2002, IRC Sec(s). 1031

## Domestic "No Rule" Areas—Exchange of Property Held for Productive Use or Investment

IRS has removed from its list of domestic "no-rule" or "limited rule" areas question of whether undivided fractional interest in real property (other than Code Sec. 614; mineral property) is an interest in a separate tax entity ineligible for tax-free exchange under Code Sec. 1031(a)(1). Topic was

added to list in 2000, with rulings and letters not to be issued pending
further guidance. *Rev Proc 2000–46,* 2000–2 CB 438, is superseded.
*Rev Proc 2002–3,* 2002–1 CB 117, is modified.

*Reference(s):* ¶ 10,315.03(40); ¶ 76,557.48(10); Code Sec. 1031

# 1. Purpose

This revenue procedure specifies the conditions under which the Internal
Revenue Service will consider a request for a ruling that an undivided fractional interest in rental real property (other than a mineral property as
defined in section 614) is not an interest in a business entity, within the
meaning of § 301.7701–2(a) of the Procedure and Administration
Regulations.

This revenue procedure supersedes Rev. Proc. 2000–46, 2002–2 C.B. 438,
which provides that the Service will not issue advance rulings or determination letters on the questions of whether an undivided fractional interest in
real property is an interest in an entity that is not eligible for tax-free
exchange under § 1031(a)(1) of the Internal Revenue Code and whether
arrangements where taxpayers acquire undivided fractional interests in real
property constitute separate entities for federal tax purposes under § 7701.
This revenue procedure also modifies Rev. Proc. 2002–3, 2002–1 I.R.B.
117, by removing these issues from the list of subjects on which the Service
will not rule. Requests for advance rulings described in Rev. Proc. 2000–46
that are not covered by this revenue procedure, such as rulings concerning
mineral property, will be considered under procedures set forth in Rev.
Proc. 2002–1, 2002–1 I.R.B. 1 (or its successor).

# 2. Background

Section 301.7701–1(a)(1) provides that whether an organization is an entity separate from its owners for federal tax purposes is a matter of federal
law and does not depend on whether the entity is recognized as an entity
under local law. Section 301.7701–1(a)(2) provides that a joint venture or
other contractual arrangement may create a separate entity for federal tax
purposes if the participants carry on a trade, business, financial operation,
or venture and divide the profits therefrom, but the mere co-ownership of

property that is maintained, kept in repair, and rented or leased does not constitute a separate entity for federal tax purposes.

Section 301.7701–2(a) provides that a business entity is any entity recognized for federal tax purposes (including an entity with a single owner that may be disregarded as an entity separate from its owner under § 301.7701–3) that is not properly classified as a trust under § 301.7701–4 or otherwise subject to special treatment under the Internal Revenue Code. A business entity with two or more members is classified for federal tax purposes as either a corporation or a partnership.

Section 761(a) provides that the term "partnership" includes a syndicate, group, pool, joint venture, or other unincorporated organization through or by means of which any business, financial operation, or venture is carried on, and that is not a corporation or a trust or estate.

Section 1.761–1(a) of the Income Tax Regulations provides that the term "partnership" means a partnership as determined under §§ 301.7701–1, 301.7701–2, and 301.7701–3.

The central characteristic of a tenancy in common, one of the traditional concurrent estates in land, is that each owner is deemed to own individually a physically undivided part of the entire parcel of property. Each tenant in common is entitled to share with the other tenants the possession of the whole parcel and has the associated rights to a proportionate share of rents or profits from the property, to transfer the interest, and to demand a partition of the property. These rights generally provide a tenant in common the benefits of ownership of the property within the constraint that no rights may be exercised to the detriment of the other tenants in common. 7 Richard R. Powell, Powell on Real Property §§ 50.01–50.07 (Michael Allan Wolf ed., 2000).

Rev. Rul. 75–374, 1975–2 C.B. 261, concludes that a two-person co-ownership of an apartment building that was rented to tenants did not constitute a partnership for federal tax purposes. In the revenue ruling, the co-owners employed an agent to manage the apartments on their behalf; the agent collected rents, paid property taxes, insurance premiums, repair and maintenance expenses, and provided the tenants with customary services, such as heat, air conditioning, trash removal, unattended parking, and maintenance of public areas. The ruling concludes that the agent's activities in providing customary services to the tenants, although imputed to the co-owners, were not sufficiently extensive to cause the co-ownership to be characterized as a partnership. See also Rev. Rul. 79–77, 1979–1 C.B. 448, which did not find a business entity where three individuals transferred ownership of a commercial building subject to a net lease to a trust with the three individuals as beneficiaries.

Where a sponsor packages co-ownership interests for sale by acquiring property, negotiating a master lease on the property, and arranging for financing, the courts have looked at the relationships not only among the co-owners, but also between the sponsor (or persons related to the sponsor) and the co-owners in determining whether the co-ownership gives rise to a partnership. For example, in *Bergford v. Commissioner*, 12 F.3d 166 (9 Cir. 1993), seventy-eight investors purchased "co-ownership" interests in computer equipment that was subject to a 7-year net lease. As part of the purchase, the co-owners authorized the manager to arrange financing and refinancing, purchase and lease the equipment, collect rents and apply those rents to the notes used to finance the equipment, prepare statements, and advance funds to participants on an interest-free basis to meet cash flow. The agreement allowed the co-owners to decide by majority vote whether to sell or lease the equipment at the end of the lease. Absent a majority vote, the manager could make that decision. In addition, the manager was entitled to a remarketing fee of 10 percent of the equipment's selling price or lease rental whether or not a co-owner terminated the agreement or the manager performed any remarketing. A co-owner could assign an interest in the co-ownership only after fulfilling numerous conditions and obtaining the manager's consent.

The court held that the co-ownership arrangement constituted a partnership for federal tax purposes. Among the factors that influenced the court's decision were the limitations on the co-owners' ability to sell, lease, or encumber either the co-ownership interest or the underlying property, and the manager's effective participation in both profits (through the remarketing fee) and losses (through the advances). *Bergford*, 12 F.3d at 169–170. *Accord Bussing v. Commissioner*, 88 T.C. 449 (1987), *aff'd on reh'g*, 89 T.C. 1050 (1987); *Alhouse v. Commissioner*, T.C. Memo. 1991–652.

Under § 1.761–1(a) and §§ 301.7701–1 through 301.7701–3, a federal tax partnership does not include mere co-ownership of property where the owners' activities are limited to keeping the property maintained, in repair, rented or leased. However, as the above authorities demonstrate, a partnership for federal tax purposes is broader in scope than the common law meaning of partnership and may include groups not classified by state law as partnerships. *Bergford*, 12 F.3d at 169. Where the parties to a venture join together capital or services with the intent of conducting a business or enterprise and of sharing the profits and losses from the venture, a partnership (or other business entity) is created. *Bussing*, 88 T.C. at 460. Furthermore, where the economic benefits to the individual participants are not derivative of their co-ownership, but rather come from their joint relationship toward a common goal, the co-ownership arrangement will be characterized as a partnership (or other business entity) for federal tax purposes. *Bergford*, 12 F.3d at 169.

## 3. Scope

This revenue procedure applies to co-ownership of rental real property (other than mineral interests) (the Property) in an arrangement classified under local law as a tenancy-in-common.

This revenue procedure provides guidelines for requesting advance rulings solely to assist taxpayers in preparing ruling requests and the Service in issuing advance ruling letters as promptly as practicable. The guidelines set forth in this revenue procedure are not intended to be substantive rules and are not to be used for audit purposes.

## 4. Guidelines for Submitting Ruling Requests

The Service ordinarily will not consider a request for a ruling under this revenue procedure unless the information described in section 5 of this revenue procedure is included in the ruling request and the conditions described in section 6 of this revenue procedure are satisfied. Even if sections 5 and 6 of this revenue procedure are satisfied, however, the Service may decline to issue a ruling under this revenue procedure whenever warranted by the facts and circumstances of a particular case and whenever appropriate in the interest of sound tax administration.

Where multiple parcels of property owned by the co-owners are leased to a single tenant pursuant to a single lease agreement and any debt of one or more co-owners is secured by all of the parcels, the Service will generally treat all of the parcels as a single "Property." In such a case, the Service will generally not consider a ruling request under this revenue procedure unless: (1) each co-owner's percentage interest in each parcel is identical to that co-owner's percentage interest in every other parcel, (2) each co-owner's percentage interests in the parcels cannot be separated and traded independently, and (3) the parcels of property are properly viewed as a single business unit. The Service will generally treat contiguous parcels as comprising a single business unit. Even if the parcels are not contiguous, however, the Service may treat multiple parcels as comprising a single business unit where there is a close connection between the business use of one parcel and the business use of another parcel. For example, an office building and a garage that services the tenants of the office building may be treated as a single business unit even if the office building and the garage are not contiguous.

For purposes of this revenue procedure, the following definitions apply. The term "co-owner" means any person that owns an interest in the Property as a tenant in common. The term "sponsor" means any person who divides a single interest in the Property into multiple co-ownership interests for the purpose of offering those interests for sale. The term "related person" means a person bearing a relationship described in § 267(b) or 707(b)(1), except that in applying § 267(b) or 707(b)(1), the co-ownership will be treated as a partnership and each co-owner will be treated as a partner. The term "disregarded entity" means an entity that is disregarded as an entity separate from its owner for federal tax purposes. Examples of disregarded entities include qualified REIT subsidiaries (within the meaning of § 856(i)(2)), qualified subchapter S subsidiaries (within the meaning of § 1361(b)(3)(B)), and business entities that have only one owner and do not elect to be classified as corporations. The term "blanket lien" means any mortgage or trust deed that is recorded against the Property as a whole.

## 5. Information to Be Submitted

.01. Section 8 of Rev. Proc. 2002–1 outlines general requirements concerning the information to be submitted as part of a ruling request, including advance rulings under this revenue procedure. For example, any ruling request must contain a complete statement of all facts relating to the co-ownership, including those relating to promoting, financing, and managing the Property. Among the information to be included are the items of information specified in this revenue procedure; therefore, the ruling request must provide all items of information and conditions specified below and in section 6 of this revenue procedure, or at least account for all of the items. For example, if a co-ownership arrangement has no brokerage agreement permitted in section 6.12 of this revenue procedure, the ruling request should so state. Furthermore, merely submitting documents and supplementary materials required by section 5.02 of this revenue procedure does not satisfy all of the information requirements contained in section 5.02 of this revenue procedure or in section 8 of Rev. Proc. 2002–1; all material facts in the documents submitted must be explained in the ruling request and may not be merely incorporated by reference. All submitted documents and supplementary materials must contain applicable exhibits, attachments, and amendments. The ruling request must identify and explain any information or documents required in section 5 of this revenue procedure that are not included and any conditions in section 6 of this revenue procedure that are or are not satisfied.

## Required General Information and Copies of Documents and Supplementary Materials

.02. Generally the following information and copies of documents and materials must be submitted with the ruling request:

(1) The name, taxpayer identification number, and percentage fractional interest in Property of each co-owner;

(2) The name, taxpayer identification number, ownership of, and any relationship among, all persons involved in the acquisition, sale, lease and other use of Property, including the sponsor, lessee, manager, and lender;

(3) A full description of the Property;

(4) A representation that each of the co-owners holds title to the Property (including each of multiple parcels of property treated as a single Property under this revenue procedure) as a tenant in common under local law;

(5)  All promotional documents relating to the sale of fractional interests in the Property;

(6)  All lending agreements relating to the Property;

(7)  All agreements among the co-owners relating to the Property;

(8)  Any lease agreement relating to the Property;

(9)  Any purchase and sale agreement relating to the Property;

(10)  Any property management or brokerage agreement relating to the Property; and

(11)  Any other agreement relating to the Property not specified in this section, including agreements relating to any debt secured by the Property (such as guarantees or indemnity agreements) and any call and put options relating to the Property.

## 6. Conditions for Obtaining Rulings

The Service ordinarily will not consider a request for a ruling under this revenue procedure unless the conditions described below are satisfied. Nevertheless, where the conditions described below are not satisfied, the Service may consider a request for a ruling under this revenue procedure where the facts and circumstances clearly establish that such a ruling is appropriate.

### Tenancy in Common Ownership

.01. Each of the co-owners must hold title to the Property (either directly or through a disregarded entity) as a tenant in common under local law. Thus, title to the Property as a whole may not be held by an entity recognized under local law.

### Number of Co-Owners

.02. The number of co-owners must be limited to no more than 35 persons. For this purpose, "person" is defined as in § 7701(a)(1), except that a husband and wife are treated as a single person and all persons who acquire interests from a co-owner by inheritance are treated as a single person.

## No Treatment of Co-Ownership as an Entity

.03. The co-ownership may not file a partnership or corporate tax return, conduct business under a common name, execute an agreement identifying any or all of the co-owners as partners, shareholders, or members of a business entity, or otherwise hold itself out as a partnership or other form of business entity (nor may the co-owners hold themselves out as partners, shareholders, or members of a business entity). The Service generally will not issue a ruling under this revenue procedure if the co-owners held interests in the Property through a partnership or corporation immediately prior to the formation of the co-ownership.

## Co-Ownership Agreement

.04. The co-owners may enter into a limited co-ownership agreement that may run with the land. For example, a co-ownership agreement may provide that a co-owner must offer the co-ownership interest for sale to the other co-owners, the sponsor, or the lessee at fair market value (determined as of the time the partition right is exercised) before exercising any right to partition (see section 6.06 of this revenue procedure for conditions relating to restrictions on alienation); or that certain actions on behalf of the co-ownership require the vote of co-owners holding more than 50 percent of the undivided interests in the Property (see section 6.05 of this revenue procedure for conditions relating to voting).

## Voting

.05. The co-owners must retain the right to approve the hiring of any manager, the sale or other disposition of the Property, any leases of a portion or all of the Property, or the creation or modification of a blanket lien. Any sale, lease, or re-lease of a portion or all of the Property, any negotiation or renegotiation of indebtedness secured by a blanket lien, the hiring of any manager, or the negotiation of any management contract (or any extension or renewal of such contract) must be by unanimous approval of the co-owners. For all other actions on behalf of the co-ownership, the co-owners may agree to be bound by the vote of those holding more than 50 percent of the undivided interests in the Property. A co-owner who has consented to an action in conformance with this section 6.05 may provide the manager or other person a power of attorney to execute a specific document with respect to that action, but may not provide the manager or other person with a global power of attorney.

## Restrictions on Alienation

.06. In general, each co-owner must have the rights to transfer, partition, and encumber the co-owner's undivided interest in the Property without the agreement or approval of any person. However, restrictions on the right to transfer, partition, or encumber interests in the Property that are required by a lender and that are consistent with customary commercial lending practices are not prohibited. See section 6.14 of this revenue procedure for restrictions on who may be a lender. Moreover, the co-owners, the sponsor, or the lessee may have a right of first offer (the right to have the first opportunity to offer to purchase the co-ownership interest) with respect to any co-owner's exercise of the right to transfer the co-ownership interest in the Property. In addition, a co-owner may agree to offer the co-ownership interest for sale to the other co-owners, the sponsor, or the lessee at fair market value (determined as of the time the partition right is exercised) before exercising any right to partition.

## Sharing Proceeds and Liabilities upon Sale of Property

.07. If the Property is sold, any debt secured by a blanket lien must be satisfied and the remaining sales proceeds must be distributed to the co-owners.

## Proportionate Sharing of Profits and Losses

.08. Each co-owner must share in all revenues generated by the Property and all costs associated with the Property in proportion to the co-owner's undivided interest in the Property. Neither the other co-owners, nor the sponsor, nor the manager may advance funds to a co-owner to meet expenses associated with the co-ownership interest, unless the advance is recourse to the co-owner (and, where the co-owner is a disregarded entity, the owner of the co-owner) and is not for a period exceeding 31 days.

## Proportionate Sharing of Debt

.09. The co-owners must share in any indebtedness secured by a blanket lien in proportion to their undivided interests.

## Options

.10. A co-owner may issue an option to purchase the co-owner's undivided interest (call option), provided that the exercise price for the call option reflects the fair market value of the Property determined as of the time the option is exercised. For this purpose, the fair market value of an undivided interest in the Property is equal to the co-owner's percentage interest in the Property multiplied by the fair market value of the Property as a whole. A co-owner may not acquire an option to sell the co-owner's undivided interest (put option) to the sponsor, the lessee, another co-owner, or the lender, or any person related to the sponsor, the lessee, another co-owner, or the lender.

## No Business Activities

.11. The co-owners' activities must be limited to those customarily performed in connection with the maintenance and repair of rental real property (customary activities). See Rev. Rul. 75–374, 1975–2 C.B. 261. Activities will be treated as customary activities for this purpose if the activities would not prevent an amount received by an organization described in § 511(a)(2) from qualifying as rent under § 512(b)(3)(A) and the regulations thereunder. In determining the co-owners' activities, all activities of the co-owners, their agents, and any persons related to the co-owners with respect to the Property will be taken into account, whether or not those activities are performed by the co-owners in their capacities as co-owners. For example, if the sponsor or a lessee is a co-owner, then all of the activities of the sponsor or lessee (or any person related to the sponsor or lessee) with respect to the Property will be taken into account in determining whether the co-owners' activities are customary activities. However, activities of a co-owner or a related person with respect to the Property (other than in the co-owner's capacity as a co-owner) will not be taken into account if the co-owner owns an undivided interest in the Property for less than 6 months.

## Management and Brokerage Agreements

.12. The co-owners may enter into management or brokerage agreements, which must be renewable no less frequently than annually, with an agent, who may be the sponsor or a co-owner (or any person related to the sponsor or a co-owner), but who may not be a lessee. The management agreement may authorize the manager to maintain a common bank account for the collection and deposit of rents and to offset expenses associated with the Property against any revenues before disbursing each co-owner's share of net revenues. In all events, however, the manager must disburse to the co-owners their shares of net revenues within 3 months from the date of receipt of those revenues. The management agreement may also authorize the manager to prepare statements for the co-owners showing their shares of revenue and costs from the Property. In addition, the management agreement may authorize the manager to obtain or modify insurance on the Property, and to negotiate modifications of the terms of any lease or any indebtedness encumbering the Property, subject to the approval of the co-owners. (See section 6.05 of this revenue procedure for conditions relating to the approval of lease and debt modifications.) The determination of any fees paid by the co-ownership to the manager must not depend in whole or in part on the income or profits derived by any person from the Property and may not exceed the fair market value of the manager's services. Any fee paid by the co-ownership to a broker must be comparable to fees paid by unrelated parties to brokers for similar services.

## Leasing Agreements

.13. All leasing arrangements must be bona fide leases for federal tax purposes. Rents paid by a lessee must reflect the fair market value for the use of the Property. The determination of the amount of the rent must not depend, in whole or in part, on the income or profits derived by any person from the Property leased (other than an amount based on a fixed percentage or percentages of receipts or sales). See section 856(d)(2)(A) and the regulations thereunder. Thus, for example, the amount of rent paid by a lessee may not be based on a percentage of net income from the Property, cash flow, increases in equity, or similar arrangements.

## Loan Agreements

.14. The lender with respect to any debt that encumbers the Property or with respect to any debt incurred to acquire an undivided interest in the Property may not be a related person to any co-owner, the sponsor, the manager, or any lessee of the Property.

## Payments to Sponsor

.15. Except as otherwise provided in this revenue procedure, the amount of any payment to the sponsor for the acquisition of the co-ownership interest (and the amount of any fees paid to the sponsor for services) must reflect the fair market value of the acquired co-ownership interest (or the services rendered) and may not depend, in whole or in part, on the income or profits derived by any person from the Property.

# 6. Effect on Other Documents

Rev. Proc. 2000–46 is superseded. Rev. Proc. 2002–3 is modified by removing sections 5.03 and 5.06.

# 7. Drafting Information

The principal authors of this revenue procedure are Jeanne Sullivan and Deane Burke of the Office of Associate Chief Counsel (Passthroughs and Special Industries). For further information regarding this revenue procedure, contact Ms. Sullivan or Mr. Burke at (202) 622–3070 (not a toll-free call).

A    P    P    E    N    D    I    X

This revenue procedure sets forth instructions for computing tax liability when the taxpayer sells property that qualifies as both a personal residence under Section 121 and investment property under Section 1031. This rev. proc. generously allows a taxpayer to take advantage of both Code sections in the same sale transaction. See Chapter 13 for further discussion of this subject.

# Rev. Proc. 2005–14, 2005–7 IRB 528, 01/27/2005, IRC Sec(s). 121

## Exclusion of Gain from Sale of Principal Residence—Single Exchange of Like-Kind Property

IRS offered guidance to taxpayers who exchange single property that meets requirements for gain exclusion under Code Sec. 121; and non-recognition of gain on like-kind exchange under Code Sec. 1031. Specific computation directions were provided: Code Sec. 121 must be applied before Code Sec. 1031, followed by application of Code Sec. 1031 to gain attributable to depreciation, with boot to be taken into account only to extent boot exceeds gain excluded under Code Sec. 121 with respect to relinquished business property. Guidance was also provided computing basis, and hypothetical illustrations were given.

*Reference(s):* ¶ 1215.01(20); Code Sec. 121; Code Sec. 1031

# 1. Purpose

This revenue procedure provides guidance on the application of §§ 121 and 1031 of the Internal Revenue Code to a single exchange of property.

# 2. Background

.01. Section 121(a) provides that a taxpayer may exclude gain realized on the sale or exchange of property if the property was owned and used as the taxpayer's principal residence for at least 2 years during the 5-year period ending on the date of the sale or exchange. Section 121(b) provides generally that the amount of the exclusion is limited to $250,000 ($500,000 for certain joint returns). Under § 121(d)(6), any gain attributable to depreciation adjustments (as defined in § 1250(b)(3)) for periods after May 6, 1997, is not eligible for the exclusion. This limitation applies only to depreciation allocable to the portion of the property to which the § 121 exclusion applies. See § 121–1(d)(1).

.02. Section 121(d), as amended by § 840 of the American Jobs Creation Act of 2004, Pub. L. 108–357, provides that, if a taxpayer acquired property in an exchange to which § 1031 applied, the § 121 exclusion will not apply if the sale or exchange of the property occurs during the 5-year period beginning on the date of the acquisition of the property. This provision is effective for sales or exchanges after October 22, 2004.

.03. Under § 1.121–1(e) of the Income Tax Regulations, a taxpayer who uses a portion of a property for residential purposes and a portion of the property for business purposes is treated as using the entire property as the taxpayer's principal residence for purposes of satisfying the 2-year use requirement if the residential and business portions of the property are within the same dwelling unit. The term "dwelling unit" has the same meaning as in § 280A(f)(1), but does not include appurtenant structures or other property. If, however, the business portion of the property is separate from the dwelling unit used for residential purposes, the gain allocable to the business portion of the property is not excludable unless the taxpayer has also met the 2-year use requirement for the business portion of the property.

.04. Section 1.121–1(e)(3) provides that, for purposes of determining the amount of gain allocable to the residential and business portions of the property, the taxpayer must allocate the basis and the amount realized using the same method of allocation the taxpayer used to determine depreciation adjustments (as defined in § 1250(b)(3)). Allocation based on the square footage of the residential and business portions of the property is an appropriate method of allocating the basis and the amount realized. *Poague v. United States*, 66 A.F.T.R.2d (RIA) 5825 (E.D. Va. 1990), *aff'd*, 947 F.2d 942 (4 Cir. 1991).

.05. Section 1031(a) provides that no gain or loss is recognized on the exchange of property held for productive use in a trade or business or for investment (relinquished property) if the property is exchanged solely for property of like kind (replacement property) that is to be held either for productive use in a trade or business or for investment. Under § 1031(b), if a taxpayer also receives cash or property that is not like-kind property (boot) in an exchange that otherwise qualifies under § 1031(a), the taxpayer must recognize gain to the extent of the boot. Section 1031 does not apply to property that is used solely as a personal residence.

.06. Section 1012 provides that the basis of property is its cost. The basis of property acquired in an exchange is its fair market value, unless otherwise provided in the Code or regulations (for example, § 1031(d)). See *Philadelphia Park Amusement Co. v. United States*, 126 F. Supp. 184 [46 AFTR 1293] (Ct. Cl. 1954).

.07. Under § 1031(d), the basis of the replacement property is the same as the basis of the relinquished property, decreased by the amount of cash received and increased by the amount of gain recognized by the taxpayer in the exchange.

.08. Neither § 121 nor § 1031 addresses the application of both provisions to a single exchange of property. Section 121(d)(5)(B), however, provides rules for applying § 121 and another nonrecognition provision, § 1033, to a single replacement of property. Under § 1033, in general, gain is recognized only to the extent the amount realized from a compulsory or involuntary conversion of property exceeds the cost of qualifying replacement property, and the basis of the replacement property is its cost reduced by the amount of the gain not recognized.

.09. Section 121(d)(5)(B) provides that, in applying § 1033, the amount realized from the sale or exchange of property is treated as the amount determined without regard to § 121, reduced by the amount of gain excluded under § 121. Under § 121(d)(5)(B), the amount realized from an exchange of a taxpayer's principal residence for purposes of applying § 1033 is the fair market value of the relinquished property reduced by the amount of the gain excluded from gross income under § 121. Thus, Congress concluded that for exchanges meeting the requirements of both § 121 and § 1033, (1) the § 121 exclusion should be applied to gain from the exchange before the application of § 1033, (2) for purposes of determining gain that may be deferred under § 1033, the § 121 exclusion should be applied first against amounts received by the taxpayer that are not reinvested in the replacement property (amounts equivalent to boot that would result in gain recognition absent the application of § 121), and (3) the gain excluded under § 121 should be added in the calculation of the taxpayer's basis in the replacement property. See S. Rep. No. 830, 88 Cong., 2d Sess. 52–53, 1964–1 C.B. (Part 2) 505, 556–7 ("the basis of the taxpayer in the newly acquired residence will be his basis for the old residence increased by any exclusion of gain obtained by him under the provision which is reinvested in the new residence"); H.R. Rep. No. 749, 88 Cong., 1 Sess. 47, 1964–1 C.B. (Part 2) 125, 171.

## 3. Scope

This revenue procedure applies to taxpayers who exchange property that satisfies the requirements for both the exclusion of gain from the exchange of a principal residence under § 121 and the nonrecognition of gain on the exchange of like-kind properties under § 1031. Thus, this revenue procedure applies only to taxpayers who satisfy the held for productive use in a trade or business or for investment requirement of § 1031(a)(1) with respect to the relinquished business property and the replacement business property (as defined below).

# 4. Application

.01. *In general.* Taxpayers within the scope of this revenue procedure may apply both the exclusion of gain from the exchange of a principal residence under § 121 and the nonrecognition of gain from the exchange of like-kind properties under § 1031 to an exchange of property by applying the procedures set forth in this section 4.

.02. Computation of gain.

(1) *Application of § 121 before § 1031.* Section 121 must be applied to gain realized before applying § 1031.
(2) *Application of § 1031 to gain attributable to depreciation.* Under § 121(d)(6), the § 121 exclusion does not apply to gain attributable to depreciation deductions for periods after May 6, 1997, claimed with respect to the business or investment portion of a residence. However, § 1031 may apply to such gain.
(3) *Treatment of boot.* In applying § 1031, cash or other non-like kind property (boot) received in exchange for property used in the taxpayer's trade or business or held for investment (the relinquished business property), is taken into account only to the extent the boot exceeds the gain excluded under § 121 with respect to the relinquished business property.

.03. *Computation of basis.* In determining the basis of the property received in the exchange to be used in the taxpayer's trade or business or held for investment (the replacement business property), any gain excluded under § 121 is treated as gain recognized by the taxpayer. Thus, under § 1031(d), the basis of the replacement business property is increased by any gain attributable to the relinquished business property that is excluded under § 121.

# 5. Examples

In each example below, the taxpayer is an unmarried individual and the property or a portion of the property has been used in the taxpayer's trade or business or held for investment within the meaning of § 1031(a) as well as used as a principal residence as required under § 121.

# Example 1

(i) Taxpayer A buys a house for $210,000 that A uses as A's principal residence from 2000 to 2004. From 2004 until 2006, A rents the house to tenants and claims depreciation deductions of $20,000. In 2006, A exchanges the house for $10,000 of cash and a townhouse with a fair market value of $460,000 that A intends to rent to tenants. A realizes gain of $280,000 on the exchange.

(ii) A's exchange of a principal residence that A rents for less than 3 years for a townhouse intended for rental and cash satisfies the requirements of both §§ 121 and 1031. Section 121 does not require the property to be the taxpayer's principal residence on the sale or exchange date. Because A owns and uses the house as A's principal residence for at least 2 years during the 5-year period prior to the exchange, A may exclude gain under § 121. Because the house is investment property at the time of the exchange, A may defer gain under § 1031.

(iii) Under section 4.02(1) of this revenue procedure, A applies § 121 to exclude $250,000 of the $280,000 gain before applying the nonrecognition rules of § 1031. A may defer the remaining gain of $30,000, including the $20,000 gain attributable to depreciation, under § 1031. See section 4.02(2) of this revenue procedure. Although A receives $10,000 of cash (boot) in the exchange, A is not required to recognize gain because the boot is taken into account for purposes of § 1031(b) only to the extent the boot exceeds the amount of excluded gain. See section 4.02(3) of this revenue procedure.

These results are illustrated as follows.

| | |
|---|---|
| Amount realized | $470,000 |
| Less: Adjusted basis | $190,000 |
| Realized gain | $280,000 |
| Less: Gain excluded under § 121 | $250,000 |
| Gain to be deferred | $ 30,000 |

(iv) A's basis in the replacement property is $430,000, which is equal to the basis of the relinquished property at the time of the exchange ($190,000) increased by the gain excluded under § 121 ($250,000), and reduced by the cash A receives ($10,000). See section 4.03 of this revenue procedure.

## Example 2

(i)   Taxpayer B buys a property for $210,000. The property consists of two separate dwelling units (within the meaning of § 1.121–1(e)(2)), a house and a guesthouse. From 2001 until 2006, B uses the house as B's principal residence and uses the guesthouse as an office in B's trade or business. Based on the square footage of the respective parts of the property, B allocates 2/3 of the basis of the property to the house and 1/3 to the guesthouse. In 2006, B exchanges the entire property for a residence and a separate property that B intends to use as an office. The total fair market value of B's replacement properties is $360,000. The fair market value of the replacement residence is $240,000 and the fair market value of the replacement business property is $120,000, which is equal to the fair market value of the relinquished business property. From 2001 to 2006, B claims depreciation deductions of $30,000 for the business use. B realizes gain of $180,000 on the exchange.

(ii)  Under § 121, B may exclude gain of $100,000 allocable to the residential portion of the house (2/3 of $360,000 amount realized, or $240,000, minus 2/3 of $210,000 basis, or $140,000) because B meets the ownership and use requirements for that portion of the property. Because the guesthouse is business property separate from the dwelling unit and B has not met the use requirements for the guesthouse, B may not exclude the gain allocable to the guesthouse under § 1.121–1(e). However, because the fair market value of the replacement business property is equal to the fair market value of the relinquished business property and B receives no boot, B may defer the remaining gain of $80,000 (1/3 of $360,000 amount realized, or $120,000, minus $40,000 adjusted basis, which is 1/3 of $210,000 basis, or $70,000, adjusted by $30,000 depreciation) under § 1031.

These results are illustrated as follows:

|  | Total property | 2/3 residential property | 1/3 business property |
|---|---|---|---|
| Amount realized | $360,000 | $240,000 | $120,000 |
| Basis | $210,000 | $140,000 | $70,000 |
| Depreciation adjustment | $30,000 |  | $30,000 |
| Adjusted basis | $180,000 | $140,000 | $40,000 |
| Realized gain | $180,000 | $100,000 | $80,000 |
| Gain excluded under §121 | $100,000 | $100,000 |  |
| Gain deferred under § 1031 | $ 80,000 | $ 80,000 |  |

(iii) Because no portion of the gain attributable to the relinquished business property is excluded under § 121 and B receives no boot and recognizes no gain or loss in the exchange, B's basis in the replacement business property is equal to B's basis in the relinquished business property at the time of the exchange ($40,000). B's basis in the replacement residential property is the fair market value of the replacement residential property at the time of the exchange ($240,000).

## Example 3

(i) Taxpayer C buys a property for $210,000. The property consists of a house that constitutes a single dwelling unit under § 1.121–1(e)(2). From 2001 until 2006, C uses 2/3 of the house (by square footage) as C's principal residence and uses 1/3 of the house as an office in C's trade or business. In 2006, C exchanges the entire property for a residence and a separate property that C intends to use as an office in C's trade or business. The total fair market value of C's replacement properties is $360,000. The fair market value of the replacement residence is $240,000 and the fair market value of the replacement business property is $120,000, which is equal to the fair market value of the business portion of the relinquished property. From 2001 to 2006, C claims depreciation deductions of $30,000 for the business use. C realizes gain of $180,000 on the exchange.

(ii) Under § 121, C may exclude the gain of $100,000 allocable to the residential portion of the house (2/3 of $360,000 amount realized, or $240,000, minus 2/3 of $210,000 basis, or $140,000) because C meets the ownership and use requirements for that portion of the property.

(iii) The remaining gain of $80,000 (1/3 of $360,000 amount realized, or $120,000, minus $40,000 adjusted basis, which is 1/3 of $210,000 basis, or $70,000, adjusted by $30,000 depreciation) is allocable to the business portion of the house (the office). Under section 4.02(1) of this revenue procedure, C applies § 121 before applying the nonrecognition rules of § 1031. Under § 1.121–1(e), C may exclude $50,000 of the gain allocable to the office because the office and residence are part of a single dwelling unit. C may not exclude that portion of the gain ($30,000) attributable to depreciation deductions, but may defer the remaining gain of $30,000 under § 1031.

These results are illustrated as follows:

| | Total property | 2/3 residential property | 1/3 business property |
|---|---|---|---|
| Amount realized | $360,000 | $240,000 | $120,000 |
| Basis | $210,000 | $140,000 | $70,000 |
| Depreciation adjustment | $30,000 | | $30,000 |
| Adjusted basis | $180,000 | $140,000 | $40,000 |
| Realized gain | $180,000 | $100,000 | $80,000 |
| Gain excluded under § 121 | $150,000 | $100,000 | $50,000 |
| Gain deferred under § 1031 | $30,000 | | $30,000 |

(iv) C's basis in the replacement residential property is the fair market value of the replacement residential property at the time of the exchange ($240,000). C's basis in the replacement business property is $90,000, which is equal to C's basis in the relinquished business property at the time of the exchange ($40,000), increased by the gain excluded under § 121 attributable to the relinquished business property ($50,000). See section 4.03 of this revenue procedure.

# Example 4

(i) The facts are the same as in *Example 3* except that C also receives $10,000 of cash in the exchange and the fair market value of the replacement business property is $110,000, which is $10,000 less than the fair market value of the business portion of the relinquished property ($120,000).

(ii) Under § 121, C may exclude the gain of $100,000 allocable to the residential portion of the house (2/3 of $360,000 amount realized, or $240,000, minus 2/3 of $210,000 basis, or $140,000).

(iii) The remaining gain of $80,000 (1/3 of $360,000 amount realized, or $120,000, minus $40,000 adjusted basis) is allocable to the business portion of the house. Under section 4.02(1) of this revenue procedure, C applies § 121 to exclude gain before applying the nonrecognition rules of § 1031. Under § 1.121–1(e), C may exclude $50,000 of the gain allocable to the business portion of the house but may not exclude the $30,000 of gain attributable to depreciation deductions. Under section 4.02(2) of this revenue procedure, C may defer the $30,000 of gain under § 1031. Although C receives $10,000 of cash (boot) in the exchange, C is not required to recognize gain because the boot is taken into account for purposes of § 1031(b) only to the extent the boot exceeds the amount of excluded gain attributable to the relinquished business property. See 4.02(3) of this revenue procedure.

These results are illustrated as follows:

|  | Total property | 2/3 residential property | 1/3 business property |
| --- | --- | --- | --- |
| Amount realized | $360,000 | $240,000 | $110,000 + 10,000 |
| Basis | $210,000 | $140,000 | $70,000 |
| Depreciation adjustment | $30,000 |  | $30,000 |
| Adjusted basis | $180,000 | $140,000 | $40,000 |
| Realized gain | $180,000 | $100,000 | $80,000 |
| Gain excluded under § 121 | $150,000 | $100,000 | $50,000 |
| Gain deferred under § 1031 | $30,000 |  | $30,000 |

(iv)  C's basis in the replacement residential property is the fair market value of the replacement residential property at the time of the exchange ($240,000). C's basis in the replacement business property is $80,000, which is equal to C's basis in the relinquished business property ($40,000), increased by the gain excluded under § 121 ($50,000), and reduced by the cash ($10,000) received. See section 4.03 of this revenue procedure.

# Example 5

(i)  The facts are the same as in *Example 3* except that the total fair market value of the replacement properties is $540,000. The fair market value of the replacement residence is $360,000, the fair market value of the replacement business property is $180,000, and C realizes gain of $360,000 on the exchange.

(ii)  Under § 121, C may exclude the gain of $220,000 allocable to the residential portion of the house (2/3 of $540,000 amount realized, or $360,000, minus 2/3 of $210,000 basis, or $140,000).

(iii)  The remaining gain of $140,000 (1/3 of $540,000 amount realized, or $180,000, minus $40,000 adjusted basis) is allocable to the business portion of the house. Under section 4.02(1) of this revenue procedure, C excludes the gain before applying the nonrecognition rules of

§ 1031. Under § 1.121–1(e), C may exclude $30,000 of the gain allocable to the business portion, at which point C will have excluded the maximum limitation amount of $250,000. C may defer the remaining gain of $110,000 ($140,000 realized gain minus the $30,000 gain excluded under § 121), including the $30,000 gain attributable to depreciation, under § 1031.

These results are illustrated as follows:

|  | Total property | 2/3 residential property | 1/3 business property |
|---|---|---|---|
| Amount realized | $540,000 | $360,000 | $180,000 |
| Basis | $210,000 | $140,000 | $70,000 |
| Depreciation adjustment | $30,000 |  | $30,000 |
| Adjusted basis | $180,000 | $140,000 | $40,000 |
| Realized gain | $360,000 | $220,000 | $140,000 |
| Gain excluded under § 121 | $250,000 | $220,000 | $30,000 |
| Gain deferred under § 1031 | $110,000 |  | $110,000 |

(iv) C's basis in the replacement residential property is the fair market value of the replacement residential property at the time of the exchange ($360,000). C's basis in the replacement business property is $70,000, which is equal to C's basis in the relinquished business property ($40,000), increased by the amount of the gain excluded under § 121 ($30,000). See section 4.03 of this revenue procedure.

## Example 6

(i) The facts are the same as in *Example 3* except that the total fair market value of the replacement properties is $750,000. The fair market value of the replacement residence is $500,000, the fair market value of the replacement business property is $250,000, and C realizes gain of $570,000 on the exchange.

(ii) The gain allocable to the residential portion is $360,000 (2/3 of $750,000 amount realized, or $500,000, minus 2/3 of $210,000 basis, or $140,000). C may exclude gain of $250,000 from gross income under § 121. C must include in income the gain of $110,000 allocable to the residential portion that exceeds the § 121(b) exclusion limitation amount.

(iii)  The remaining gain of $210,000 (1/3 of $750,000 amount realized, or $250,000, minus $40,000 adjusted basis) is allocable to the business portion of the house. C may defer the $210,000 of gain, including the $30,000 gain attributable to depreciation, under § 1031.

These results are illustrated as follows:

|  | Total property | 2/3 residential property | 1/3 business property |
|---|---|---|---|
| Amount realized | $750,000 | $500,000 | $250,000 |
| Basis | $210,000 | $140,000 | $70,000 |
| Depreciation adjustment | $30,000 | $30,000 |  |
| Adjusted basis | $180,000 | $140,000 | $40,000 |
| Realized gain | $570,000 | $360,000 | $210,000 |
| Gain excluded under § 121 | $250,000 | $250,000 |  |
| Gain deferred under § 1031 | $210,000 | $210,000 |  |
| Gain recognized | $110,000 | $110,000 |  |

(iv) C's basis in the replacement residential property is the fair market value of the replacement residential property at the time of the exchange ($500,000). C's basis in the replacement business property is $40,000, which is equal to C's basis in the relinquished business property at the time of the exchange.

## 6. Effective Date

This revenue procedure is effective January 27, 2005. However, taxpayers may apply this revenue procedure in taxable years for which the period of limitation on refund or credit under § 6511 has not expired.

## Drafting Information

The principal author of this revenue procedure is Sara Paige Shepherd of the Office of Associate Chief Counsel (Income Tax & Accounting). For further information regarding this revenue procedure, contact Ms. Shepherd at (202) 622–4960 (not a toll free call).

A Delaware statutory trust is a special entity created under Delaware law to hold title to real estate. This revenue ruling authorizes the use of a Delaware statutory trust as the entity to hold the replacement property in a 1031 exchange under the specific circumstances described. It is unclear until further rulings are issued how widespread the use of a DST will be. This is discussed in Chapter 12.

# Rev. Rul. 2004–86, 2004–33 IRB 191, 07/20/2004, IRC Sec(s). 7701

**Entity Classification—Trust Created under Delaware Law to Hold Real Property for Investment—Like-Kind Exchange Treatment of Real Property for Trust Interest Exchanges**

IRS provided guidance on tax classification of Delaware statutory trust (DST) created to hold real property for investment, and how taxpayer may exchange real property for interest in trust without recognition of gain or loss under like-kind exchange rules of Code Sec. 1031. Since all interests in DST were of single class representing undivided beneficial interests in assets of DST and DST's trustee had no power to vary investment of certificate holders to benefit from variations in market, DST was investment trust under Code Sec. 7701; entity regs that was classifiable as trust for tax purposes. IRS further determined that taxpayer would be permitted to exchange real property for interest in trust without recognizing gain under Code Sec. 1031, provided other requirements of Code Sec. 1031 were met.

*Reference(s):* ¶ 77,015.18(15); Code Sec. 7701

## ISSUE(S)

(1) In the situation described below, how is a Delaware statutory trust, described in Del. Code Ann. title 12, §§ 3801 – 3824, classified for federal tax purposes?

(2) In the situation described below, may a taxpayer exchange real property for an interest in a Delaware statutory trust without recognition of gain or loss under § 1031 of the Internal Revenue Code?

## Facts

On January 1, 2005, A, an individual, borrows money from BK, a bank, and signs a 10-year note bearing adequate stated interest, within the meaning of § 483. On January 1, 2005, A uses the proceeds of the loan to purchase Blackacre, rental real property. The note is secured by Blackacre and is nonrecourse to A.

Immediately following A's purchase of Blackacre, A enters into a net lease with Z for a term of 10 years. Under the terms of the lease, Z is to pay all taxes, assessments, fees, or other charges imposed on Blackacre by federal, state, or local authorities. In addition, Z is to pay all insurance, maintenance, ordinary repairs, and utilities relating to Blackacre. Z may sublease Blackacre. Z's rent is a fixed amount that may be adjusted by a formula described in the lease agreement that is based upon a fixed rate or an objective index, such as an escalator clause based upon the Consumer Price Index, but adjustments to the rate or index are not within the control of any of the parties to the lease. Z's rent is not contingent on Z's ability to lease the property or on Z's gross sales or net profits derived from the property.

Also on January 1, 2005, A forms DST, a Delaware statutory trust described in the Delaware Statutory Trust Act, Del. Code Ann. title 12, §§ 3801 – 3824, to hold property for investment. A contributes Blackacre to DST. Upon contribution, DST assumes A's rights and obligations under the note with BK and the lease with Z. In accordance with the terms of the note, neither DST nor any of its beneficial owners are personally liable to BK on the note, which continues to be secured by Blackacre.

The trust agreement provides that interests in DST are freely transferable. However, DST interests are not publicly traded on an established securities market. DST will terminate on the earlier of 10 years from the date of its creation or the disposition of Blackacre, but will not terminate on the bankruptcy, death, or incapacity of any owner or on the transfer of any right, title, or interest of the owners. The trust agreement further provides that interests in DST will be of a single class, representing undivided beneficial interests in the assets of DST.

Under the trust agreement, the trustee is authorized to establish a reasonable reserve for expenses associated with holding Blackacre that may be payable out of trust funds. The trustee is required to distribute all available cash less reserves quarterly to each beneficial owner in proportion to their respective interests in DST. The trustee is required to invest cash received from Blackacre between each quarterly distribution and all cash held in reserve in short-term obligations of (or guaranteed by) the United States, or any agency or instrumentality thereof, and in certificates of deposit of any bank or trust company having a minimum stated surplus and capital. The trustee is permitted to invest only in obligations maturing prior to the next distribution date and is required to hold such obligations until maturity. In addition to the right to a quarterly distribution of cash, each beneficial owner has the right to an in-kind distribution of its proportionate share of trust property.

The trust agreement provides that the trustee's activities are limited to the collection and distribution of income. The trustee may not exchange Blackacre for other property, purchase assets other than the short-term investments described above, or accept additional contributions of assets (including money) to DST. The trustee may not renegotiate the terms of the debt used to acquire Blackacre and may not renegotiate the lease with Z or enter into leases with tenants other than Z, except in the case of Z's bankruptcy or insolvency. In addition, the trustee may make only minor non-structural modifications to Blackacre, unless otherwise required by law. The trust agreement further provides that the trustee may engage in ministerial activities to the extent required to maintain and operate DST under local law.

On January 3, 2005, B and C exchange Whiteacre and Greenacre, respectively, for all of A's interests in DST through a qualified intermediary, within the meaning of § 1.1031(k)–1(g). A does not engage in a § 1031 exchange. Whiteacre and Greenacre were held for investment and are of like kind to Blackacre, within the meaning of § 1031.

Neither DST nor its trustee enters into a written agreement with A, B, or C, creating an agency relationship. In dealings with third parties, neither DST nor its trustee is represented as an agent of A, B, or C.

BK is not related to A, B, C, DST's trustee or Z within the meaning of § 267(b) or § 707(b). Z is not related to B, C, or DST's trustee within the meaning of § 267(b) or § 707(b).

## Law

Delaware law provides that a Delaware statutory trust is an unincorporated association recognized as an entity separate from its owners. A Delaware statutory trust is created by executing a governing instrument and filing an executed certificate of trust. Creditors of the beneficial owners of a Delaware statutory trust may not assert claims directly against the property in the trust. A Delaware statutory trust may sue or be sued, and property held in a Delaware statutory trust is subject to attachment or execution as if the trust were a corporation. Beneficial owners of a Delaware statutory trust are entitled to the same limitation on personal liability because of actions of the Delaware statutory trust that is extended to stockholders of Delaware corporations. A Delaware statutory trust may merge or consolidate with or into one or more statutory entities or other business entities.

Section 671 provides that, where the grantor or another person is treated as the owner of any portion of a trust (commonly referred to as a "grantor trust"), there shall be included in computing the taxable income and credits of the grantor or the other person those items of income, deductions, and credits against tax of the trust which are attributable to that portion of the trust to the extent that the items would be taken into account under chapter 1 in computing taxable income or credits against the tax of an individual.

Section 1.671–2(e)(1) of the Income Tax Regulations provides that, for purposes of subchapter J, a grantor includes any person to the extent such person either creates a trust or directly or indirectly makes a gratuitous transfer of property to a trust.

Under § 1.671–2(e)(3), the term "grantor" includes any person who acquires an interest in a trust from a grantor of the trust if the interest acquired is an interest in certain investment trusts described in § 301.7701–4(c).

Under § 677(a), the grantor is treated as the owner of any portion of a trust whose income without the approval or consent of any adverse party is, or, in the discretion of the grantor or a nonadverse party, or both, may be distributed, or held or accumulated for future distribution, to the grantor or the grantor's spouse.

A person that is treated as the owner of an undivided fractional interest of a trust under subpart E of part I, subchapter J of the Code (§§ 671 and following), is considered to own the trust assets attributable to that undivided fractional interest of the trust for federal income tax purposes. See Rev. Rul. 88–103, 1988–2 C.B. 304; Rev. Rul. 85–45, 1985–1 C.B. 183; and Rev. Rul. 85–13, 1985–1 C.B. 184. See also § 1.1001–2(c), Example 5.

Section 761(a) provides that the term "partnership" includes a syndicate, group, pool, joint venture, or other unincorporated organization through or by means of which any business, financial operation, or venture is carried on, and that is not a corporation or a trust or estate. Under regulations the Secretary may, at the election of all the members of the unincorporated organization, exclude such organization from the application of all or part of subchapter K, if the income of the members of the organization may be adequately determined without the computation of partnership taxable income and the organization is availed of (1) for investment purposes only and not for the active conduct of a business, (2) for the joint production, extraction, or use of property, but not for the purpose of selling services or property produced or extracted, or (3) by dealers in securities for a short period for the purpose of underwriting, selling, or distributing a particular issue of securities.

Section 1.761–2(a)(2) provides the requirements that must be satisfied for participants in the joint purchase, retention, sale, or exchange of investment property to elect to be excluded from the application of the provisions of subchapter K. One of these requirements is that the participants own the property as co-owners.

Section 1031(a)(1) provides that no gain or loss is recognized on the exchange of property held for productive use in a trade or business or for investment if such property is exchanged solely for property of like kind that is to be held either for productive use in a trade or business or for investment.

Section 1031(a)(2) provides that § 1031(a) does not apply to any exchange of stocks, bonds or notes, other securities or evidences of indebtedness or interest, interests in a partnership, or certificates of trust or beneficial interests. It further provides that an interest in a partnership that has in effect a valid election under § 761(a) to be excluded from the application of all of subchapter K shall be treated as an interest in each of the assets of the partnership and not as an interest in a partnership.

Under § 301.7701–1(a)(1) of the Procedure and Administration Regulations, whether an organization is an entity separate from its owners for federal tax purposes is a matter of federal tax law and does not depend on whether the organization is recognized as an entity under local law.

Generally, when participants in a venture form a state law entity and avail themselves of the benefits of that entity for a valid business purpose, such as investment or profit, and not for tax avoidance, the entity will be recognized for federal tax purposes. See Moline Properties, Inc. v. Comm'r, 319 U.S. 436 [30 AFTR 1291](1943); Zmuda v. Comm'r, 731 F.2d 1417 [53 AFTR 2d 84–1269](9th Cir. 1984); Boca Investerings P'ship v. United States, 314 F.3d 625 [91 AFTR 2d 2003–444](D.C. Cir. 2003); Saba P'ship v. Comm'r, 273 F.3d 1135 [88 AFTR 2d 2001–7318](D.C. Cir. 2001); ASA Investerings P'ship v. Comm'r, 201 F.3d 505 [85 AFTR 2d 2000–675](D.C. Cir. 2000); Markosian v. Comm'r, 73 T.C. 1235 (1980).

Section 301.7701–2(a) defines the term "business entity" as any entity recognized for federal tax purposes (including an entity with a single owner that may be disregarded as an entity separate from its owner under § 301.7701–3) that is not properly classified as a trust under § 301.7701–4 or otherwise subject to special treatment under the Code. A business entity with two or more owners is classified for federal tax purposes as either a corporation or a partnership. A business entity with only one owner is classified as a corporation or is disregarded.

Section 301.7701–3(a) provides that an eligible entity can elect its classification for federal tax purposes. Under § 301.7701–3(b)(1), unless the entity elects otherwise, a domestic eligible entity is a partnership if it has two or more owners or is disregarded as an entity separate from its owner if it has a single owner.

Section 301.7701–4(a) provides that the term "trust" refers to an arrangement created either by will or by an inter vivos declaration whereby trustees take title to property for the purpose of protecting and conserving it for the beneficiaries. Usually the beneficiaries of a trust do no more than accept the benefits thereof and are not voluntary planners or creators of the trust arrangement. However, the beneficiaries of a trust may be the persons who create it, and it will be recognized as a trust if it was created for the purpose of protecting and conserving the trust property for beneficiaries who stand in the same relation to the trust as they would if the trust had been created by others for them.

Section 301.7701–4(b) provides that there are other arrangements known as trusts because the legal title to property is conveyed to trustees for the benefit of beneficiaries, but that are not classified as trusts for federal tax purposes because they are not simply arrangements to protect or conserve the property for the beneficiaries. These trusts, which are often known as business or commercial trusts, generally are created by the beneficiaries simply as a device to carry on a profit-making business that normally would have been carried on through business organizations that are classified as corporations or partnerships.

Section 301.7701–4(c)(1) provides that an "investment" trust will not be classified as a trust if there is a power under the trust agreement to vary the investment of the certificate holders. See Comm'r v. North American Bond Trust, 122 F.2d 545 [27 AFTR 892](2d Cir. 1941), cert. denied, 314 U.S. 701 (1942). An investment trust with a single class of ownership interests, representing undivided beneficial interests in the assets of the trust, will be classified as a trust if there is no power to vary the investment of the certificate holders.

A power to vary the investment of the certificate holders exists where there is a managerial power, under the trust instrument, that enables a trust to take advantage of variations in the market to improve the investment of the investors. See Comm'r v. North American Bond Trust, 122 F.2d at 546.

Rev. Rul. 75–192, 1975–1 C.B. 384, discusses the situation where a provision in the trust agreement requires the trustee to invest cash on hand between the quarterly distribution dates. The trustee is required to invest the money in short-term obligations of (or guaranteed by) the United States, or any agency or instrumentality thereof, and in certificates of deposit of any bank or trust company having a minimum stated surplus and capital. The trustee is permitted to invest only in obligations maturing prior to the next distribution date and is required to hold such obligations until maturity. Rev. Rul. 75–192 concludes that, because the restrictions on the types of permitted investments limit the trustee to a fixed return similar to that earned on a bank account and eliminate any opportunity to profit from market fluctuations, the power to invest in the specified kinds of short-term investments is not a power to vary the trust's investment.

Rev. Rul. 78–371, 1978–2 C.B. 344, concludes that a trust established by the heirs of a number of contiguous parcels of real estate is an association taxable as a corporation for federal tax purposes where the trustees have the power to purchase and sell contiguous or adjacent real estate, accept or retain contributions of contiguous or adjacent real estate, raze or erect any building or structure, make any improvements to the land originally contributed, borrow money, and mortgage or lease the property. Compare Rev. Rul. 79–77, 1979–1 C.B. 448 (concluding that a trust formed by three parties to hold a single parcel of real estate is classified as a trust for federal income tax purposes when the trustee has limited powers that do not evidence an intent to carry on a profit making business).

Rev. Rul. 92–105, 1992–2 C.B. 204, addresses the transfer of a taxpayer's interest in an Illinois land trust under § 1031. Under the facts of the ruling, a single taxpayer created an Illinois land trust and named a domestic corporation as trustee. Under the deed of trust, the taxpayer transferred legal and equitable title to real property to the trust, subject to the provisions of an accompanying land trust agreement. The land trust agreement provided that the taxpayer retained exclusive control of the management, operation, renting, and selling of the real property, together with an exclusive right to the earnings and proceeds from the real property. Under the agreement, the taxpayer was required to file all tax returns, pay all taxes, and satisfy any other liabilities with respect to the real property. Rev. Rul 92–105 concludes that, because the trustee's only responsibility was to hold and transfer title at the direction of the taxpayer, a trust, as defined in § 301.7701–4(a), was not established. Moreover, there were no other arrangements between the taxpayer and the trustee (or between the taxpayer and any other person) that would cause the overall arrangement to be classified as a partnership (or any other type of entity). Instead, the trustee was a mere agent for the holding and transfer of title to real property, and the taxpayer retained direct ownership of the real property for federal income tax purposes.

## Analysis

Under Delaware law, DST is an entity that is recognized as separate from its owners. Creditors of the beneficial owners of DST may not assert claims directly against Blackacre. DST may sue or be sued, and the property of DST is subject to attachment and execution as if it were a corporation. The beneficial owners of DST are entitled to the same limitation on personal liability because of actions of DST that is extended to stockholders of Delaware corporations. DST may merge or consolidate with or into one or more statutory entities or other business entities. DST is formed for investment purposes. Thus, DST is an entity for federal tax purposes.

Whether DST or its trustee is an agent of DST's beneficial owners depends upon the arrangement between the parties. The beneficiaries of DST do not enter into an agency agreement with DST or its trustee. Further, neither DST nor its trustee acts as an agent for A, B, or C in dealings with third parties. Thus, neither DST nor its trustee is the agent of DST's beneficial owners. Cf. Comm'r v. Bollinger, 485 U.S. 340 [61 AFTR 2d 88–793](1988).

This situation is distinguishable from Rev. Rul. 92–105. First, in Rev. Rul. 92–105, the beneficiary retained the direct obligation to pay liabilities and taxes relating to the property. DST, in contrast, assumed A's obligations on the lease with Z and on the loan with BK, and Delaware law provides the beneficial owners of DST with the same limitation on personal liability extended to shareholders of Delaware corporations. Second, unlike A, the beneficiary in Rev. Rul. 92–105 retained the right to manage and control the trust property.

## Issue 1. Classification of Delaware Statutory Trust

Because DST is an entity separate from its owner, DST is either a trust or a business entity for federal tax purposes. To determine whether DST is a trust or a business entity for federal tax purposes, it is necessary, under § 301.7701–4(c)(1), to determine whether there is a power under the trust agreement to vary the investment of the certificate holders.

Prior to, but on the same date as, the transfer of Blackacre to DST, A entered into a 10-year nonrecourse loan secured by Blackacre. A also entered into the 10-year net lease agreement with Z. A's rights and obligations under the loan and lease were assumed by DST. Because the duration of DST is 10 years (unless Blackacre is disposed of prior to that time), the financing and leasing arrangements related to Blackacre that were made prior to the inception of DST are fixed for the entire life of DST. Further, the trustee may only invest in short-term obligations that mature prior to the next distribution date and is required to hold these obligations until maturity. Because the trust agreement requires that any cash from Blackacre, and any cash earned on short-term obligations held by DST between distribution dates, be distributed quarterly, and because the disposition of Blackacre results in the termination of DST, no reinvestment of such monies is possible.

The trust agreement provides that the trustee's activities are limited to the collection and distribution of income. The trustee may not exchange Blackacre for other property, purchase assets other than the short-term investments described above, or accept additional contributions of assets (including money) to DST. The trustee may not renegotiate the terms of the debt used to acquire Blackacre and may not renegotiate the lease with Z or enter into leases with tenants other than Z, except in the case of Z's bankruptcy or insolvency. In addition, the trustee may make only minor nonstructural modifications to Blackacre, unless otherwise required by law.

This situation is distinguishable from Rev. Rul. 78–371, because DST's trustee has none of the powers described in Rev. Rul. 78–371, which evidence an intent to carry on a profit making business. Because all of the interests in DST are of a single class representing undivided beneficial interests in the assets of DST and DST's trustee has no power to vary the investment of the certificate holders to benefit from variations in the market, DST is an investment trust that will be classified as a trust under § 301.7701–4(c)(1).

## Issue 2. Exchange of Real Property for Interests under § 1031

B and C are treated as grantors of the trust under § 1.671–2(e)(3) when they acquire their interests in the trust from A. Because they have the right to distributions of all trust income attributable to their undivided fractional interests in the trust, B and C are each treated, by reason of § 677, as the owner of an aliquot portion of the trust and all income, deductions, and credits attributable to that portion are includible by B and C under § 671 in computing their taxable income. Because the owner of an undivided fractional interest of a trust is considered to own the trust assets attributable to that interest for federal income tax purposes, B and C are each considered to own an undivided fractional interest in Blackacre for federal income tax purposes. See Rev. Rul. 85–13.

Accordingly, the exchange of real property by B and C for an interest in DST through a qualified intermediary is the exchange of real property for an interest in Blackacre, and not the exchange of real property for a certificate of trust or beneficial interest under § 1031(a)(2)(E). Because Whiteacre and Greenacre are of like kind to Blackacre, and provided the other requirements of § 1031 are satisfied, the exchange of real property for an interest in DST by B and C will qualify for nonrecognition of gain or loss under § 1031. Moreover, because DST is a grantor trust, the outcome to the parties will remain the same, even if A transfers interests in Blackacre directly to B and C, and B and C immediately form DST by contributing their interests in Blackacre.

Under the facts of this case, if DST's trustee has additional powers under the trust agreement such as the power to do one or more of the following: (i) dispose of Blackacre and acquire new property; (ii) renegotiate the lease with Z or enter into leases with tenants other than Z; (iii) renegotiate or refinance the obligation used to purchase Blackacre; (iv) invest cash received to profit from market fluctuations; or (v) make more than minor non-structural modifications to Blackacre not required by law, DST will be a business entity which, if it has two or more owners, will be classified as a partnership for federal tax purposes, unless it is treated as a corporation under § 7704 or elects to be classified as a corporation under § 301.7701–3. In addition, because the assets of DST will not be owned by the beneficiaries as co-owners under state law, DST will not be able to elect to be excluded from the application of subchapter K. See § 1.761–2(a)(2)(i).

## Holdings

(1) The Delaware statutory trust described above is an investment trust, under § 301.7701–4(c), that will be classified as a trust for federal tax purposes.

(2) A taxpayer may exchange real property for an interest in the Delaware statutory trust described above without recognition of gain or loss under § 1031, if the other requirements of § 1031 are satisfied.

## Effect on Other Revenue Rulings

Rev. Rul. 78–371 and Rev. Rul. 92–105 are distinguished.

## Drafting Information

The principal author of this revenue ruling is Christopher L. Trump of the Office of Associate Chief Counsel (Passthroughs and Special Industries). For further information regarding this revenue ruling, contact Christopher L. Trump on (202) 622–3070 (not a toll-free call).

This is the Internal Revenue Code section that provides for an exclusion from income of a portion of the sale proceeds of a personal residence. The exclusion amount is $250,000 per person, or $500,000 for a married couple. The home must have been used as the taxpayer's personal residence for two of the prior five years before the exemption may be taken. See further discussion in Chapter 13.

# § 121 Exclusion of Gain from Sale of Principal Residence

**(a) Exclusion.**

Gross income shall not include gain from the sale or exchange of property if, during the 5-year period ending on the date of the sale or exchange, such property has been owned and used by the taxpayer as the taxpayer's principal residence for periods aggregating 2 years or more.

**(b) Limitations.**

**(1) In general.**

The amount of gain excluded from gross income under subsection (a) with respect to any sale or exchange shall not exceed $250,000.

**(2) Special rules for joint returns.**

In the case of a husband and wife who make a joint return for the taxable year of the sale or exchange of the property—

(A) $500,000 limitation for certain joint returns. Paragraph (1) shall be applied by substituting "$500,000" for "$250,000" if—

(i) either spouse meets the ownership requirements of subsection (a) with respect to such property;

(ii) both spouses meet the use requirements of subsection (a) with respect to such property; and

(iii) neither spouse is ineligible for the benefits of subsection (a) with respect to such property by reason of paragraph (3).

(B) Other joint returns. If such spouses do not meet the requirements of subparagraph (A), the limitation under paragraph (1) shall be the sum of the limitations under paragraph (1) to which each spouse would be entitled if such spouses had not been married. For purposes of the preceding sentence, each spouse shall be treated as owning the property during the period that either spouse owned the property.

**(3) Application to only 1 sale or exchange every 2 years.**

(A) In general. Subsection (a) shall not apply to any sale or exchange by the taxpayer if, during the 2-year period ending on the date of such sale or exchange, there was any other sale or exchange by the taxpayer to which subsection (a) applied.

(B) Pre-May 7, 1997, sales not taken into account. Subparagraph (A) shall be applied without regard to any sale or exchange before May 7, 1997.

**(c) Exclusion for taxpayers failing to meet certain requirements.**

**(1) In general.**

In the case of a sale or exchange to which this subsection applies, the ownership and use requirements of subsection (a), and subsection (b)(3), shall not apply; but the dollar limitation under paragraph (1) or (2) of subsection (b), whichever is applicable, shall be equal to—

(A) the amount which bears the same ratio to such limitation (determined without regard to this paragraph) as

(B)

    (i) the shorter of—

        (I) the aggregate periods, during the 5-year period ending on the date of such sale or exchange, such property has been owned and used by the taxpayer as the taxpayer's principal residence; or

        (II) the period after the date of the most recent prior sale or exchange by the taxpayer to which subsection (a) applied and before the date of such sale or exchange, bears to

    (ii) 2 years.

**(2) Sales and exchanges to which subsection applies.**

This subsection shall apply to any sale or exchange if—

(A) subsection (a) would not (but for this subsection) apply to such sale or exchange by reason of—

    (i) a failure to meet the ownership and use requirements of subsection (a), or

    (ii) subsection (b)(3), and

(B) such sale or exchange is by reason of a change in place of employment, health, or, to the extent provided in regulations, unforeseen circumstances.

**(d) Special rules.**

**(1) Joint returns.**

If a husband and wife make a joint return for the taxable year of the sale or exchange of the property, subsections (a) and (c) shall apply if either spouse meets the ownership and use requirements of subsection (a) with respect to such property.

**(2) Property of deceased spouse.**

For purposes of this section, in the case of an unmarried individual whose spouse is deceased on the date of the sale or exchange of property, the period such unmarried individual owned and used such property shall include the period such deceased spouse owned and used such property before death.

**(3) Property owned by spouse or former spouse.**

For purposes of this section —

(A) Property transferred to individual from spouse or former spouse. In the case of an individual holding property transferred to such individual in a transaction described in section 1041(a), the period such individual owns such property shall include the period the transferor owned the property.

(B) Property used by former spouse pursuant to divorce decree, etc. Solely for purposes of this section, an individual shall be treated as using property as such individual's principal residence during any period of ownership while such individual's spouse or former spouse is granted use of the property under a divorce or separation instrument (as defined in section 71(b)(2)).

**(4) Tenant-stockholder in cooperative housing corporation.**

For purposes of this section, if the taxpayer holds stock as a tenant-stockholder (as defined in section 216) in a cooperative housing corporation (as defined in such section), then—

(A) the holding requirements of subsection (a) shall be applied to the holding of such stock, and

(B) the use requirements of subsection (a) shall be applied to the house or apartment which the taxpayer was entitled to occupy as such stockholder.

**(5) Involuntary conversions.**

(A) In general. For purposes of this section, the destruction, theft, seizure, requisition, or condemnation of property shall be treated as the sale of such property.

(B) Application of section 1033. In applying section 1033 (relating to involuntary conversions), the amount realized from the sale or exchange of property shall be treated as being the amount determined without regard to this section, reduced by the amount of gain not included in gross income pursuant to this section.

(C) Property acquired after involuntary conversion. If the basis of the property sold or exchanged is determined (in whole or in part) under section 1033(b) (relating to basis of property acquired through involuntary conversion), then the holding and use by the taxpayer of the converted property shall be treated as holding and use by the taxpayer of the property sold or exchanged.

**(6) Recognition of gain attributable to depreciation.**
Subsection (a) shall not apply to so much of the gain from the sale of any property as does not exceed the portion of the depreciation adjustments (as defined in section 1250(b)(3)) attributable to periods after May 6, 1997, in respect of such property.

**(7) Determination of use during periods of out-of-residence care.**
In the case of a taxpayer who—

(A) becomes physically or mentally incapable of self-care, and

(B) owns property and uses such property as the taxpayer's principal residence during the 5-year period described in subsection (a) for periods aggregating at least 1 year,

then the taxpayer shall be treated as using such property as the taxpayer's principal residence during any time during such 5-year period in which the taxpayer owns the property and resides in any facility (including a nursing home) licensed by a State or political subdivision to care for an individual in the taxpayer's condition.

**(8) Sales of remainder interests.**
For purposes of this section —

(A) In general. At the election of the taxpayer, this section shall not fail to apply to the sale or exchange of an interest in a principal residence by reason of such interest being a remainder interest in such residence, but this section shall not apply to any other interest in such residence which is sold or exchanged separately.

(B) Exception for sales to related parties. Subparagraph (A) shall not apply to any sale to, or exchange with, any person who bears a relationship to the taxpayer which is described in section 267(b) or 707(b).

**(9) Members of uniformed services and foreign service.**

(A) In general. At the election of an individual with respect to a property, the running of the 5-year period described in subsections (a) and (c)(1)(B) and paragraph (7) of this subsection with respect to such property shall be suspended during any period that such individual or such individual's spouse is serving on qualified official extended duty as a member of the uniformed services or of the Foreign Service of the United States.

(B) Maximum period of suspension. The 5-year period described in subsection (a) shall not be extended more than 10 years by reason of subparagraph (A).

(C) Qualified official extended duty. For purposes of this paragraph —

   (i) In general. The term "qualified official extended duty" means any extended duty while serving at a duty station which is at least 50 miles from such property or while residing under Government orders in Government quarters.

   (ii) Uniformed services. The term "uniformed services" has the meaning given such term by section 101(a)(5) of title 10, United States Code, as in effect on the date of the enactment of this paragraph.

   (iii) Foreign Service of the United States. The term "member of the Foreign Service of the United States" has the meaning given the term "member of the Service" by paragraph (1), (2), (3), (4), or (5) of section 103 of the Foreign Service Act of 1980, as in effect on the date of the enactment of this paragraph.

   (iv) Extended duty. The term "extended duty" means any period of active duty pursuant to a call or order to such duty for a period in excess of 90 days or for an indefinite period.

(D) Special rules relating to election.

   (i) Election limited to 1 property at a time. An election under subparagraph (A) with respect to any property may not be made if such an election is in effect with respect to any other property.

   (ii) Revocation of election. An election under subparagraph (A) may be revoked at any time.

**(10) Property acquired in like-kind exchange.**

If a taxpayer acquires property in an exchange with respect to which gain is not recognized (in whole or in part) to the taxpayer under subsection (a) or (b) of section 1031, subsection (a) shall not apply to the sale or exchange of such property by such taxpayer (or by any person whose basis in such property is determined, in whole or in part, by reference to the basis in the hands of such taxpayer) during the 5-year period beginning with the date of such acquisition.

**Caution:** Para. (d)(11), redesignated as such by Sec. 403(ee)(1) of P.L. 109–135, is effective for estates of decedents dying after 12/31/2009 as enacted by Sec. 542(c) of P.L. 107–16. Para. (d)(11) was originally enacted as para. (d)(9) by Sec. 542(c) of such Act and later redesignated as para. (d)(10) by Sec. 101(a) of P.L. 108–121.

**(11)  Property acquired from a decedent.**
The exclusion under this section shall apply to property sold by—

(A)  the estate of a decedent,

(B)  any individual who acquired such property from the decedent (within the meaning of section 1022), and

(C)  a trust which, immediately before the death of the decedent, was a qualified revocable trust (as defined in section 645(b)(1)) established by the decedent,
determined by taking into account the ownership and use by the decedent.

**(e)  Denial of exclusion for expatriates.**
This section shall not apply to any sale or exchange by an individual if the treatment provided by section 877(a)(1) applies to such individual.

**(f)  Election to have section not apply.**
This section shall not apply to any sale or exchange with respect to which the taxpayer elects not to have this section apply.

**(g)  Residences acquired in rollovers under section 1034.**
For purposes of this section, in the case of property the acquisition of which by the taxpayer resulted under section 1034 (as in effect on the day before the date of the enactment of this section) in the nonrecognition of any part of the gain realized on the sale or exchange of another

residence, in determining the period for which the taxpayer has owned and used such property as the taxpayer's principal residence, there shall be included the aggregate periods for which such other residence (and each prior residence taken into account under section 1223(6) in determining the holding period of such property) had been so owned and used.

A P P E N D I X    X

This is the Internal Revenue Code section that deals with deductible expenses when a portion of a residence is used for business purposes. The most common example is where a taxpayer has a room dedicated solely to office use. Another example would be a home day-care business. This section is also cited as authority on the subject of vacation homes and whether they qualify as 1031 property. See Chapter 13 for a more thorough discussion.

# § 280A Disallowance of Certain Expenses in Connection with Business Use of Home, Rental of Vacation Homes, etc.

**(a) General rule.**

Except as otherwise provided in this section, in the case of a taxpayer who is an individual or an S corporation, no deduction otherwise allowable under this chapter shall be allowed with respect to the use of a dwelling unit which is used by the taxpayer during the taxable year as a residence.

**(b) Exception for interest, taxes, casualty losses, etc.**
Subsection (a) shall not apply to any deduction allowable to the taxpayer without regard to its connection with his trade or business (or with his income-producing activity).

**(c) Exceptions for certain business or rental use; limitation on deductions for such use.**

**(1) Certain business use.**
Subsection (a) shall not apply to any item to the extent such item is allocable to a portion of the dwelling unit which is exclusively used on a regular basis—

(A) as the principal place of business for any trade or business of the taxpayer,
(B) as a place of business which is used by patients, clients, or customers in meeting or dealing with the taxpayer in the normal course of his trade or business, or
(C) in the case of a separate structure which is not attached to the dwelling unit, in connection with the taxpayer's trade or business.

In the case of an employee, the preceding sentence shall apply only if the exclusive use referred to in the preceding sentence is for the convenience of his employer. For purposes of subparagraph (A), the term "principal place of business" includes a place of business which is used by the taxpayer for the administrative or management activities of any trade or business of the taxpayer if there is no other fixed location of such trade or business where the taxpayer conducts substantial administrative or management activities of such trade or business.

**(2) Certain storage use.**
Subsection (a) shall not apply to any item to the extent such item is allocable to space within the dwelling unit which is used on a regular basis as a storage unit for the inventory or product samples

of the taxpayer held for use in the taxpayer's trade or business of selling products at retail or wholesale, but only if the dwelling unit is the sole fixed location of such trade or business.

**(3) Rental use.**
Subsection (a) shall not apply to any item which is attributable to the rental of the dwelling unit or portion thereof (determined after the application of subsection (e)).

**(4) Use in providing day care services.**

(A) In general. Subsection (a) shall not apply to any item to the extent that such item is allocable to the use of any portion of the dwelling unit on a regular basis in the taxpayer's trade or business of providing day care for children, for individuals who have attained age 65, or for individuals who are physically or mentally incapable of caring for themselves.

(B) Licensing, etc., requirement. Subparagraph (A) shall apply to items accruing for a period only if the owner or operator of the trade or business referred to in subparagraph (A)—

(i) has applied for (and such application has not been rejected),

(ii) has been granted (and such granting has not been revoked), or

(iii) is exempt from having,

a license, certification, registration, or approval as a day care center or as a family or group day care home under the provisions of any applicable State law. This subparagraph shall apply only to items accruing in periods beginning on or after the first day of the first month which begins more than 90 days after the date of the enactment [5/23/77] of the Tax Reduction and Simplification Act of 1977.

(C) Allocation formula. If a portion of the taxpayer's dwelling unit used for the purposes described in subparagraph (A) is not used exclusively for those purposes, the amount of the expenses attributable to that portion shall not exceed an amount which bears the same ratio to the total amount of the items allocable to such portion as the number of hours the portion is used for such purposes bears to the number of hours the portion is available for use.

**(5) Limitation on deductions.**

In the case of a use described in paragraph (1), (2), or (4), and in the case of a use described in paragraph (3) where the dwelling unit is used by the taxpayer during the taxable year as a residence, the deductions allowed under this chapter for the taxable year by reason of being attributed to such use shall not exceed the excess of—

(A) the gross income derived from such use for the taxable year, over

(B) the sum of—

    (i) the deductions allocable to such use which are allowable under this chapter for the taxable year whether or not such unit (or portion thereof) was so used, and

    (ii) the deductions allocable to the trade or business (or rental activity) in which such use occurs (but which are not allocable to such use) for such taxable year.

Any amount not allowable as a deduction under this chapter by reason of the preceding sentence shall be taken into account as a deduction (allocable to such use) under this chapter for the succeeding taxable year. Any amount taken into account for any taxable year under the preceding sentence shall be subject to the limitation of the 1st sentence of this paragraph whether or not the dwelling unit is used as a residence during such taxable year.

**(6) Treatment of rental to employer.**

Paragraphs (1) and (3) shall not apply to any item which is attributable to the rental of the dwelling unit (or any portion thereof) by the taxpayer to his employer during any period in which the taxpayer uses the dwelling unit (or portion) in performing services as an employee of the employer.

**(d) Use as residence.**

**(1) In general.**

For purposes of this section, a taxpayer uses a dwelling unit during the taxable year as a residence if he uses such unit (or portion thereof) for personal purposes for a number of days which exceeds the greater of—

(A) 14 days, or

(B) 10 percent of the number of days during such year for which such unit is rented at a fair rental.

For purposes of subparagraph (B), a unit shall not be treated as rented at a fair rental for any day for which it is used for personal purposes.

**(2) Personal use of unit.**

For purposes of this section, the taxpayer shall be deemed to have used a dwelling unit for personal purposes for a day if, for any part of such day, the unit is used—

(A) for personal purposes by the taxpayer or any other person who has an interest in such unit, or by any member of the family (as defined in section 267(c)(4)) of the taxpayer or such other person;

(B) by any individual who uses the unit under an arrangement which enables the taxpayer to use some other dwelling unit (whether or not a rental is charged for the use of such other unit); or

(C) by any individual (other than an employee with respect to whose use section 119 applies), unless for such day the dwelling unit is rented for a rental which, under the facts and circumstances, is fair rental.

The Secretary shall prescribe regulations with respect to the circumstances under which use of the unit for repairs and annual maintenance will not constitute personal use under this paragraph, except that if the taxpayer is engaged in repair and maintenance on a substantially full time basis for any day, such authority shall not allow the Secretary to treat a dwelling unit as being used for personal use by the taxpayer on such day merely because other individuals who are on the premises on such day are not so engaged.

**(3) Rental to family member, etc., for use as principal residence.**

(A) In general. A taxpayer shall not be treated as using a dwelling unit for personal purposes by reason of a rental arrangement for any period if for such period such dwelling unit is rented, at a fair rental, to any person for use as such person's principal residence.

(B) Special rules for rental to person having interest in unit.

    (i) Rental must be pursuant to shared equity financing agreement. Subparagraph (A) shall apply to a rental to a person who has an interest in the dwelling unit only if such rental is pursuant to a shared equity financing agreement.

    (ii) Determination of fair rental. In the case of a rental pursuant to a shared equity financing agreement, fair rental shall be determined as of the time the agreement is entered into and by taking into account the occupant's qualified ownership interest.

(C) Shared equity financing agreement. For purposes of this paragraph, the term "shared equity financing agreement" means an agreement under which—

    (i) 2 or more persons acquire qualified ownership interests in a dwelling unit, and

    (ii) the person (or persons) holding 1 or more of such interests—

        (I) is entitled to occupy the dwelling unit for use as a principal residence, and

        (II) is required to pay rent to 1 or more other persons holding qualified ownership interests in the dwelling unit.

(D) Qualified ownership interest. For purposes of this paragraph, the term "qualified ownership interest" means an undivided interest for more than 50 years in the entire dwelling unit and appurtenant land being acquired in the transaction to which the shared equity financing agreement relates.

## (4) Rental of principal residence.

(A) In general. For purposes of applying subsection (c)(5) to deductions allocable to a qualified rental period, a taxpayer shall not be considered to have used a dwelling unit for personal purposes for any day during the taxable year which occurs before or after a qualified rental period described in subparagraph (B)(i), or before a qualified rental period described in subparagraph (B)(ii), if with respect to such day such unit constitutes the principal residence (within the meaning of section 121) of the taxpayer.

(B) Qualified rental period. For purposes of subparagraph (A), the term "qualified rental period" means a consecutive period of—

(i)  12 or more months which begins or ends in such taxable year, or

(ii) less than 12 months which begins in such taxable year and at the end of which such dwelling unit is sold or exchanged, and

for which such unit is rented, or is held for rental, at a fair rental.

## (e) Expenses attributable to rental.

### (1) In general.

In any case where a taxpayer who is an individual or an S corporation uses a dwelling unit for personal purposes on any day during the taxable year (whether or not he is treated under this section as using such unit as a residence), the amount deductible under this chapter with respect to expenses attributable to the rental of the unit (or portion thereof) for the taxable year shall not exceed an amount which bears the same relationship to such expenses as the number of days during each year that the unit (or portion thereof) is rented at a fair rental bears to the total number of days during such year that the unit (or portion thereof) is used.

### (2) Exception for deductions otherwise allowable.

This subsection shall not apply with respect to deductions which would be allowable under this chapter for the taxable year whether or not such unit (or portion thereof) was rented.

## (f) Definitions and special rules.

### (1) Dwelling unit defined.

For purposes of this section—

(A) In general. The term "dwelling unit" includes a house, apartment, condominium, mobile home, boat, or similar property, and all structures or other property appurtenant to such dwelling unit.

(B) Exception. The term "dwelling unit" does not include that portion of a unit which is used exclusively as a hotel, motel, inn, or similar establishment.

**(2) Personal use by shareholders of S corporation.**

In the case of an S corporation, subparagraphs (A) and (B) of subsection (d)(2) shall be applied by substituting "any shareholder of the S corporation" for "the taxpayer" each place it appears.

**(3) Coordination with section 183.**

If subsection (a) applies with respect to any dwelling unit (or portion thereof) for the taxable year—

(A) section 183 (relating to activities not engaged in for profit) shall not apply to such unit (or portion thereof) for such year, but

(B) such year shall be taken into account as a taxable year for purposes of applying subsection (d) of section 183 (relating to 5-year presumption).

**(4) Coordination with Section 162(a)(2).**

Nothing in this section shall be construed to disallow any deduction allowable under section 162(a)(2) (or any deduction which meets the tests of section 162(a)(2) but is allowable under another provision of this title) by reason of the taxpayer's being away from home in the pursuit of a trade or business (other than the trade or business of renting dwelling units).

**(g) Special rule for certain rental use.**

Notwithstanding any other provision of this section or section 183, if a dwelling unit is used during the taxable year by the taxpayer as a residence and such dwelling unit is actually rented for less than 15 days during the taxable year, then—

(1) no deduction otherwise allowable under this chapter because of the rental use of such dwelling unit shall be allowed, and

(2) the income derived from such use for the taxable year shall not be included in the gross income of such taxpayer under section 61.

# Index

Boldface numbers indicate illustrations and tables.

Access to exchange funds, restrictions
  to, 57–59
Accommodator, 16. *See also* Qualified
  intermediaries (QIs)
Adjusted tax basis, 21, 22–23, **22**.
  *See also* Basis
Alienation, fractional ownership and,
  restrictions on, 202
All-inclusive deeds of trust (AITDs),
  seller financing and, 83–84, **84**
American Jobs Creation Act of 2004,
  10
Amount realized, 21–22
Animals and livestock as personal
  property, 155, 179
Appurtenances, construction
  exchanges and, 128–130

Backdating of property identification,
  xx
Basic concept of exchange, 7
Basis, 21–23, **22**, 179
  carryover, 23–24, **24**

involuntary conveyances (Section
  1033) and, carryover of, 169
personal residence sales (IRC
  Section 121) and, 211, 212, **212**,
  213–218, **213, 215–218**
related-party exchange and, 65
shifting of, 65
stepped-up, 25
Bonds, 30
Boot, xii, xviii,16, 73
  carryover basis and, 76
  cash, 73–74, **73**
  mortgage type, 16, 74–75, **74**
  netting, 24, 76–77
  "other nonqualifying property" as,
    74
  personal residence sales (IRC
    Section 121) and, 211
  reverse exchanges and, 147–148
Brokerage agreements, fractional
  ownership and, 204
Build-to-suit exchange, 125. *See also*
  Construction exchange

Building on exchange property. *See*
    Construction exchange
Bulletins (IRS), 8
Business use of home, 119
Business as personal property, 155
Business activities, fractional
    ownership and, 203
    expenses associated with, 239–246

Cancelling and exchange, recouping
    money from, xviii
Capital gain, 7, 23
    personal residence sales (IRC
        Section 121) and, 207–208,
        211–218, **212, 213, 215, 218,**
        231–238
Capital loss, 23
Capitalization of expenses, reporting
    the exchange and, for tax
    purposes, 161
Carryback. *See* Seller financing
Carryover basis, 21, 23–24, **24.** *See*
    *also* Basis
    boot receipt and, 76
Cash boot, 73–74, **73**
Cash substituted for debt,
    reinvestment amount and, 75
Casualty loss, xii
    involuntary conveyances (Section
        1033) and, 168
Certificates of trust, 31
Changing identified properties for
    exchange, xxi
Children, gifting to, xix
Choses in action, 31
Closing, 17
    interest earnings and, 171–172
    processing of exchange funds by
        QI at, 54–55
    settlement statement, prorations,
        security deposits and, 104–106,
        **105, 106**
Closing costs, xvii, 17

Closing date, 17
Combining multiple properties in
    exchange, xvii
Community property, 48
Concurrent exchange, 15, 137
Condemnation, involuntary
    conveyances (Section 1033) and,
    168
Construction exchange, xix, 125–135
    appurtenances versus incidental
        property issues in, 128–130
    currently owned property in, 132
    documenting exchange value in,
        134
    exchange accommodation
        titleholder (EAT) in, 126, 133
    general concepts of,, 125
    improvements during, time
        constraints on, 126–127,
        130–131
    improvements versus construction
        in, 131
    lease with option to buy and,
        131–132
    like-kind issues and, real versus
        personal property in, 128
    "parking transaction" in, 126,
        186–187
    process or mechanics of, 132–133
    qualified intermediary selection
        for, 126
    replacement property identification
        for, 127, **127**
Constructive receipt, 15
Cooperative apartments (coops), 48
Corporation as owner, 40, 45. *See also*
    Same taxpayer rule
Cost of replacement property in
    exchange, xvi–xvii
Cost basis, 22
Crown Zellerback Corporation. *See*
    Starker v. United States
    landmark legislation

Death of taxpayer during exchange, 42, 180

Debt/equity ratio in exchange, xvii

Deductible expenses, reporting the exchange and, for tax purposes, 160–163, **161**, 239–246

Deeds, reverse exchanges and, producing and recording, 149–150

Delaware statutory trusts (DSTs), 49, 113–114, 219–230
  classification of, 227–228
  drafting information for, 230
  entity classification for, 219
  general concepts of, 220–222
  holdings defined for, 220–230
  issues relevant to, 220–222
  laws pertaining to, 222–227
  like-kind exchanges under, 219–220
  real property exchange for interests under, 228–229

Delayed exchange, 14–15, 137
  partial reverse-partial delayed exchanges in, 150–151
  reverse exchanges and, 150–151

Deposits, 101. *See also* Earnest money

Depreciation, 22
  personal residence sales (IRC Section 121) and, 211
  recapture of, 25–26

Disposition of note through exchange, 81

Disqualified person, defined, 16
  replacement property identification and, 89–90

Disregarded entities, 42, 46

Documentation of exchange, 57
  construction exchanges and, 134
  by QI, 54

Due-on-sale provisions, reverse exchanges and, 143

Early release money, 100

Earnest money, 101–103
  exchange funds used as, 101
  nonexchange funds used as, 102–103, **102**

Easements, as real property, 29

Eminent domain, xii. *See also* Involuntary conveyances (Section 1033)

Entities
  defined, 40
  pass-through, 40

Entity structures. *See* Vesting issues and entity structures

Escrow, 17

Estates, 40

Exchange
  basic concept of, 7
  defined, 14
  "gray areas" of, 12
  Partial. *See* Partial exchange
  pros and cons of, 6
  value of, 3–12

Exchangor, defined, 14

Exchange accommodation titleholder (EAT)
  construction exchanges and, 126, 133
  reverse exchanges and, 139–140, 145–147, 149

Exchange-first structure, 142–143. *See also* Reverse exchanges

Exchange funds, access to, restrictions to, 57–59

Exchange groups, 35

Exchange-last structure, 141–142. *See also* Reverse exchanges

Exchange period, 17–18

Exchange value, 22
  reinvestment amount and, 71–72, **72**

Exclusion of gain from sale of principal residence. *See* Personal residence sales (IRC Section 121), gain and, exclusion of

Expenses, 239–246
  business use of home and, 239–246
  capitalization of, 161
  deductible, 160–163, **161**, 239–246
  nondeductible, 162, **163**
  operating costs versus, 162
  rental units, 239–246
  vacation homes and, 239–246
Facilitator, 16. *See also* Qualified
    intermediaries (QIs)
Failed exchange, installment sale
    election for, 172–173
Fair market value, 34
Family. *See* Related-party exchange
Federal statutes applicable to
    exchanges, 8–9
Federation of Exchange
    Accommodators, 7, 116
Fee interests, as real property, 28
Financing, reverse exchanges and, 147
"Flipping" property, xviii–xix
Foreign or foreign-held property, 30,
    31, 181
Foreign Investment in Real Property
    Tax Act (FIRPTA), reporting the
    exchange and, for tax purposes,
    163–164
Foreign persons, reporting the
    exchange and, for tax purposes,
    163
Forward exchange, 15, 138
Fractional ownership, 139–205. *See
    also* Tenancies-in-common;
    Vesting issues
  alienation and, restrictions on, 202
  business activities and, 203
  co-ownership agreements in, 201
  court rulings pertaining to, 196–197
  drafting information for, 205
  entity treatment of, 201
  general concepts in, 194–197
  information required for
    submission of, 198–200
  leasing arrangements and, 204
  loan agreements and, 205
  management and brokerage
    agreements in, 204
  number of co-owners in, 200
  obtaining rulings on, conditions
    for, 200
  options and, 203
  scope of legislation for, 197
  sharing of proceeds and liabilities
    in, 202–203
  sharing of profits and losses in,
    202–203
  sponsors and, payments to, 205
  submission guidelines for, 197–198
  tenancy-in-common and, 200
  voting in, 201–202
Frequently asked questions (FAQs),
    xv–xxii

Gain. *See* capital gain
Gifting to children, xix
"Gray areas" of exchanges, 12
Guam, 11, 31

History of exchange legislation, xv
Holding periods, qualified property,
    35–36

Identification of property, 56
Identification of QIs, xx
Identification of replacement property,
    87–98. *See also* Replacement
    property, identification of
Identification period, 17
Improvements, xii, 125. *See also*
    Construction exchanges
  construction exchanges and,
    126–131
    improvements verus
    construction in, 131
    time constraints on, 126–127,
    130–131

Incidental property, construction exchanges and, 128–130
Installment sale election for failed exchanges, 172–173
Intangible property as qualified property, 31–32
Interest earnings, 171–172
Internal Revenue Code (IRC) and exchanges, 6–8, 21–26. *See also* Reporting the exchange
Investment intent for qualified property, 35–36
Involuntary conveyances (Section 1033), 167–170
  basis carryover and, 169
  casualty loss and, 168
  condemnation and, 168
  identification period in, 169
  qualified intermediaries (QIs) and, 169
  replacement period allotted in, 168–169

Joint tenancy, joint tenancy with right of survivorship, 47–48
Joint ventures versus TIC, 110–111

Land contracts, 48–49
Land trusts, 49
Lease with option to buy, construction exchanges and, 131–132
Leasehold interests, as real property, 28–29
Leasing arrangements, fractional ownership and, 204
Leasing to relatives, xx
Like-kind exchange, 13, 14, 31, 128, 177–179
  Delaware statutory trusts (DSTs) and, 219–220
  personal property and, 154
Limited liability companies (LLCs), 40, 42–43, 45–46, 112

Limited partnerships, 40
Livestock as personal property, 155, 179
Loan agreements, fractional ownership and, 205
Loss of identified property before exchange, xxii
Losses, 179
Management and brokerage agreements, fractional ownership and, 204
Mineral rights, 114–115
Mortgage boot, 16, 74–75, **74**
Mortgage payoff from proceeds of exchange, xx
Multiple properties from exchange, xvii, 24, 33–35, **34**

Net sale price, 21–22
Netting, boot, 24, 76–77
Ninety-five percent rule, replacement property identification, 92
Nondeductible expenses, 162, **163**
Nonentity types of ownership, 47–48
Nonqualifying property, 30–32
  as boot, 74
Notes, 30
  assignment to seller of replacement property, 82
  disposition of, through exchange, 81
  QI sale of, in seller financing, 83
  short-term, in exchange, 81–82
  third-party sale of, in seller financing, 82
Notices (IRS), 8

Oil and gas investments, 114–115
Operating costs versus expenses, 162
Options, 33
  fractional ownership and, 203
Orchestration and documentation of exchange by QI, 54

"Other nonqualifying property" as boot, 74
Ownership. *See* Vesting issues and entity structures

Paperwork Reduction Act, qualified exchange accommodation agreement (QEAA) and, 191
"Parking transaction," construction exchanges and, 126, 133, 186–187
Partial exchange
  reinvestment amount and, 72–73, **73**, 76
  seller financing and, 80–81, **80**
Partnership interests, 30, 40, 43–44. *See also* Fractional ownership; Tenancies-in-common
  exchanges within, 43–44
  individual partners versus, distinction between, 44–45
  refinancing and, 123
Pass-through entities, 40
Personal property, xii, 8, 28–30, 33, 153–156, 181–182
  animals and livestock as, 155, 179
  businesses as, 155
  construction exchanges and, 128
  identification of, 155–156
  like-kind concepts in, 154
Personal residence sales (IRC Section 121), xii, xvi, 117–120, 207–218
  application of, 211
  basis and, computation of, 211, 212, **212**, 213–218, **213, 215, 216, 217, 218**
  boot and, 211
  court rulings pertaining to, 209–210
  depreciation and, 211
  drafting information for, 218

dual use as primary residence and business/investment for, 119
gain and
  computation of, 211, 212, **212**, 213–218, **213, 215, 216, 217, 218**
  exclusion of, 207–208, 212, **212**, 213–218, **213, 215–218**, 231–238
  general concepts of, 208–210
  primary residence converted to rental and, 118–119
  rental unit converted to, 120
  scope of legislation pertaining to, 210
Pledge of exchange proceeds, 58
Pledging property held by QI, 172
Pooling of funds, in TICs, 110
Power of attorney as signer, xx–xxi, 96
Private Letter Ruling (PLR), 8
Process of exchange, 3–6, 55–57, 132–133
Processing of exchange funds by QI, 54–55
Profits and losses, sharing, in fractional ownership, 202–203
Prorations, 103–104
Pros and cons of exchange, 6

Qualified exchange accommodation agreement (QEAA), 183–191
  definition of, 188–189
  drafting information for, 191
  effective date for, 191
  exchange accommodation titleholder (EAT), 185–187
  general concepts of, 187–188
  noncompliance with, 187
  Paperwork Reduction Act and, 191
  parking transaction in, 186–187
  permissible agreements under, 189–190
  permissible treatment under, 190

qualified indicia of ownership in, 188

reverse exchanges and, 145, 183–191

time constraints on, 188–189

Qualified indicia of ownership, qualified exchange accommodation agreement (QEAA) and, 188

Qualified intermediaries (QIs), xii, xx–xxii, 15–16, 51–61

access to exchange funds and, restrictions to, 57–59

changing, during exchange process, 60–61

communicating with, 60

construction exchanges and, 126

exchange process and, 55–57

identification of, xx

identification of property and, 56

involuntary conveyances (Section 1033) and, 169

note purchase from, in seller financing, 83

orchestration and documentation of exchange by, 54

pledging of property held by, 172

principal activities of, 52

processing of exchange funds by, 54–55

safe harbor and, 51–53

selection of, 59–60

Qualifying properties for exchange, xvi, xviii, 7, 8, 13, 27–38

appurtenances versus incidental property issues in, 128–130

construction exchanges and, 128

cooperative apartments (co-ops) as, 48

definition of, 29–32

Delaware statutory trusts (DSTs) and, 49, 113–114, 219–230

easements as, 29

exchange groups as, 35

fair market value of, 34

fee interests as, 28

foreign or foreign-held property as, 30, 31, 181

holding periods for, 35–36

intangible property as, 31–32

investment intent for, 35–36

land contracts as, 48–49

land trusts as, 49

leasehold interests as, 28–29

like-kind property in, 31

multiple properties as, 33–35, **34**

nonqualifying property versus, 30–32

options to buy property and, 33

"other nonqualifying property" as boot in, 74

personal property and, 28, 29

personal residence and, 30, 33

qualifying use and, 32–33

real estate investment trust (REIT) and, 31, 49, 115

real property as, 27, 28–29. *See also* Real property

reverse exchanges and, 138–139

state-to-state property in, 31

timeshares as, 32

types of, 27–28

vacation homes and, 32

Virgin Islands and Guam in, 31

Qualifying use, 32–33. *See also* Qualifying properties for exchange

reverse exchanges and, 138–139

Real estate investment trust (REIT), 31, 49, 115

Real property, 27–29, 181

appurtenances versus incidental property issues in, 128–130

construction exchanges and, 128

easements as, 29

Real property (*Cont.*)
fee interests as, 28
leasehold interests as, 28–29
like-kind, 31
tenancies-in-common (TIC) and,
determining status of, 113
Recapture of depreciation, 25–26
Refinancing, xii, 121–124
as alternative to Section 1031,
121–122
before versus after exchange, 122
limited tax authority available for,
122–124
partnerships and, 123
step-transaction doctrine and, 123
Reinvesting profits from exchange,
xvii
Reinvestment amount, 71–78. *See also*
Boot
boot in, 73
boot netting and, 76–77
carryover basis and boot in, 76
cash boot in, 73–74, **73**
cash substituted for debt in, 75
exchange value and, 71–72, **72**
mortgage boot in, 74–75, **74**
"other nonqualifying property" as
boot in, 74
partial exchanges and, 72–73, **73**,
76
timing for receipt of boot and,
75–76
Related-party exchange, xii, 65–69,
180
basis and, 65
basis shifting and, 65
buying from, consequences of,
66–68
definition of "related" in, 66
leasing to, xx
multiple exchanges within, 68–69
two-year rule in, 66
Relatives. *See* Related-party exchange

Relinquished property, 14
Rental units
conversion to primary residence of,
120
expenses associated with,
239–246
primary residence converted to,
118–119
as residence, xvi, 2
Replacement property, xii, 14
identification of, 56, 87–98, 178
ambiguity avoided in, 97–98
common issues, questions,
problems in, 95
construction exchanges and, 127,
**127**
disqualified persons for, 89–90
document for, 91
fractional interests and, 96
invalid, 92–93, **93**
involuntary conveyances (Section
1033) and, 169
methods of, 91–93
modifying, amending, revoking list
of, 96
ninety-five percent rule in, 92
person providing, 89
personal property and, 155–156
power of attorney as signer, 96
precision in, 97
purchase of, mandatory nature of,
96
reverse exchanges and, 144–145
rule selection for, 95
specificity of, 90
substitutes for formal identification
in, 97
tenancies-in-common (TIC) and,
112
three-property rule in, 91
time constraints on, 88–90, 95, 97
timeliness of, 90
two-hundred percent rule in, 92, **94**

valid form of, 89, 93–94, **94**
verifying, 98
involuntary conveyances (Section
    1033) and, 168–169
modifying, amending, revoking list
    of, 96
note assigned to seller of, in seller
    financing, 82
personal property as, 87
purchase of, mandatory nature of,
    96
real property as, 87
Reporting the exchange, xii, xviii,
    159–166
capitalization of expenses for,
    161
deductible expenses in, 160–163,
    **161**, 239–246
documentation needed for, 57
Foreign Investment in Real
    Property Tax Act (FIRPTA) and,
    163–164
foreign persons and, 163
nondeductible expenses and, 162,
    **163**
operating costs versus expenses in,
    162
submission of, to IRS, 166
withholding certificates (Form
    8288-B) and, 164–165
withholding taxes and, 164
Residence from exchange, time to
    wait, xix
Revenue Procedure (Rev. Proc.), 8
Rev. Proc. 2000-37, 2000-2 CB
    308, 9/18/2000, IRC Sec(s).
    1031 (text), 183–191
Rev. Proc. 2002-22, 2002-1 CB
    733, 03/19/2002, IRC Sec(s).
    1031 (text), 193–205. *See also*
    Fractional ownership
Rev. Proc. 2005-14, 2005-7 IRB
    528, 01/27/2005, IRC Sec(s).

121 (text), 207–218. *See also*
    Personal residence sales
Revenue Rulings (Rev. Rul.), 8
Rev. Rul. 2004-86, 2004-33 IRB
    191, 07/20/2004, IRC Sec(s).
    7701 (text), 219–230. *See also*
    Delaware statutory trusts
Reverse exchanges, xii, xvi, 15,
    137–151
boot and, 147–148
concurrent exchange and, 137
deeds and, producing and recording
    of, 149–150
delayed exchange and, 137
documentation for, 145–146
double transfer tax problems in,
    148–149
due on sale provisions and, 143
exchange accommodation
    titleholder (EAT) in, 139–140,
    145–147, 149
exchange-first structure in,
    142–143
exchange-last structure in,
    141–142
fees for, 140–141
financing and, 147
forward exchange and, 138
general concepts of, 137–139
multiple properties involved in,
    150
partial reverse-partial delayed
    exchanges in, 150–151
problems in, 146–151
process or mechanics of, 145–146
qualified exchange accommodation
    agreement (QEAA) in, 145,
    183–191
qualifying property in, 138–139
qualifying use in, 138–139
replacement property identification
    and, 144–145
reverse exchanges and, 150–151

Reverse exchanges (*Cont.*)
 single-purpose entities (SPEs) in,
  139
 structuring of, two options for,
  141–144
 title insurance and, 147
Risk, diminution of, 181

Safe harbor, 16, 51–53
Sale versus exchange, **4**, 4
Sale price, 21–22
Same taxpayer rule (corporation as
  owner), xix
Section 453, seller financing and,
  80–81
Section 1031 Exchange of Property
  Held for Productive Use or
  Investment (text), 177–182
Section 1033. *See* Involuntary
  conveyances
Securities, 30, 113
Security deposits, 103–104
Seller financing, 79–85
 all-inclusive deeds of trust (AITDs)
  in, 83–84, **84**
 general issues of, 79–80
 note assignment to seller of
  replacement property in, 82
 note disposition through, 81
 note purchased from QI in, 83
 note sold to third party in, 82
 partial exchange and, 80–81, **80**
 planning for, 84–85
 Section 453 and Section 1031
  applicable to, 80–81
 short-term notes in, 81–82
 "wraps" in, 83
Settlement statement, prorations and
  security deposits in, 104–106,
  **105, 106**
Sharing of proceeds and liabilities,
  fractional ownership and,
  202–203

Shifting of basis, 65
Short sales, 173–174, **174**
Short-term notes in exchange, 81–82
Signed sales contract versus
  identification of property,
  xxi–xxii
Simultaneous exchange, 15
Single-purpose entities (SPEs), 46,
  112
 exchange accommodation
  titleholder (EAT) as, 139–140,
  145–147, 149
 reverse exchanges and, 139
 sponsors, fractional ownership and,
  payments to, 205
 spousal changes, in vesting issues,
  41–42
 Starker v. United States landmark
  legislation, 9–10, 171
 state-to-state exchanges, xv, 11, 31
 step-transaction doctrine,
  refinancing, 123
 stepped-up basis, 25
 stocks, 30
 structure of an exchange, **18**
 subsidiaries, corporate, 40
 substitution of other properties in
  exchange, xxi

T. J. Starker v. United States landmark
  legislation. *See* Starker v. United
  States landmark legislation
Tax basis. *See* Basis
Tax code regulations pertaining to
  exchanges, 6–7, 8, 21–26. *See
  also* Reporting the exchange
Tax deferment, 8–9
Technical Advice Memorandum
  (TAM), 8
Tenancies-in-common (TIC), xii, xxi,
  7, 43, 47, 49, 109–111, 115–116,
  200. *See also* Fractional
  ownership; Vesting issues

TIC (*Cont.*)
  identification of a transaction
    involving, 112
  joint ventures versus, 110–111
  limited liability companies (LLCs)
    and, 112
  ownership in, 111–112
  pooling of funds in, 110
  real estate versus security and,
    determining, 113
  replacement property identification
    and, 96
  representative organizations for, 7,
    116
  single-purpose entities (SPEs) and,
    112
  TIC deal and, 110
  vesting in, 112
Tenant-in-Common Association, 7,
  116
Terminology, 13–19
Third-party sale of notes, in seller
  financing, 82
Three-property rule, replacement
  property identification, 91
TIC deal, 110. *See also* Tenancies-in-
  common
Timber rights, 114–115
Time constraints in exchanges,
  xv–xvi, 11–12
  concurrent exchange and, 15,
    137
  delayed exchange and, 14–15,
    137
  exchange period in, 17–18
  forward exchange and, 15, 138
  holding periods for qualified
    property and, 35–36
  identification period in, 17
  improvements during construction
    exchange and, 126–127, 130–131
  involuntary conveyances (Section
    1033) and, 168–169

qualified exchange accommodation
  agreement (QEAA) and,
  188–189
  receipt of boot and reinvestment
    amounts in, 75–76
  replacement property identification
    and, 88–95, 97
  reverse exchange and, 15, 137–151
  simultaneous exchange and, 15
  structure of an exchange within, **18**
  vesting and, 41
Timeshares, 32
Title, xii
Title insurance, reverse exchanges
  and, 147
Trade organizations for tenant-in-
  common exchanges, 7, 116
Transfer taxes, reverse exchanges and,
  double taxation in, 148–149
Treasury regulations pertaining to
  exchanges, 10. *See also*
  Reporting the exchange; Tax
  code regulations
Trusts, 40, 46
  all-inclusive deeds of trust (AITDs)
    in, 83–84, **84**
Two-hundred percent rule,
  replacement property
  identification, 92, **94**
Two-year rule, related-party exchange
  and, 66

Vacation homes, xix, 32
  expenses associated with,
    239–246
Value of exchange, 3–12
Vesting issues and entity structures,
  39–50. *See also* Fractional
  ownership
  community property and, 48
  cooperative apartments (co-ops)
    and, 48
  corporations and, 40, 45

Vesting issues and entity structures
    (*Cont.*)
  death of taxpayer during exchange
    and, 42, 180
  Delaware statutory trusts (DSTs)
    and, 49, 113–114, 219–230
  disregarded entities and, 42, 46
  entities defined for, 40
  exchange accommodation
    titleholder (EAT), 138, 145–147,
    149, 185–187
  joint tenancy or joint tenancy with
    right of survivorship in, 47–48
  land contracts and, 48–49
  land trusts and, 49
  limited liability companies (LLCs)
    and, 40, 42–43, 45–46, 112
  nonentity types of ownership and,
    47–48
  partnerships in, 40, 43–44
  permissible changes to, 42–43

  real estate investment trusts
    (REITs) and, 49, 115
  special-purpose entities (SPEs)
    and, 46, 112, 139
  spousal changes in, 41–42
  tenancy-in-common (TIC) and, 43,
    47, 49, 112
  timing of changes in, 41
  trusts and, 40, 46
  vesting defined for, 39–41
Virgin Islands, 11, 31
Voting, fractional ownership and,
    201–202

Withholding certificates (Form 8288-
    B), 164–165
Withholding taxes, reporting the
    exchange and, for tax purposes,
    164
W-9 form, 56
Wraps, 83. *See also* Seller financing

# About the Authors

**Timothy S. Harris** has served as President of TIMCOR Exchange Corporation since 1982. During his tenure, TIMCOR has grown to become one of the nation's leading 1031 exchange accommodators. TIMCOR currently handles approximately 7,500 exchanges per year and has offices in Los Angeles, Houston, Chicago, Richmond, Phoenix and Miami. An attorney at law, Mr. Harris is a member of both the State Bar of California and the State Bar of Texas. He received his Bachelor of Arts in Economics from Cornell University in 1971, his Juris Doctor from Cornell Law School in 1974, and his Master of Science in Taxation from Northrop University in 1980. Mr. Harris is a Certified Exchange Specialist™.

Mr. Harris lectures nationwide on the topic of 1031 exchanges, most frequently in California, Texas, and Florida. He has taught courses on 1031 exchanges for various professional organizations, including the Los Angeles Chapter of the California Society of CPAs and the Arizona Escrow Association.

His articles on 1031 exchanges have appeared in such publications as the NJPA Real Estate Journal and the New England Real Estate Journal.

**Linda Monroe** is Executive Vice President and corporate counsel to TIMCOR Exchange Corporation. She has worked with Mr. Harris for 17 years, and has been associated with TIMCOR since early 2000.

Ms. Monroe has been a member of the State Bar of California since 1976. She received her Bachelor of Arts in Psychology from Pitzer College, in Claremont, California, and her Juris Doctor from Loyola Law School of Los Angeles. She has practiced law with the firm of Harris & Monroe, specializing in estate planning, business and real estate since 1989. From 1979 to 1989, she was Vice President and corporate counsel to a property management firm in Beverly Hills, California. She is a recipient of the Benjamin A. Aranda III Outstanding Public Service Award from the Los Angeles County Bar Association.

Ms. Monroe lectures in Southern California on the topic of 1031 exchanges to various professional organizations and investor groups. She appears regularly as a guest lecturer at UCLA Extension. Ms. Monroe is a Certified Exchange Specialist™.